Flashes and Sparks

A Memoir

Kate Peters

This book is a work of nonfiction. Some names and identifying details of people described in this book have been altered to protect their privacy.

Copyright © 2020 by Kate Peters

All rights reserved. This book may not be reproduced or stored in whole or in part by any means without the written permission of the author except for brief quotations for the purpose of review.

ISBN: 978-1-7357280-6-3

Peters. Kate.
Flashes and Sparks.

Edited by: Melissa Long

Published by Warren Publishing
Charlotte, NC
www.warrenpublishing.net
Printed in the United States

*For my love, Tom;
for Michael;
and in eternal memory of Doug*

PART I

1990

Mother

For as long as I can remember, I've been an observer. I wake up each day in a play I forgot to rehearse. There's little conversation but lots of reaction. I act. They react. The tension builds as my palms sweat and I wing it.

This is, by the way, the exact premise of one of my recurring nightmares. I'm thrown center stage into the climax of a production. I can't understand what's at stake or what's driving these characters. I stand still in the bright lights, trying not to giggle because it's tense and awkward, and people seem really serious about it. I have no idea what I'm doing here.

But, the thing about bright lights is they make you squint and look inward, make you see things in slow motion. In the bright clarity that comes with darkness, you see things, perhaps as they really are.

To me, most people are like those Disneyland animatrons; they do a dance, sing a song, say lines they don't have the capacity to understand and certainly don't believe. I imagine their circuitry can be hijacked, and the robots will come for me. All through the Small World ride, I see phoney, plaster mountainsides and animatronic robots covered in bright felt and dust. I'm just thirteen, already jaded and full of distrust.

⁓

My brothers are barging down the hall toward the den where I've been hiding with a magazine. I hear the pressure of their hollow basketball ping loudly. It rattles the hardwood and reverberates off the walls to the roots of my teeth. Doug is fifteen and six feet tall. His nine-year-old sidekick, Brian, has a blonde mop of surfer hair and an eagerness to please our big brother.

Brian beckons to me in excitement, "We're going surfing, Kate. Grab your board!"

Doug throws the basketball at the couch, like maybe this will inspire me to move. It lands right next to where I'm sitting and reading the latest issue of Dad's *Psychology Today*, and trying to figure out, once and for all, if it's nature or nurture.

"Yeah," says Doug. "Get up!"

"You guys go," I plead with them to leave.

"You're a nerd," Doug chides and stomps away. On his way out, he throws the door wide open. Brian gives me a snot-faced look before following his big bro out.

Not thirty seconds later, the phone rings, and it rings. After the third round, it stops.

"Kate! Kate!" Mom calls from the other side of the house. "Pick up the phone. It's Grandmama."

Oh, crap—here we go. I pick up the receiver. "Hello?"

"Hellooo ..." Grandma says nothing more, but this is my cue to dance.

"Hey, Grandma. How's it going?"

Mom walks in and stands above me to observe. Her hovering and the half-open drawer across the room are making me twitch. "Tell her you love her," Mom whispers.

I wait for a lull in Grandma's diatribe to say, like a moron, "I love you, Grandmama." I'm instantly a phoney because my tone and words don't match this feeling in my gut.

Mom continues to hover and hold her hand out for the receiver, a surgeon waiting for a sterile tool, but I'm not at liberty to pass the phone just yet.

"I saw you skate right by my house. You couldn't even be bothered to knock?" Grandma presses for the third time. "Don't you respect your grandmother?"

"I'm sorry, Grandmama, I was just getting some quick exercise down the boardwalk. I'll be sure to see if you're home next time."

"Put your mother back on the phone." I hand the cordless to Mom. I can't help but feel sorry for her. She just takes it, submissively pressing the receiver to her ear, offering herself up as a ready reception. She listens to Grandma's complaints and walks quietly down the hall.

I've lost my place in the magazine, so I flip to the table of contents. My eyes get stuck on another article, "How to Find Calm When You Don't Have Control." I toss it aside and head over to close the half-open drawer that's been bugging me all afternoon.

When I slam it shut, the drawer beneath pops open just enough to pique my curiosity. I've never looked inside this bureau before. With two hands, I pull the handles past patches of resistance and get the drawer open. It's full of loose papers, a picture book about ancient Rome, and a glass bead necklace. At the bottom is an envelope with a cassette tape labeled "Psychic Reading: Linda Brewer." The outside is scrolled with Grandma's cursive, "Happy Birthday, Linda!" At the very bottom of the drawer is something else, a manila folder with a typed label: "Brewer, Katherine; 1977." Inside the folder are documents on stationery from the UCLA Paranormal Psychology Clinic. I read the first page.

> Subject, Katherine Brewer, is an eleven-month-old female, born by natural birth. Her development has been unremarkable, and milestones have been met in average time.
>
> On February 25, 1978, subject's parents inquired with UCLA PPC because, as of yet, nonverbal subject awakened from a daytime nap, sat upright in her crib, and uttered, in a deepened voice and with easily comprehensible English, "I need complete silence."
>
> Subject's parents expressed concerns of paranormal possession over subject's physical body.

I can't feel my face, but my fingers work fast, and I flip to another sheet of paper. It's biofeedback readings, electromagnetic field studies, and FLIR thermal camera recordings, whatever those are. I flip to the last page of the stack.

Dear Mrs. and Mr. Brewer,

    As discussed on the telephone, we regret to inform you that our lab will be shutting down effective May 1. We would like to thank you for entrusting us with your remarkable daughter and for allowing us to continue our research in the important field of paranormal psychology. We do believe that we will get our funding replenished in the near future, and we encourage you to stay in contact with the university and to get updates on the status and the future of our clinic.

    As regards to Katherine, be assured that she is a bright and healthy baby girl with whom we would be interested in working in the future. As for our current research into her spontaneous speech and the possibility that she is or has been possessed, our research is inconclusive. If it is any consolation to you, Dr. Harbolden has stated that he believes perhaps she is just "an old soul."

With very best regards,
The UCLA PPL Team

Mom calls from the kitchen, "Kate! I need to talk to you."

I'm shaking and fumbling to return the items to the drawer when I find a loose photo of my brothers and me from 1981. We have bowl cuts and corduroy pants. This simple, family image is suddenly overshadowed by big-picture questions. Why didn't anyone ever mention I was part of a paranormal study?

I've always thought I don't belong in this family of chaos and drama, as if there was a crack in the time-space continuum and my soul has been misplaced.

I slam the album shut and toss it in the drawer on top of the UCLA file and the "Psychic Reading" audio tape before heading out to have this conversation with Mom about Grandma … again.

So, it's chicken or the egg, I guess—whether Grandma's multigenerational henpecking has turned me off to lighthearted human interactions, or I was just born this way.

⁂

There's no question, though—this is the birthplace of my nervous tic. I crank my neck abruptly to the left and Grandma is alerted. "What's wrong with you? Are you nervous?" She smirks, and her eyes fix on me. I can see she's inspired—like Gargamel or a James Bond villain. She's in leopard pants with gold, Hermes flats and a neon blue sweater. She's clutching her white Maltese, Picoleto, under the ribs with one hand and stroking it with the other.

Mom makes us attend Grandma's four o'clock cocktail hour a few times a week. My brothers and I sit around her coffee table while she paces. Mom's in a long white cotton dress. She's silent and dutiful, sitting oddly upright in her leather recliner, while Grandma is clearly deciding who to pick on next.

We're surrounded; the side tables and coffee table are covered in dishes of mini pickles, bowls of pearl onions, and trays of cold cuts and cheese. The walls and bookshelves are adorned with a globetrotter's gallery of powers. Thai spirit houses, Cambodian wood carvings, and a shrunken monkey head—appropriations with esoteric significance not even she understands. Nonetheless, their purpose is well-served. By her possession of these spiritual items, we are to understand Grandma is rich, omniscient, and superior to us all. Here, backed by her gallery of evil and benevolent spirits, Grandma holds court.

"So … Doug, your sister said that your girlfriend is stupid."

"No," I say, calmly. I strain to sound emotionless as this yearning swells in my throat. Still, my face betrays me. I feel it turn red. "I said she goes to St. Catherine's—"

"Right," interrupts Grandma, "the school for the slow girls."

Doug's eyes hold mine in solidarity. My big brother is supportive and steady. His six-foot frame sits upright in Grandma's leather occasional chair. We won't let her break us.

But still, that's one point for Grandma. She's thrilled. She serves again, this time right between me and Brian.

"Brian ... didn't you tell Kate that you don't like it when Doug is home from boarding school?"

"No!" he fires back, snide and petulant. He tosses his head to the side to get locks of grown-out, beach-blonde hair out of his eyes. Brian doesn't yet understand Grandma's games. "That's not true!" he argues.

Doug and I share a strategic glance. *Keep it together, little bro!* we plead with only our eyes. We don't move a muscle.

Through it all, we're bros, my brothers and me—*hermanos*, as we say in Spanish. The fact that I'm a girl is irrelevant.

Grandma moves on to the subject of a friend's granddaughter, a woman we've never met. "In my day, breastfeeding was for the poor. It's vulgar! I guess she's a real earth mama now, probably strung out on drugs." Her eyes are wide as she studies my face. When her direct attacks don't work, Grandma moves on to anecdotes about strangers. They can elicit the same controversy if we bite. Instead, I fix my eyes on the carpet. I'm careful not to look as if I've got an opinion.

Nonetheless, Grandma's glare finds me, and I'm up next. "Kate ... Margie saw you walking in front of the library ... with oily hair?"

I swallow hard and listen closely. I have inadvertently compromised Grandma's fancy public image, and this is very bad. She stops pacing and just stands above me and stares. She's going in for the kill. "Why were you walking around town in front of my friends looking like a homeless person?"

I wrap my hair around my neck to conceal the quickening of my pulse. "Uh ... I read that olive oil is good for your hair—"

"What?"

"I said I had read that olive oil was good for your hair, so I was conditioning my hair with olive oil. I had it up in a bun—"

"What?" Grandma interrupts again, just for fun. When she sees my nerves are sufficiently fried, she casually changes the subject to the Memorial Day sale at Macy's. "They are giving it all away! Here. Here!" I reach out, not fast enough, for the bulk mail ads she's shoved in my face. "Here. Take them, Kate! Look!" With the flick of a sharply filed fingernail, she points. Her acrylic tips rattle the roots of my teeth.

"They're giving it all away!" Through her Long Island accent and excited intonation, we are to understand that this is a very good thing. We must acquire more. We must fill the void. We must inspire jealousy in our friends and foes alike.

"Oh, cool!" I fake enthusiasm, however poorly. I scan the room. In corners and on countertops, there are shopping bags Grandma has yet to unpack. There are lots of little dolls and other creepy knickknacks with faces. Several solar-powered dancing flowers start to move behind me when the wind blows the sun shade from the window. The light bombards the room like a flashbulb.

I think of that old black and white movie the boys and I watched one night like a train wreck we just had to see, a revelation that might explain how we ended up on this wild track. Ingrid Bergman is manipulated into thinking she's the only one who sees the lights flicker, and she slowly goes insane. Around the same time *Gaslight* came out in the theaters, Grandma married Grandpa Becker, and the legacy of our family dysfunction began. We think it's no coincidence. Grandma's mind games come straight from this playbook. The old gas lamps flicker, the breeze blows Grandma's flapping shade. I look covertly over my shoulder at the dancing, solar-powered flowers with faces.

"Aren't they cheerful?" Grandma grins. This is not a question; she's telling me to smile for her, to dance. She keeps her eyes on me and takes another sip of her scotch.

"Oh, yes! Very!"

I roll my neck to the left. Brian rolls his to the right. Then one of us bobs our head up and down as if we're trying to dislodge water from an ear. Doug's tic is different. He breathes hard out of his nostrils, blinks, and then raises his chin to the ceiling to stretch his jaw muscles. I pulse a crossed leg up and down over my left knee. We look like lunatics, but we're doing well under the circumstances.

We sit in her beachfront windows, sipping our sodas, surrounded by her hordes of things. Grandma's scotch ebbs and flows over her rocks. Meanwhile, our nervous tics are orchestrated like the gears of a cuckoo clock.

After half an hour, Grandma's still gossiping and barking orders. Mom is politely obedient. She's just putting in her time.

"Linda, you'd be an idiot if you didn't get a sweater like mine. You should get one. Coogi. Australian. Very expensive." She shakes her old-fashioned glass, and the ice jingles. "All the rage."

Grandma talks sassy, like a 1950s movie star. She calls this affectation "continental," but my brothers and I have never heard anyone else talk exactly this way. We assume she's being fancy.

"Over the moon ... hot and heavy," she reports. The neighbor is having an affair, and it's steamy. "Oh, the wuata!" The Caribbean is where to be. You're an idiot if you're not there, she insists. A nobody. "They are all wearing leopard this season." The holy grail, the September issue of *Vogue*, appears right before my nose. "Hum? What?" she implores, though I've said nothing.

I've been commanded to speak, so I focus. I get back in the game. "Oh yes, they are, Grandmama!" I make a face like I am really studying the page and planning how I, too, will pull it off. I can feel Doug looking at me, as if maybe I'm overdoing it. I don't dare look his way because she's said the buzzword, and I won't be able to keep it together if I do.

They.

They are all wearing leopard, paying cash, cheating on their spouses. *They* are the subject of endless entertainment for my brothers and me. We wonder if *they* appear to Grandma merely as figures of speech, or if *they* truly live in her mind as delusions or hallucinations. One thing is clear, though: to Grandma, appearances are everything. I've often thought her reliance on external appearances could be explained by her utter lack of substance within.

Nonetheless, if *they* bully her half as much as she does us, we'll wear leopard to appease them. We'll bow down to their judgment and do anything to not get on their bad side. We imagine *they* lurk in dark corners and have elaborate reporting systems, and when the coast is clear of Grandma, we laugh because the thought of them thrills us and fuels our paranoia.

But during cocktail hour, we play our parts. We pretend to savor her every word. We practice restraint. Mom listens to the gossip and becomes dramatic and sort of bitchy herself. Of course, she doesn't have a bitchy bone in her body. She's acting. She placates—all of us do. But mostly, we try to make ourselves small so we're not Grandma's next target.

Picoleto is wagging his tail furiously and heading my way. When Grandma turns for her scotch, I toss a tiny piece of a Ritz cracker behind the coffee table. "Treats! Treats," I whisper, but he doesn't see it and just keeps coming. I try to shoo him with mind control, but it's too late; he's here, and he's called attention to me again.

"Well! Give him some, Kate. He wants your turkey!"

"Oh, yeah. Sorry." I hand him my food and try to look adoringly at the Maltese as he salivates on my fingers and bites at my thumb.

Pico's a VIP. We show him the utmost respect. In front of Grandma, we feign profound affection for the dog, but at home, Doug jokes that Grandma's a mob boss and Pico's her muscle. Even Brian gets this joke because he's seen *The Godfather*. And just like Mafia muscle, Pico can be shut down in an instant, caged at Grandma's whim. He's helpless and dependent on his master, and that's just the way she likes it.

I shake my knee up and down, bounce the ball of my foot off the floor to burn nervous energy.

"Why are you wearing boys' shoes?" Grandma says. I stare at my Vans sneakers and buy some time as I formulate an answer. "Don't you ever want to get married? The gays wear those sneakers, you know. Isn't Britt gay? And what's this lumberjack shirt?"

"You mean Quinn?" I say. By "forgetting" her name, Grandma belittles my best friend. She "forgets" the names of all our best friends, as only she is allowed in the sphere of influence. "Nope. Straight," I add.

"Huh?" She dares me to repeat myself. I don't. "Well … they will think you are gay." Grandma waits for me to bite. Instead, I bite my lip and crank my neck to the right. I see Mom sitting there. She's holding her breath.

"I knew your father's aunt," Grandma says. None of us says a word. "Mary." Yes, we know. We nod solemnly.

We've heard it many times before. Aunt Mary played bridge with Grandma in the sixties and seventies. Across a card table, they decided to introduce my parents to each other. This was most likely so they'd have something to gossip about at their card games. Nonetheless, my parents got married in 1975, and Mom gave birth to us three. Aunt Mary never had any children of her own. Her frenemy, our Grandma, mentions this over and over, implying that we should infer something scathing from this little fact. And though Mary isn't around to explain this or anything else about the past, Mary remains a go-to source of Grandma's hearsay.

Doug readies himself for the retelling by slumping a bit in his chair. I sit like an expressionless yogi and engage in a time-passing exercise where I listen for inconsistencies in her story. I breathe slowly, methodically. I refuse to engage.

"You know ... your Grandma Grace ... well, she was fast and loose with the sailors during the war. Haven't you ever noticed your dad has red hair, but your Grandpa Bill's hair was brown?"

We nod as if we are accepting tragic news. Not one of us looks up. There is no right facial expression for this conversation. I've tried out inquisitiveness and failed. I've tried to make my eyes big, like suspense, but she's snapped at me for that too. She's not stupid. She knows when we're faking it. After all, it's because of her that we're such phonies, such actors. So, we just sit here. We let her rant and hold court, which is exactly what she wants.

"They all know it. Your dad is the love child of your Grandma Grace and a longshoreman." The evidence for this is the fact that longshoremen are redheaded—of course they are; they are from Norway—and Grandpa Bill was dark-haired. Grandpa simply could not have been his father. Further supporting the longshoreman theory is Grandma's signature use of hearsay. "According to some of the bridge ladies," she says, "Grandma Grace needed to trap a man into marriage and fast."

Unlike Doug and me, Brian hasn't mastered the art of listening without reacting. I see him in the chair across from me, rolling his neck, blinking hard. He flares his nostrils and looks down at the Persian rug. This sets off Doug, who is a sensitive and fiercely loyal big brother. He's had enough. I look at the two of them and see their disgust, and I panic. All I can think is that we need to get them some acting lessons.

I've lost track of where she is in this story about Dad's alleged true paternity. Grandma is full of denial and good at casting wild accusations. It makes me wonder if she was the one who was actually fast and loose during the war. It's classic projection. *Look away. Nothing to see here,* I think. Then I nod, all naïve and wide-eyed and innocent, but she glares at me, and I can tell she's not really buying it.

The sun's going down on the beach just outside. It radiates under Grandma's dark screen. I'm sweating in here on her leather chair and mourning the lost opportunity to live this day in goodness and light. A hundred yards out, I see a family building a sandcastle. I hear their laughter. I see the flares of joy surrounding them as the sunlight dances, and the wind whips through their hair. The hazard flag flaps violently on the lifeguard tower. I need to get out of here, to barrel out the door and join them, into the torrent of sunshine, into the sea foam and the crashing waves. I want to lose myself in earth and sky, to dive in, and make snow angels in the sand with the happy family outside. But I pull it together. I focus my attention on Grandma. I do my job.

"That's why I'm a good swimmer," I say at the end of her story, playing two very useful cards, lighthearted and dumb, "because we are descendants of longshoremen." But I don't put the proper effort into the lighthearted part. Instead, I'm deadpan, snarky, and rebellious.

Oops.

In my peripheral view, I see Doug and Brian are on the verge of nervous laughter. *Be careful; you'll get us all in trouble,* they say with their eyes. I'm at once terrified and humored. My face muscles start to twitch. Brian's leg shakes up and down like a time bomb ticking down, and I twist my neck to the left.

Mom has sat quietly through all this. She appears emotionless but attentive. She's just putting in her time. She gingerly puts down her plate of hors d'oeuvres and excuses herself to the restroom.

Grandma takes every opportunity she has with a more intimate audience to say things even she doesn't dare say to the larger group. In few ways is she this predictable. Doug glances over at me. His eyes say, *Here it goes.*

"Fraaaankly …"

We breathe in and don't breathe out. "Frankly" is never good. "Frankly" means that even Grandma realizes the potentially harmful content of what she's about to say. And her suggestion of candor means this one's a real doozy, a fabrication that she wants us to buy into wholeheartedly.

"Frankly," she repeats, "Brian was unwanted … you know. I had arranged for your mother to have an abortion, and right when I was in the alley to pick her up, your dad called and gave her a hard time about it."

She looks eagerly to each of us for a response. This is her favorite game, and she's thrilled to be playing it. But there's something else too. It's that look from the old movies, the subdued afterglow of a fiery broad just before she lights up a cigarette. It appears that by running her mouth and letting some of the demoness out, she has relieved a bit of the tension.

"Wow," I say. I nod in what I hope looks like surprise but also acceptance. Grandma studies my face for earnestness, and I try not to flinch.

"Hmm," says Doug, looking thoughtful and solemn, but he's overdoing it. I see him lower his brow and make a face as if he's doing calculus in his head.

It's not rocket science, my eyes tell him. *Knock it off. She'll suspect all of us.*

Meanwhile, Brian's eyes have welled up with tears he will refuse to shed. His hand is balled into a fist. I think he's not even aware of it. Doug notices the balled-up pain in Brian's fist, and he turns, enraged, to Grandma.

"Ha!" she cackles. She's broken us, and she's loving it. She smirks, as if to say, "Bring it on!"

I'm paralyzed as I listen to the pounding of my heart. But in my mind's eye, I see the three of us wearing old-timey sailor outfits, white origami hats and all. Grandma keeps jabbing until Doug slams his shot glass onto the bar and bursts out in pained violence. Grandma cackles. Brian and I hold our impassioned big brother back. "Doug, don't worry, man. Forget her. She's not worth it …"

This is my brothers and me on the rocky seas. Nauseated, lonely, and hurt. At least, that's how I see it.

And, just like that, the moment is over. Grandma shoves a coat hanger in my direction. "Here! You need some pizzazz in your wardrobe, Kate. I bought it for you at Macy's. You can wear it to your school cotillion."

"Oh, thank you!" I gush, my heart still pounding in my neck. The dress is fluorescent pink with a feathered hem. I reach for the flamboyant garment, careful to look appreciative while she studies my face.

"Well! Go try it on!"

"Thank you, Grandma. It's getting late. I'll try it later." I'm exhausted and already feel too exposed to strip down to my underwear.

"Later? Why later? Try it now, Kate!"

I just shrug. Doug looks down at his watch. He stands up and paces back and forth, then peers down the hall for Mom to rescue us. But, apparently, there is time for another story.

"I set your dad up with your mom because I thought he was going to amount to something," Grandma says.

We don't say what we're all thinking. He's a nice man, a successful attorney, a good father. Those are fighting words, so we say nothing. This story always ends the same: "I should have put your mother on a couch with the first rich man I could find."

Mom walks in somewhere around "I should have." We look to her for a rebuttal. It's as if she hasn't heard a thing. She sits back down in her Knoll chair and casually picks up *Time* magazine for a closer look at the cover photo of George and Barbara Bush. Mom has learned not to argue. She has learned to deny herself a voice. Damn, she's good.

The air cools. And then, just as casually as Mom sat down, she stands and says, "Well, Mom, I think we should head home." She's slow and steady, careful not to arouse suspicion. Grandma expects submissiveness from Mom. Mom is trained, raised just like the dog. But Grandma sniffs the necks of us three, looking for signs of revolt.

By our insurgency, we put Mom at risk. Nonetheless, we siblings feel reckless today, impenetrable and united like sailors. In my imagination, we slam our whiskeys down on her enamel coffee table. "Let's roll!" says Doug, and we stand to leave. Our possibly longshoreman blood courses furiously through our veins.

Outside Grandma's gate, Doug and Brian race up the boardwalk. Shades of peach and blue hover under the darkening clouds, and shadows form under the streetlamps at the corner of each block. I see Doug's imposing figure push Brian into the beach wall at the corner as he runs ahead. But Brian's back on his feet and apparently winning the race as they approach the lifeguard tower at 12th Street. He shrieks in victory.

Mom and I walk side by side. I grab her chunky sweater around the waist. "Well, she's fun, anyway," says Mom, but the air between us is heavy and awkward.

"She's really controlling and mean, Mom."

Mom is silent. I watch our shadows on the boardwalk as we make our way home.

She had gotten all dressed up for Grandma. Over her dress, she wears an open cardigan and a wide, leather belt that lends a glamorous silhouette to the dusk. She doesn't say a word about my Vans sneakers, Doug's hand-me-down board shorts, or my lumberjack shirt.

At 29th Street, the darkness amplifies my hearing, and the sounds seem to come out of nowhere. I'm startled by the heavy breath of joggers, the light buzz of music streaming from headphones, and the chitchat of friends on roller skates.

"I have to read an essay for history class over the weekend," a girl says, skating so close I feel as though she's talking to me.

"Ugh! That sucks," a second girl responds in my other ear. In the lamplight, I see they're wearing bright lipstick and bikini tops with shorts under open hoodie sweatshirts.

"Oh my God! It's supposed to be overcast tomorrow!"

"Ew!" says the second girl.

There's only so much manic sunshine I can take. So I, for one, am thrilled.

Mom and I walk another block together in silence. At the turn for our street, she says, "Grandmama means well." But I hear her breath catch deep within her lungs as she says it.

Through the dusk, I see Brian is perched on a branch of our magnolia tree. Maria's walking barefoot in the grass, a stack of folded laundry on her head. She doesn't use her hands except to hold the hem of her skirt below the knee. She's beautiful, ageless, with high cheek bones and a demeanor that slows my pulse in an instant. She doesn't speak any English, but quick Mayan Spanish comes out in thick layers of love. She waves to us as we approach, and the hem of her Guatemalan skirt falls midcalf in a brush of teal, black, and yellow textile. From where we stand, she's a worry doll in waist-length braids.

"Brianquito, ven aca," Maria beckons to Brian warmly.

My brothers and I have grown up with two mothers. As a young child, I considered nanny and housekeeper as fighting words. Even now, there are times I can hardly believe Maria is a paid employee.

Brian drops to the ground and juts forward onto one knee in the grass. He takes off running to the door, where the five of us enter the house together. The smell of mole greets us like an ancient spirit, spreading joy in our home and adding flavor to our otherwise WASPy lives.

I'm surprised to see Dad here before dinner. Usually, he comes in halfway through, exasperated from heavy Los Angeles traffic. He places his loose change in a bowl on the kitchen counter and drops his monogrammed leather briefcase, full of what we assume are important, stress-inducing papers on the floor. He's normally in a charcoal gray suit and a wide, serious tie. Tonight, it's sweats and his red Stanford cap. He's a kid excited for tee-ball practice.

"Come on, Doug! Grab your mitt. Let's play ball!"

Doug is athletic and has what Dad calls "good instincts." Dad treats him like a star recruit and Brian, a minor league prospect. He rubs my head and walks right past me. Mom said that since I'm turning into a woman, Dad no longer knows how to interact with me. I think Mom is very kind, always explaining away others' failures. And though her explanation falls short of the fact that Dad never played sports with me and doesn't even touch upon the generations of gender socialization we have to contend with, I appreciate her attempts to raise a daughter free of daddy issues.

Dad and Doug head happily through the living room toward the back door to play catch. Brian trails behind.

"Hey, Doug, catch!" Dad tosses a baseball in Doug's direction. It flies right over his shoulder and cracks Mom's antique lamp, which slides off the lid of our piano and lands in a heap of shards on the floor. Daisy, the dog, lays just five feet from the crash. She looks mostly unfazed, like only a golden retriever can.

"James!" Mom yells at Dad. She tears up the stairs in a dramatic tantrum.

"Linda, wait!" Dad chases behind. Dad usually consoles Mom after she's been upset by Grandma. In tonight's odd twist, he's the bad guy as well as her consolation.

For a while, Doug, Brian, and I just stand here in the dark. The sun has set, our light switches, neglected. Maria's in her private quarters watching telenovelas on Univision. The house is now quiet, save for that cued-up laughter. So, the three of us shuffle down the hall and file into her TV-lit space.

Maria outstretches her arms to us, tossing aside a roll of packing tape and some scissors. On my way to her, I trip on a box at her bedside. Every month, she uses her paycheck to mail these boxes of our castoff T-shirts and shorts back home to Guatemala. Brian climbs onto her bed and slides under an arm. Doug flops beside her, and I nestle in too. Here, in the flicker of a slapstick comedy, we watch *Chavo* until it's time for dinner.

"Doug! Kate! Brian! Dinner!" Dad calls. He's seated at the table with a stern look on his face. He's in character. When we take our seats, he begins, taking his cue from Mom. He reads her face like a teleprompter. "We are never to throw a baseball in this house. Do you all understand me?" But he's the one who threw the baseball. None of us let on. We're skilled actors, trained for this kind of hypocrisy and twisted logic. "Do you understand?"

We're unsure if it's a confession or an accusation, so we keep our faces down, into bowls of mole—large chunks of carrot and potato swim in an earthy sauce of such substance and character, it's hard to take the baseball conversation seriously. Doug kicks me under the table and tries to make me laugh, but I'm emotionally exhausted and can't muster the strength to even smile.

"After dinner, you are to go upstairs and brush your teeth, put on your PJs, and get to bed," says Mom.

"But it's Memorial Day weekend," I argue. "There's no school tomorrow, and we don't leave for San Francisco until Saturday."

"Fine, then. Go clean up the den."

On our way, we cross paths with Maria, who is whistling on her way to the kitchen to clean up our mess.

಄

After twenty minutes of Doug flipping through the TV channels and Brian driving his Matchbox cars through the frontier town he's built with Lincoln Logs, Brian ravages his structures and starts putting away the pieces. Each wooden log clangs loudly in its aluminum bucket and startles Brian into moving faster. In Spanish, his hurry is "prisa." We hear it like a firecracker lit under our butts, a tidying frenzy we fall into when Maria has let us slack and Mom is on her way home. We'd better clean up for Maria's sake as well as our own.

I crawl across the carpet and help Brian toss the wooden blocks back in the bucket. He stands up on the couch and dances to the clangs, then jumps down to put the cushions back up. To the beat of my drum, the two of us tidy the room. Doug's just standing at the bookshelf, looking through a photo album.

"Doug!" I yell at him to help clean.

He leans against a wall of encyclopedias and flips through the pages, his lanky right leg crossed over his left. "Dude! Brian, Kate—come over here!" Once we're at his attention, he points to an old photo of Grandma and gets into character. "Fraaaaankly!" The three of us laugh a hysterical, stress-induced laugh. We make our eyes big and grit our teeth. We crack up some more.

Brian points down at the album. "Dude, she looks scared!" We see a young Grandma looking like a deer in headlights. She's wearing dowdy clothing and her hair, photographed in black and white, looks ... brown.

Grandma's a blonde with arctic blue eyes. Never in our lives did we consider that her hair might actually be gray. Gray-haired grannies are a different breed. We see them as knitters, porch-rockers, speakers of kind words, and doers of kind deeds. We don't have that kind of luck. Our grandma is vain and cold, a platinum-blonde destroyer of morale and spirit.

"Graduation, Bay Shore High School." I read the faded black cursive in a whisper. Doug turns the page.

"Look! She's changing into Cruella DeVille." Brian points to a forty-something Grandma Barbara in a fur coat, now dripping in jewels. Her deer-in-headlights expression now the driver barreling recklessly down the road. She's turned her vulnerability into power and intimidation. I look back and forth between the pages, seeing the before and after, catching the very moment those genes, that would be Mom's—which are now mine, mutated and set us all off on a path of fight or flight. I crank my neck to the right.

"Wow!" Brian points to a photo of Grandma and Grandpa Becker in an old Studebaker. "Cool, fancy old car!" says Brian.

I'm sure the car is cool, but I just can't shake the witchy look on Grandma's face. She looks utterly victorious, but not the happy-go-lucky kind, more like vengeful.

Grandma doesn't believe she could have "landed" my grandfather all on her own. She doesn't believe a woman can achieve any form of success without employing a fierce sexuality and some black magic. And, since Grandpa Frank came from a prominent and wealthy family, Grandma considers herself extremely successful in life. She hides her own poor upbringing and credits her fellow witches for her good fortune.

Grandma suggests that I, too, should try to master the craft, in the case it's inherited or catching. She denounces organized religion as for the others, the poor and the weak. Instead, she suggests taking matters into your own hands. That is, if like her, you possess that kind of talent. For the boys and me, the jury is still out on whether she's a legitimate witch or not, but under the tribal masks and the sacred objects in Grandma's living room, we're careful not to upset the spirits.

In rare moments of modesty or mistake, Grandma alludes to her meager upbringing. She lets it slip, that which she expends so much energy to hide. "You buy a tiny bottle of your expensive signature scent and you ration it," she says. "Sneak just a dab under his nose." Her scent followed him everywhere. In this way, she bewitched Grandpa Becker, one frugal drop at a time.

To Grandma, hard work is stupid. Smart is sneaky, and you get a thrill out of getting away with it. Best of all, she insists, "You do it right under his nose!" Whatever Grandma lacked in social status or pedigree, she made up for with a tiny dab of perfume, some magical thinking, and a little voodoo.

Brian pulls down another album and points to a Christmas photo, "Long Island, 1953." Grandma and Grandpa Frank are sitting on a Persian carpet in front of a tinseled Christmas tree. Uncle Frankie and Mom look to be four and six, and they're playing with blocks in the foreground. Our very own enamel lamp lights their formal living room. It sits on our present-day piano, precisely where it sat tonight, forty years later, before landing in a heap of shards on the floor.

Grandpa Frank passed away when Mom was sixteen. And, though we never knew him, I felt the loss of him when I walked by the vase on the piano. I'm glad it's gone, happy to start new and infuse our space with life. But to Mom, preserving our fancy home décor is a serious obligation. At times, I think it's all for *they*.

Our home is immaculate, with few creature comforts. We live with the delicate Becker antiques that Maria keeps shiny and polished. We're nervous about bumping them and breaking the legs of rickety wooden chairs when we sit on their silk upholstered cushions. Our fancy museum-like artifacts cause Mom to tread lightly too. She tiptoes through her days, trapped in the past, preserving the polish on her codependency and grief. One day, I will own a comfortably tattered throw blanket and an old farm table with peeling paint and a good patina.

Doug slams the album shut. Brian takes a cushion from the couch we've just put back together and pelts Doug square in the back with it. This means war. I stand back and avoid getting pummeled by a seat cushion that flies overhead. When it lands at my feet, I grab a blanket I've just put away and drape it over the coffee table to make an enclosure. Brian lays the rest of the seat cushions out to make walls and forms a roof out of the back cushions. We crawl commando-style through the tunnels toward the coffee table to safety.

Just when we think we've made it, Doug goes nuclear and jumps on top of our structure. It collapses and traps my left leg and Brian's right arm. We surrender to Doug and quickly put the couch back together before the boys run happily upstairs to bed. I watch a feather from the couch float slowly to the floor. The room is joyful and full of life. Our togetherness has awakened this spirit.

༺✺༻

In the morning, the smells of fresh coffee and sunny linens permeate my dreams. I open my eyes, take a whiff of the nutty roast and the warmth of my sheets, and realize it's real. The boys must still be asleep. Otherwise, I would have awakened to their shouts intertwined with my dreams.

In late spring, the heat of inland California evaporates the Pacific. The morning fog hovers where hot meets cold. We live right in the convergence zone. I love this dark energy, this June gloom.

In my favorite Surfrider Foundation sweatshirt and Jimmy'z shorts, I stumble into the kitchen where Maria's warming a tortilla on the burner.

"Mis hermanos?" I ask.

She makes a sleepy gesture with her two hands in a praying formation, her eyes closed and head tilted to one side. I can't tell if she's praying I'll keep quiet or just insinuating my brothers are still asleep.

"Cállate," (Quiet), Maria chuckles quietly. I keep quiet as I tiptoe to the fruit bowl and grab a banana. Then, I take my roller skates from the coat closet and take off out the door.

The crowds stay away on these yucky days. The shiny, happy people of Southern California hide indoors, taking refuge from the fifty-degree temperatures and overcast skies. They console one another in coffee shop lines and assure one another that the sun will return tomorrow.

But not me. I walk two blocks in my socks, downhill to the boardwalk, where I sit on the concrete and lace my skates. Mine are the real deal. They're heavy with high-end German bearings. I like to feel their soft polyurethane wheels roll over the sidewalk like a rolling pin over fresh dough.

I stand up and take flight on eight wheels, down the concrete strip, into dense clouds of the morning. I fly through these daydreams, my feet vibrating on the pavement. Save for the squawk of a seagull or the boom of a rogue wave, there is just the world whirling past. Block by block I skate. I imagine sandcastles at the water's edge crumbling under the force of the waves, and everything is new again.

This beach town is basically a playground for grown-ups. The Pacific Ocean has churned out the softest sand in a wide band that hugs the shore. I like the natural order of things here. Early-morning dolphins bob up and down like merry-go-round horses. They take turns surfing the waves. Seals swim right up to greet surfers propped up on their boards. A lone pelican—or sometimes an entire flock of seagulls—takes flight. I love everything about this beach, but not necessarily the people.

"I need complete silence," I say out loud, recalling that letter from the paranormal psychology lab. I laugh a quiet, maniacal laugh, glad that nobody's around to hear it.

At Pier Avenue, I stop in at Sponda and use a five-dollar bill from my sock for a green tea. The clerk asks, "Why the frown?" He suggests I try to smile, as if it's the new cool thing. "Don't worry," he assures me, "the clouds will burn off." But I'm not the one who's concerned.

"Hi! How are you?" he greets the next customer with his perfectly calibrated, upbeat tone. It's as though he's got short-term memory loss. I blink. I imagine for a second that he's a Beach Bot, programmed to serve coffee and mania.

"How are you?" the patron dutifully chirps before he gets to order his latte. It cracks me up that neither regards the other as having actually asked a question. I skate carefully to the counter, snap a lid onto my cup, and head for the door.

"Bye!" the clerk calls expectantly to me through the line of waiting customers. It feels passive-aggressively SoCal, like the hazy sunshine that just won't quit.

I skate on with my paper cup. I breathe and think … it's appropriate that Grandma ended up here, on this boardwalk, in this town. The superficial values of Southern California beach life and the faux happiness are just her speed. In 1963, within a year of Grandpa Frank's passing, Grandma and her second husband moved to this beach town. She vowed she'd never again shovel snow, weather sleet, or feel sorrow.

At 16th Street, her big boardwalk home looms. I speed up my pace because I'm not here for cocktail hour. I throw my arms out, one at a time, and propel the opposite skate forward until I feel the windchill increase on my cheeks and legs. When I pass house number 1600, I feel the grasp of her demons, so I skate even faster.

A jogger shuffles slowly to my left. I fly by, breathing in the life of the sea. The fog ahead looks like rice paper. I think of that episode of *Kung Fu* my brothers and I like to reenact. Doug plays the blue-eyed shogun. He sits in contemplation in his palace. Meanwhile, Brian is a visitor, so he kneels, and ever so slowly, slides the rice paper wall. Before he utters a word or makes eye contact, he bows and turns to close the door behind him. He waits there on his knees to be called to his master. He plays it so well—so aware of his own energy and so careful not to disturb the shogun's chi.

In our world, Mom calls to us from many rooms away. The vibrations of her voice ride waves of despair. They penetrate our skin and send chills down our spines. And she has no idea. "Doug, Kate, Brian! Dinner!" We three are always on alert. We hold our breath.

I wish I lived in a rice paper house.

But as persecuted as my brothers and I feel, the tension between Grandma and Mom has permeated just about everything. Mom has always brushed it off by saying that Grandma is "Old World," which we assume has something to do with obligation, immigration, and New York. But out here, out West, we are new. The laissez-faire West Coast frees us of this discord and abuse, and the sand on the beach provides our daily meditation and escape. "The beach has always been my therapist," Mom told me before I was aware enough to think she needed one.

And so, by my nature-loving nature or by Mom's nurturing suggestion, I have retreated to the sand. I make snow angels in it and have molded my little feet in its enveloping form, size by size, all these years of my youth. I dig my feet to where it's cool and sheltered on those sweltering days when the surface burns, and I take refuge down there. And I dig with my hands and make moats for the tides and rivers and swimming pools for the colonies of little sand crabs. I build bridges they can cross and sandcastles where they may live. Mom encourages us to commune with nature, to retreat to the beach. Never mind that Grandma is the reigning queen of the boardwalk.

Where the boardwalk ends, I spin. My feet slide into the only position I can remember from those days of pigtails and tutus. In ballet position number one, I glide, and my wheels turn me home. At the base of 30th Street, I sit on the cool concrete and take off my skates. I tie their laces together and throw one over my shoulder to wear them like a purse. The wheels press hard into the flesh of my shoulder blade and into my back. I don't care. I've got skater's high. I walk up the hill wearing bare feet in socks and a smile.

When I get home, Brian whacks Doug with his rash guard and winds up in a headlock.

"Kate!" It sounds like a cry for help, but then Brian yells, "Grab your board!"

I'm wearing my bathing suit under my shorts, so I grab my Body Glove spring suit from the coat closet and my surfboard from under the living room stairs and meet them outside.

Two blocks down the hill, I cross Hermosa Avenue again to the boardwalk. This time, we hop over the beach wall and onto the sand. We run like warriors to the berm. By now, the fog has lifted, and I can see clear to the ocean floor, past beds of kelp to a few rocks down there at the bottom. White foam rolls gently over the crest of the berm and over our feet.

"About fifty-eight degrees," says Doug.

"Not too bad," Brian assures me.

We look out to the break to see if it's a left or a right. We scan the horizon to see who's out there. Mom warns us to stay out of Blue Pacific's turf. She read us an article one time called "Surf Wars" about the surf gangs using switch blades to cut leashes and slash tires if someone drops in on one of their waves. Mom says we're young, so it's unlikely to happen to us, but still, we avoid the surf gangs at all costs.

There's a Mohawk bobbing up and down on the horizon. It's Todd, who lives on the corner of our block. He must have just paddled out because his hair is still high and dry.

When Doug's in waist-deep, he throws his board down, hops on, and paddles out to sea. Brian and I watch him duck dive under white breakers and glide over blue swells. We prepare for the shock of the cold and follow him out.

Across the crest of a wave, Brian gives me a frown and shakes his head. "Wheesh!" he yells through the rustle, but I take it anyway and give him a "na-na na-na na-na" face. He's right, though. It fizzles out after about ten feet, so when he's not looking, I bail and head back to the lineup. I splash water over my fiberglass board and bob over the swells like a rider on horseback.

I'm the only girl out here, but I don't think about that often. My brothers and I skateboard, surf, and play basketball on the sidewalk in front of our house. We play ding-dong ditch 'em down the block and throw water balloons over the brick walls and around the stucco corners of our neighborhood.

At night, we watch classic surf movies like *Big Wednesday* and *Endless Summer*. Throughout it all, we're sure to pelt each other with Nerf guns to dispel any bad juju.

༄

Saturday morning, the bright light radiates around the edges of my curtains. White flecks of feather and dust hover in the light. I take in the sounds of Daisy barking and my parents packing us up for our drive north to San Francisco. A pair of birds sing in the magnolia tree outside, and soft Santa Anas blow its leaves against my window.

Doug and Brian are roughing each other up in some manner or other. Their crashes and thumps startle me as they wrestle each other up against walls and onto the ground. I hide under my covers in case they head my way.

I'm lazy and content this morning. Out of another dimension, the rotary phone bubbles and shrieks. Nobody's in a hurry to answer. It rings three times again, and I hear Doug yell, "Mom, it's Grandma!"

The house goes quiet, and my adrenaline kicks in. I jump out of bed—my trunk strangled in a twist of

PJs—and head toward the kitchen. Doug and Brian are now eating cereal side by side at the table. They take turns elbowing one another and roughing up each other's hair. Mom takes the phone receiver from the hallway telephone nook.

"Hi, Mom."

She's silent for a few minutes, then she hangs up and approaches Dad, who's reading the paper. "Mom wants us to replace that window in the boardwalk house. She says it's embarrassing, that people walking by can see it's cracked. She says it looks like we spent our last dime, and now we're destitute."

Dad spits a venom he reserves only for conversations about Grandma. "That's ridiculous. She knows we're tearing all the windows out soon."

Though we live just three blocks from the boardwalk, we are "inland"—as we say in coastal California—and this is not as fancy. So, last month, Grandma convinced Mom that she and Dad were "idiots" if they didn't buy the house three doors south of her. I sat out of view on the stairwell and listened. Because we are WASPs, my parents don't raise their voices during disagreements. Instead, the tension builds up until Mom cries.

Dad sees her display of emotion as a type of manipulation. "Did your mother tell you to come crying to me about this?" he asks her. "Is this your mom's idea or yours?" But we kids know her emotion is genuine. It's a primal reaction she has—in lieu of rational conversation—when her position in the disagreement can only be justified by Grandma's preference. Grandma has inserted herself into my parents' marriage this way, and there is no room for compromise.

In the end, Dad's calm, lawyer demeanor is no match for Mom's emotional state. Within a few weeks, they have refinanced our home, taken out a construction loan, and bought a really expensive piece of beachfront property just a few doors down from Grandma. It sits empty, awaiting our next move. Whether we occupy the house now or redevelop it first is an argument for another day.

But for now, just two blocks up the hill, our sweet family home is framed by a white picket fence and a magnolia tree. Up here, we have distance from the chaos and the spectacle that takes place down on the boardwalk, refuge from prying eyes and the constant chatter of looky-loos and rowdy beachgoers. In our comfortable, middle-class home just a few blocks inland, we are underrated, and living within our budget. More importantly, we have a little distance from Grandma.

While Mom and Dad talk about whether to replace the window, the boys place their empty bowls in the sink. "What would *they* think?" I quietly say to Doug as he passes me on his way out. He picks up a basketball, bounces it, and laughs out loud. I drag a wooden chair across the floor and hop up to reach the last cereal bowl that's way up on the top shelf.

I'm up here for just a second when I notice my parents' voices have disintegrated into white noise. Up here, I'm above the room, above the drama, and somehow, above even myself.

The kitchen's quiet, and suddenly I realize Mom's talking to me. "Kate … what are you doing?"

"I was getting a bowl. It's just really nice up here. It clears my mind."

Now I'm unsure about her look, but Mom focuses in on me. Whether it's out of pride or love or sadness, she approaches me teary-eyed, and we share an awkward hug from my seven-foot height. I get this feeling that she's sending me over a border to a better life. She will stay behind to fight, content that her progeny will live on and prosper. And I think, maybe, she needs this altitude the most.

"Mom? What's that folder about me in the bottom drawer of the den? It's labeled Paranormal Psychology."

She looks startled. She pauses thoughtfully. "It's about you and your connection to truth."

"Oh." I have no idea what she means. "What's that tape that says, Psychic Reading?"

This time, her answer is immediate, spontaneous. It shows up on her face as an epiphany. "It's about me and my ability to choose for myself."

"Oh. And can you? Can you choose for yourself?"

"I'm working on it, Kate. But maybe, I can tap into your truth sometime."

We laugh dismissively. What fools we are—weirdos saying nonsense things. But I feel a truth lurking somewhere beneath the judgment and in those spaces high above the room. I eat my cereal, thinking, *Just kidding, but not really.*

After breakfast, we throw our bags into the trunk of Dad's Baltic Blue BMW sedan and we drive. The roads are wide open. The air is warm and blustery, the Santa Ana winds bringing a soft and dry touch to our typically briny breeze. Palm fronds light up a fiery orange as we pass. Flashes of white light illuminate waxy branches that dance and wave to us as we roll by. We're stars riding on a float in the Rose Parade.

Mom's voice floats somewhere between the light and the breeze. "If we need to go three hundred miles, and we're driving sixty miles per hour, how long will it take us to get there?"

"Ten!" yells Brian.

"Good guess, Brian!" says Mom. "Doug, what do you think?"

We happily hunker down for what we decide is our six-hour drive to San Francisco.

This sedan is my favorite place. The five of us are warm and snug and secure inside. We're moving together toward a common goal. There's no past or real anticipation of future events. There is just now, and we experience life as it comes, each mile a paradigm shift that delights as it happens upon us.

We pass through our small, LA beach town, past rectangular structures that sit in heavily paved yards. Our town came of age in the eighties, that era of bright red lips and form-morphing shoulder pads. The sharp right angles have prevailed, announcing man's dominion over nature. Gone are the wooden hippie bungalows and untamed lots full of grass and weeds.

There isn't a lot of green in Los Angeles. I was born into this drought-plagued land and can barely recall a time when water fell from the sky. The drought, and our trendy 1980s postmodern architecture, has virtually eradicated natural landscapes from this town—and, for those of us born here, from our consciousness. But instinct dies hard, and my ancestral subconscious yearns for dirt, water, and roots.

As we ascend the Grapevine of Interstate 5 and head into the Tehachapi Mountains, the façade of concrete that smothers earth begins to crack and fall away. Mile by mile, the dirt wins over, and by the time we reach Tejon Pass, Earth is breathing like an old, musty wine. The land fills our noses with the nuance of flora past and seasons of varying solar intensity. There's the faint remembrance of a foggy morning wafting from this dirt and of one scalding afternoon when the grass became hay.

After a while, we're outside the concrete basin, out of the constant temperatures of our marine climate. Up here, there's evidence of frost, a die-out, and a reset. I marvel at the grasses and shrubs. Nobody fertilized them or confined them to a planter box. They've been guided so intimately by the seasons, but they grow so free. I feel a natural rhythm, even if my experience down in the concrete basin doesn't lend me the history to understand it.

We're officially out of LA. I breathe a sigh of relief and let my guard down. I relax into these natural surroundings and drink in each scene without hesitation because Mother Earth doesn't manipulate.

Fancy This

When I was five, I was obsessed with the *Emperor's New Clothes*. I'd riffle through the pages to see the image of the child in the crowd who refused to be deceived. I was inspired by this child.

But mostly, I felt sorry for the Emperor. Alienated by his own fanciness, he stood inauthentic and exposed. It seemed Grandma must feel this way, a fraud under the eyes of God and the old souls of Earth who threaten to reveal her.

Time on the beach is measured by the big party weekends. In sixteen months, another Memorial Day weekend has passed, and Labor Day weekend is just around the corner. This year, I'm dreading it. We've moved into our very public teardown on the beach, and now there's nowhere to hide. All summer, this last hurrah has caused me a low-grade anxiety. Now it's Friday, and I'm on edge, wide-eyed in the face of the oncoming storm.

A few scouts have come to observe. One guy in a black trucker hat and a Descendants hoodie stands on the beach wall, sipping a beer. He'll report back like an ant, and overnight, they'll mobilize and multiply. Tomorrow morning, I'll awaken to an entire colony of them outside my window.

The pane of glass in the living room is still cracked, so we just leave it open all the time. Aside from the fact that we live on the boardwalk, it feels like we actually *live* on the boardwalk. I hear a guy whistling, like for a dog, then he calls, "Adam! Hey!"

Mom says it's Murphy's Law that the back-ordered window will arrive just in time for our demolition and remodel. I think it's actually Grandma's law since she's the one who insists that our home can't have a visibly cracked window, not for one hour or minute. I wonder who this "Murphy" guy is, why he's always playing the victim, and why anything that could go wrong in his world inevitably does. I heard Murphy's Law is a plain consequence of hurry or worry—Mom's hurry to replace the window, her worry over Grandma's wrath. I like the alliteration, anyway, and think it pretty much explains our situation, down here in this house with our back-ordered window.

A skateboard thrashes over the pavement. It sounds as if it's taken flight from our living room slate. There's a three-second delay before it comes crashing back down. I hear a succession of four ollies then, "Hey, dickhead!"

From the hallway, I see Dad on the floor of our small home office. He's slumped over a box of legal documents all marked "COPY" in red ink. He looks up at me with a theatrically pissed-off face, but I know his sentiment is genuine.

"What are those idiots yelling about now? I don't even like the beach!"

"Careful, Dad." And Dad knows just what I mean. It's a very unpopular thing to admit around here. "As they say, Dad,"—and I make *they* come out really nasal and witchy to conjure up Grandma—"life's a beach."

"Yeah, or the other word," he says, pursing his lips and furling his brow for effect.

I brace myself with my right hand against the doorjamb as I laugh and roll my eyes. It's true. All this is for Mom or for her mom. We aren't really sure.

Before I go to bed, I hallucinate a deluge. The beachgoers start running for higher ground, and we're left here in peace. But alas, the weather forecast calls for perfect, and the mania of the weekend has just begun.

༺༻

In the morning, just as I manage to put two feet on the ground, a woman's voice rises above the boardwalk and blows into my window.

"I would *kill* to live here!"

Even in its current state, the location of our home inspires envy and hatred from passersby. Quite possibly, this woman doesn't realize how sound carries. But I take her utterance as a verbal assault and duck under the windowsill to avoid enemy eyes.

When the coast sounds clear, I shimmy the wall with my back. Then I turn to peer around the edge of the window frame. It's just as I expected; they have come in droves. Ghetto blasters blare out from the back of bikes, where they're bound on cargo racks with bungee cords. Car radios sound at full volume as vehicles full of half-clothed people look for parking in our back alley.

A hoard of men in their twenties performs a sort of rebel yell before crossing the boardwalk to the surf. They look like half-peeled bananas, legs in and tops out of their wetsuits. Limp, neoprene arms dangle at their sides. But when their feet hit the sand, they take off running. They morph into barbarians storming the Pacific. Their sharply-styled short boards become spears under their arms. Zinc oxide war paint marks their cheeks, tribal band tattoos encircle biceps. They disappear over the berm to the crashing waves and valiantly, they throw themselves in.

A swarm of G-string-clad women in pink lipstick and crimped hair emerge from the south on roller skates. They bound by, one hip at a time. These bare-butt salutations seem like a cheeky "eff you" as they skate off into the distance.

"You, you, you!" The resident volleyball players chime in. It's a group of professionals and local wannabes. The ball lands in the sand of the back court. "Shit!" someone says on the north side of the net. The team on the south slaps high fives as they pass the ball and position for another round.

These voices carry down the boardwalk. They echo up our streets. Skateboard wheels collide with the edges of boardwalk pavers like percussion instruments. "Ka-thlunk, ka-thlunk ..."

"Hey, bro!" yells someone who appears from the south. He tosses the butt of his cigarette to the ground. I watch, and against my will, I listen. I organize my books from tall to small. I am a grumpy princess in my tower of cracked glass.

☙

On Tuesday, I will start high school. This fact clashes in my snarky soul as another little annoyance. I'm certain I'll find our public high school dull. I'm just thankful that Quinn is coming with me. Never has it occurred to me to want a sister, and Quinn would make a tyrant of one, but she's a pretty awesome best friend. I pick up the phone and dial the Heisers' home. Quinn answers on the second ring.

"I'll meet you at the Sandcastle," I say.

"Give me ten," she says and slams the receiver down.

I throw on the plaid boxer shorts I carefully curated from the men's underwear department at Target. I look down to ensure that the stitches I added to close the fly are holding up. I zip my favorite hoodie over my wifebeater before passing Mom and Brian in the living room on my way out.

"Headed to Quinn's!" The door slams closed.

The town is vibrating with noise and sunlight and some other manic energy that makes me queasy. Twin-engine banner planes cruise up and down the beach. They drag advertisements for Gillette razors and Sunkist soda. The air's a mess with news helicopters buzzing over airwaves about the perfect weather. The excitement level out here has clearly reached nine, and I'm having none of it. I escape the boardwalk by beelining down a cut through to the back alley.

Every block of Beach Drive is barricaded. It's a quiet thoroughfare in this war zone—my shaded oasis. But even Eden has its serpent. When I was five, Mom told me these barriers were put up in the seventies to keep the Hell's Angels from cruising the beach on their motorcycles. Now, I see angels flying like bats out of hell as I pass each barricade. On occasion, I give myself a small panic attack by envisioning a herd of chopper bikes revving in unison. I'm not really sure if the Hell's Angels are good or bad, so I accept them as a sort of gray area and proceed with my typical neurotic caution. In this town where people live to be seen, I find the back alley and hide at each turn.

Beach Drive alley opens up at Pier Avenue. Mom's "Fancy This" sign hangs above her storefront on this main drag. This old-fashioned brick façade is one of Grandma's investment properties. On my way across the street, my inner agoraphobe surfaces. I imagine Grandma peering out at me from the tiny attic window above the street. I scan my surroundings for a parked car to crouch behind, though I know nobody's actually watching.

The little gift shop at street level is intended to give Mom "something to do," to keep her contained. So, into the minutiae of inventory lists and packing slips, Mom's days are spent here. Here, she unpacks boxes of Styrofoam packing chips and small, fancy things. Here, she adorns her perfectly gift-wrapped packages with curling ribbon, so expertly scoured with the edge of her scissor blade.

Meanwhile, Doug, Brian, and I are raised by Maria. She arrived at our doorstep from Huehuetenango the year before I was born. My parents showed her to her room on the first floor near the laundry and handed over one-year-old Dougie. A couple years later, she was braiding my fine toddler hair into indigenous Mayan strands and teaching us kids to eat green apples with lime and salt.

It's been fifteen years, and still she's "the housekeeper." Mom keeps a polite distance from us kids and the housework and the cooking, opting to nibble on Weight Watchers bars behind the wheel of her car. We kids are clad in overwashed beach wear that Maria repeatedly stain treats and tumbles dry. We're fed generous portions of American PB and J and Guatemalan stews. Meanwhile, Mom is on the go in silk.

Unbound from us three, Mom is Grandma's constant companion and codependent. She returns home late each day with a headache and passes quickly through the kitchen, where the boys and I eat our dinner with Maria. Mom retires immediately to the privacy of the master bedroom. There can be one woman of the house, and she's given that role to Maria.

However, Mom owns the public spaces of our lives—the soccer fields, the school parking lot, grocery stores, and the mall. There, she mimics mannerisms and patterns of speech, searching for common ground with the other moms. I feel her alienation by fanciness. Last week, she threw out a "y'all" to Mrs. Durgin from

Nashville, who might not have the means or inclination to hire another woman to feed, clothe, and bathe her children. On the edge of the soccer field, the moms had gathered for pickup in shorts and sweatshirts, some in elastic waist pants and tunic sweaters I've seen in the *Lands' End* catalog where Mom buys our apres ski boots. I observed them, looking my own mother up and down as she spoke, clad in a fur coat and leaning casually against her white Mercedes. It was a display of tolerance of Mom, clearly the outsider trying to work her way in. I heard Mom concur, meal preparation is "so hard, with laundry and carpool." Lord help us, she said with a twang. She pretends, of course, because she's good at acting and because we have Maria.

This phoniness of appearances is endlessly confusing to me. In my toddler days, I dubbed myself "Katie the Cleaning Lady." I wiped down countertops and swept floors with my toy broom as if it were my job. When asked by strangers how it was that I spoke Spanish, I told them I was Guatemalan. "Watermelon!" they'd repeat in hysterics, clearly misunderstanding.

Grandma maintains that walking around town "like a frumpy nursemaid" is beneath Mom or any of the Beckers. We are, after all, fancier than that. And so, Fancy This has given Mom an excuse to prefer shiny objets d'art over soiled diapers and task Maria with the dirty work. But to us three, the glory is in the small things, the little acts of devotion. A powerful bond forms when Maria sparks the kitchen burner to fry up a plantain or draws us a bath and smothers our little bodies in Ivory soap. So much love and culture has been conveyed in these little acts of our early care. Because of them, we are authentically hers.

Doug's on sports fields all over the South Bay this summer. Mom whisks him down the alley and onto Pacific Coast Highway in her oversized sunglasses. Her permed hair is tousled dramatically around her shiny, red lips. Her *Flashdance* cassette tape feeds slowly through her Bose sound system. What a feelin' as she grips the wheel and assumes the aggressor stance in traffic. Just like Grandma's, Mom's driving style is pure New York.

Maria, and I continue to walk this little beach town. We take ten-year-old Brian to the park. We pick up Mom's dry cleaning and do other errands. Maria has never driven a car. But through the small alleys of our town she ushers us, conversing with us in Spanish and digging through alleyway garbage bins, collecting aluminum cans for their redemption value.

We, too, are skilled rubbish rummagers. This fact is ignored by Mom and Grandma even when we show up to the stockroom of the shop, smelling of sunshine and sweat, with dirt-marked shins and Maria's large black trash bag clanging and crunching loudly in a heap on the floor. It continues to chime until finally it settles awkwardly into the middle of our conversation. We never speak of our rubbish-rummaging with Mom or Grandma, but the embarrassing schism of our two worlds is an irreconcilable fact.

Through the storefront window, Waterford crystal shines in the beachy sun. Royal Copenhagen china, Lladró porcelain, and Anri wood carvings dare the occasional beachgoer to go inside and take a closer look.

But mainly, the gift shop is a quiet stronghold of uppity taste and knickknack worship in our otherwise laid-back town. I look in the shop window and cringe because the crystal reflects on me in an offensive and embarrassing way. I hurry past and duck into the back alley at last.

On the dark pavement in the shade, I spot a few white cigarette butts. I can almost hear the tapping of the box, smell the heavy must of her Marlboro Reds. For a while, Mom employed a shop girl we called "Auntie Anne." She took her smoke breaks out here in the shade, in the relative quiet I've grown to love. Anne was sophisticated enough to peddle Mom's goods to the occasional fancy lady about town. She dressed the part, with her neat silk scarf tied around her neck like a jetliner stewardess. Her clean, 1970s bob hairstyle framed her face just so. On the inside, however, we knew she was a free spirit—earthy and gritty. Implied in her words and mannerisms was, perhaps, her own voodoo. I imagined she drew pentagrams with sticks in the sand.

Grandma hated Anne, but I forget exactly why. I search the dark spaces of my mind for a second until I get a chill that has nothing to do with the shade of the alley or the breeze off the Pacific. Oh my God! Was it … that Anne called me … an "old soul"?

Now, I remember Grandma telling the story. I can feel the spit flying from her mouth, a venomous utterance, "In a stroller, no less!" The audacity, we are to understand, the gall, we are to believe, of this woman. How dare she make such a proclamation about toddler me.

Anne spent quiet hours in the shop with Mom. If anyone could threaten Grandma's capture-bonding regimen, it would have been Anne. But if anyone was born to reveal Grandma as an imposter, it very well might be … me.

My old soul might contrast with hers, making its newness all too clear. This is especially true since the halls of science have apparently bestowed on me these credentials. To Grandma, power is intimidation, and I might present her with a threat from within the ranks.

In the early days of the shop, Fancy This attracted one woman in town who did in fact fancy Mom's fancy things. And that is how Mom met Margaret Heiser and her two-year-old daughter, Quinn. Quinn and I were born in the same month of the same year. As Mom struggled to find her voice and distinguish herself from Grandma, Margaret had struggles of her own. In and out of clinical depression trials, she sought to alter her internal chemistry and find joy.

Paying witness to these existential battles of codependency and depression, Quinn and I are perhaps darker than we'd like to be. So, we inject humor and cope in various sarcastic ways. Quinn calls her mother "Margie" as a small act of rebellion and puts sand in empty milk containers in the refrigerator. Margaret's seemingly emotionless demeanor frustrates Quinn, so she works overtime to make her mom smile, or crack, or something … anything. Margaret spends an inordinate amount of time sleeping, and we have come to accept that as uniquely Margaret.

I retreat to my room and organize my toys and trinkets. I exert dominion over what I can. My books are organized from small to tall, my clothes from light to dark. I feel Mom's struggles with Grandma in my bones. It's a disorganization of emotions, a love-hate or a hate-love. So, I spend my free time sorting and shuffling, trying to make orderly these conflicted feelings. I organize my things. Mom spends her days shopping with Grandma. She returns with more and more junk.

Quinn and I like to simultaneously yell, "No wire hangers!" As daughters of unstable mothers, we find it cathartic to ally ourselves with Joan Crawford's daughter in *Mommy Dearest*, perhaps callously so since our mothers have never abused us. But we find it hysterically funny, and it expresses just the right tangle of obsessiveness and lack of control.

"Jinx!" Quinn says, upon our simultaneous utterance. She punches my arm. She's slaphappy and competitive, but I'm lucky to have her because she understands me and will nestle into the dark side with me. It's within the protective vortex of this snarky snobbery that Quinn and I were destined to be friends.

I reach our halfway point at 19th Street, where Quinn is sitting on the beach wall, waiting for me. We laugh as our eyes meet because it's already funny. We're silent and content together the rest of the way to her house.

Through the small, cottagey kitchen and into the quaint hallway that makes up the laundry room, I greet Mrs. Heiser. Quinn's recently retired Lycée Français uniform hangs there on the dryer. I see that Quinn's choice to attend the public school and give up Le Lycée is a bittersweet one since Margaret never leaves objects of clothing to hang within view. Everything is whisked off promptly to its proper place. I, of course, love that. Here, there's no pesky little brother to trail behind us, no big brother to call me by an unflattering pet name or throw a soccer ball in my direction. There's just Quinn and John and Margaret and their impeccably organized home.

"Oh, Jesus." Quinn rolls her eyes at me. She hates that I love the compulsive cleaning. In my life, emotional voids are filled with lots and lots of stuff, so I admire the sparsity and organization here. I also love the understated nature of this beachy cottage home. Nobody gawks through the windows or threatens to kill to live here. This little cottage is my safehouse, my refuge.

Quinn's matching twin beds have been reshuffled to the adjacent wall. I nod approvingly at the new configuration.

"Oh, it gets better." She rolls her eyes and opens a white shiplap cabinet door to show me how the board game boxes have all been stacked, big to small.

"Brilliant!" I say. "I love your mom because she reminds me of me."

"I'm glad you said it and not me."

From the bottom of the stack, Quinn grabs Monopoly and takes it to the coffee table in the little sitting room. I dislike games of any kind. It seems to me, there's enough scheming and trickery in life. But I'll play Monopoly with Quinn. Quinn is thin and naturally blonde with light brunette eyebrows. She's the only child her parents tried for over a decade to conceive. She's had epilepsy since her seizures began when we were eight. Ever since then, I've seen her as electrically charged, maybe able to access other realms. Quinn is feisty and smart and competitive. In many ways, she's my polar opposite, which is another reason we work. She steals Monopoly money under the table for the win and I let her.

We walk to Might-T-Mart and buy Twinkies. We make grilled cheese sandwiches on the apartment-sized range in her tiny kitchen and eat them outside on the concrete stoop. After a dessert of Red Vines, we settle in for more Monopoly. Quinn reads the classified ads in the *Los Angeles Times* during my turn. She's trying to throw me off, but I think she genuinely finds the "Apartment for Rent" section amusing.

"'Two-bedroom apartment in Hawaiian Gardens available for sublease. Seven hundred dollars per month,'" she reads aloud.

"I'm sure it's lovely. Just like a little slice of Hawaii in the inner city," I say, paying the banker. "Your turn."

The sun creeps underneath their Levelor blinds. It casts an orange glow in my eyes. I throw down my stack of fake money and hug my friend awkwardly around the neck. It makes me laugh because she hates affection.

"Bye. See you tomorrow," she mumbles. I half run and half walk home the exact route that brought me here. But this time, the sunset glows orange, and my neurotic phobias are replaced by a great sense of happiness.

Doug and Brian are downstairs, impressing each other with guitar chords. Brian's a bit of a musical prodigy, and with his grown-out surfer hair, he's the quintessential grunge-era kid. In his khaki corduroy jacket and black Dickies work pants, he grabs the guitar and plays our preppy older brother a Pearl Jam riff.

Doug goes back to his Massachusetts boarding school this week. In his pleated khaki pants and brown braided belt, he looks ready. His white baseball cap—covering that grown-out, good-ole-boy hair—makes him stick out like a sore thumb around here. It's endlessly amusing to Brian and me.

"Hey, Kate!" Doug must have heard the door. I quickly shuffle up the stairs. "Come here!"

"No." I hear it in his voice. They're launching an attack. It usually starts with a comment about my attire. I'm certainly not the Ann Taylor-wearing girl that Doug is used to at school.

I keep walking toward my room, but my attempt at escape is futile. Within seconds, my brothers are running up the stairs in my direction. Doug chases Brian to the top landing and assaults him with the guitar. He swings, and it hits the wall. The wooden vessel lets out a loud crack and continues to vibrate until all three of us are begging for some discipline.

"Doug!" Mom shouts at him. "The statue!"

Mom has a Rodin bronze mounted to a riser on our stairwell. We are well-versed in its provenance. It's an original copy of *The Age of Bronze,* one of a hundred that Rodin commissioned during his lifetime. It's fancy and ostentatious, a far cry from cozy home decor. We find it oppressive because it's "important" and embarrassing because it's naked. But mostly it's alienating because it was placed here to prove how fancy we are.

Doug ignores Mom's pleas about the statue and comes after me. "So, are you the janitor?" He grabs my wallet on a chain from my pocket. "Good thing you have those work boots on." He kicks the toe of my Dr. Martens.

I say nothing, but I'm glad that my wallet's on a chain and my boot has a steel toe.

My brothers lose interest in me and just walk away. "Hey, Mom, what's for dinner?"

"Oh, I'm sure we'll find something in the freezer."

It's Maria's day off, and Mom has just gotten home from a day of shopping with Grandma.

"Kate, come look!" I'm beckoned to marvel at the treasures of the day. The glass coffee table that houses our zoo full of crystal animals is now covered in loot. Scattered around the zoo are a few leather belts, a furry vest, and some heavy costume jewelry necklaces made out of plastic, animal-shaped beads. I think these are hardly improvements on God's creations.

With her retail license for Fancy This, Grandma takes Mom downtown to the wholesale markets. At the Giftmart and the Clothing Mart, they buy samples of the newest styles going to market next season. I've been sworn to secrecy about this fact. When I was ten, I saw Grandma's retail license on the counter next to a parking receipt from the Clothing Mart. I was cornered and got a stern talking-to about the importance of image and keeping up with the Joneses. "We want people to think we spend more money on our clothes than we actually do." I was forced to swear that I would never reveal this secret to anyone. Their deceit is all for show. And of course, they are thrilled to be getting away with it.

However, underlying their thrill lurks the stench of desperation and inauthenticity. It's laughable, except that I'm truly scared of them. I'm happy that I don't have any lies to cover up myself. I'm paranoid enough as it is.

Voice Lessons

In freshman algebra, Alden's making those bong water sounds with his mouth, which is apparently hilarious because he won't stop laughing. I whip around to catch a quick glance. He's hunched over his desk with his face burrowed in his arms. His beet-red, sunburned complexion appears between locks of salt-crisp, blond hair. The audible bong simulation is impressive, especially since he's probably actually stoned.

At the front of the room, Mr. N's droning on about linear equations. Shelby, who's sitting in the back row, lets out a quick laugh. But Mr. N goes on teaching algebra, pretending he doesn't hear the bubbling saliva bong water or the intermittent rounds of laughter.

Quinn fumbles and drops her pencil onto the desk in front of her. We watch it roll slowly to the edge of the table and fall to the floor. She swoops down to grab it. "Please, oh please, don't tear me away from this." She's sarcastic and upside down. She grabs her desk to right herself, and her hair swooshes and flops back into place. Involuntarily, I laugh out loud.

The two of us have just tested into the advanced placement track, so we won't be attending class with Alden or many of his surfer friends or the class clowns anymore. "No, really. I'll miss it," Quinn mumbles. I agree; our days here in general population are filled with such spontaneity and art.

It's been two months since we started high school—forty ascents up the sand dune and into the eucalyptus grove to the big public school. It's a nice walk, even if I am relegated to pedestrian status. I get a nice view of where the South Bay plateau crests and dips at Pacific Coast Highway, the curve of the shore and Catalina Island in the distance.

On my treks in and out of school, I clutch my backpack straps tight for moral support. Meanwhile, shiny-sexy upperclassmen buzz past in hand-me-down sedans and SUVs. In a dark corner of my mind, I imagine they gesture as they pass me, awkward and adolescent, "Seeya, loser!" Their puberty is cast off like snake molt. But just under my blemished face and baby fat lies an explosion of adult life. Inside, imprisoned, lies the shiny-sexy me.

Today, Quinn and I are getting a ride with our new friend, Jenny, and her older brother, Matt. Quinn picked Jenny up in the locker hall somewhere. At first, I was suspicious of her and jealous, like I was being replaced. But, behind soft brown locks that flank her face, Jenny's warmth bubbles over. It floats softly like soap suds catching rainbows in the light. I can't help but like her. Her brother's a soft-spoken musician type who sorta looks like Jesus. The distinctive whirr of his 1975 VW bus is an integral part of the 3:20 p.m. ode to joy in the student lot. The twenty-year-old starter strains to turn over, finally bubbling to life, a percussion instrument, adding a heartbeat to the symphony of the dismissal hour. Today, it's my anthem, ours.

Aside from the cruelty of freshmanhood and the hazing of our imminent physical maturity, Quinn and I are actually having fun. As it turns out, there's a place for snarky introverts like us in the halls of the American high school. Our call for independence is answered here. Our sardonic attitude and flannel-clad, Dr. Martens-wearing angst has found a home. And because of Mom's codependency and Margaret's depression, Quinn and I are left to our own devices. We're pretty much poster children for the cause.

"ACES. ACES. ACES," I repeat as I follow Quinn to her locker.

"OCD much? What the hell are you saying?" She pelts me lightly with her backpack. What is ACES?"

"It's my list. Apple core. Swim Cap, Enrollment papers, and *Siddhartha*. Throw away, find it, fill them out, read it. You owe me a quarter for saying hell."

Being feral daughters of fancy, refined mothers, we try to raise one another as our mothers would please. We started charging each other for swear words about a year ago, but no money has actually changed hands and no fewer expletives uttered. Having seen a lot of bad-doers with impeccable lexical hygiene, I have a hard time with the idea that some words are innately bad. In protest of this hypocrisy, I contine to swear. I tell Quinn I'm conducting a study in etymology and authority and continue to challenge this phony concept. Oh, and I continue to charge Quinn each time she swears.

"Yeah, yeah. Put in on my bill," she says. "Oh, and add C for chill out. You really are insane."

"Maybe so," I agree.

I feel like I'm undercover. At any given moment, the mothership might return, and I'll be reabsorbed by the great vibration. The superficial and material interests of high school kids make me squirm. I'm a skeptic and would-be nihilist, except I'm starting to think that what seems to matter is what we make of matter. The stuff of the world agitates. It motivates me to act. I clean, I sort, I align; on all sides, the edges of my books are equidistant to the corners of the tabletop. The world is beautifully malleable, here for world-building. This might be my new religion.

Quinn, on the other hand, observes her OCD with caution. After all, it could be a symptom of inherited cortisol and serotonin imbalances. But, we concur, cleaning and sorting are feel-good activities. On occasion, I'll dare her to leave that drawer across the room slightly ajar, just to see how long we can both stand it.

"Over here!" Jenny's waving to us from across the parking lot, the lone girl in a gaggle of boys. She's all little-sister sweetness, sitting on the floor of the VW bus with the sliding door open. The Allman Brothers jam in the background. A hacky sack flies over the vehicle and lands on the windshield. Within the frame of this scene, Jenny looks connected to community and carefree. She's quite unlike me. I'm drawn to her, like she holds the key to lessons I have yet to learn.

Our group of friends is made up mostly of Jenny's brother's friends, a bunch of shaggy-haired juniors. We know them by their last names and by their cars. As world-building goes, these lifelong friends have built a cozy one, full of hygge. Quinn and I are from the town next door and are just now making inroads. I'm honored to be in the presence of their kinship and comfort, the inside jokes, and folklore of over a decade. Even if I don't understand what they're talking about, their warmth and humor washes over me all the same. This group isn't the cool kids in the quad. Their bonds go beyond all the high school posturing and competition. These are real friends with no popularity contest to win and nothing to prove. Quinn and I are on the inside of the outsiders, and there's no place I'd rather be.

This could be the year I was born. Jenny's 1970s bell-bottom cords grace her brown, suede Clarks Wallabees. Her tie-dye T-shirt is thin from decades of air-drying on a clothesline. I look across the parking lot, into the cloth, to the innocence and softness of a time I could not possibly remember but which I so thoroughly crave—an era when we toddled for the first time over shag carpets, bringing new promise and joy to the world. Unlike the predictable plaid flannel shirts and jeans of this grunge era, our little group's aesthetic is retro and nostalgic. We are the children of the flower children, our origination date frozen in time.

But, not actually me. I carry the legacy of the space-age square—of fitting into that man-made box of chaste debutante expectation. Dad, who was a junior at Stanford, escaped the draft by volunteering for a desk job to which he was never called. Mom kept her hair short and continued to wear a bra, big curlers, and pearls. And though both my parents actually objected to the war, they were decidedly establishment.

An El Segundo Blue butterfly flaps her wings in my view. Quinn and I make our way past the dissipating group to Jenny and Matt Cipriani, another junior, Ross, and the orange VW bus.

Inside, I'm fumbling with a heavy, metal, seatbelt buckle on a limp webbing of black nylon. This vehicle smells like old vinyl, motor oil, and recklessness. Jenny giggles at my failed attempts to buckle. She reaches over and cinches me. She's got an easy smile and a soft flower-child vibe that goes beyond her style choices. Before I ever saw her parents, I knew her dad must be tall and have long hair and wear Birkenstocks and that her mom parts her naturally gray hair carelessly down the middle.

Jenny and Matt were molded by this ease. This hand-me-down vehicle of Matt's is definitely not my Mom's white Mercedes or Dad's Baltic Blue Beemer. As I sink into the awkward squeak of the springboard seat, I feel out of place, like uptight yuppie scum.

The bus whirs alive and jerks out of the parking lot and onto Pacific Coast Highway. Matt turns up Blind Melon. The huge, roll-down windows let in a torrent of wind, and I can't hear what anyone's saying, but I see lips moving and golden hair flying around in the sunny head room.

༄༅

"Hi, Kate! How was school?" I'm irritated by the intrusion and startled to hear Mom's voice. She's not usually here when I get home. I relish in that hour or so before anyone but Maria is around, when Mom is still doing whatever she's been doing with Grandma. I would put on my sweats and sit on the couch, pretending to do my homework, but really I just gaze out at the pier and the bay and enjoy the silence.

"Mom? What are you doing here? No charity group meeting, no shopping expedition? Where's Grandma?"

"I thought I'd be here when you got home from school."

"Why?"

She doesn't answer. She just watches as I dump out my backpack on the kitchen counter. I get straight to my acronym—tossing the apple core, locating my swim cap around the corner in the laundry room, and tossing *Siddhartha* on the countertop. Of course, I'm sure to align the horizontal and vertical corners of the paper even with the edges of the counter.

"What are you up to?"

"Choosing an elective, Mom. These are my reenrollment forms." She hovers over me and surveys my choices. I roll my eyes. I look out the window at the pier and catch the very moment the lights flicker on.

"There is a window of opportunity for everything," says Mom. "Don't miss your opportunity to find your voice."

"What?" I mumble. I tap my pencil on the granite.

Mom points to the word "drama."

"I feel like acting is your thing, not mine ... really?" I roll my eyes all huffy and sigh.

"Yes!" She doesn't flinch, and because shop and home economics hold no cache for me, I check the box.

⁘

It's November, and I'm standing under hot stage lights during fourth-period drama. "I don't believe you, Ophelia, again!" Mrs. Basure yells from the front row of the school auditorium. I say my line again, louder.

"But, good my brother, do not as some ungracious pastors do, show me the steep and thorny way to heaven, whiles, like puff'd and reckless libertine, himself the primrose path of dalliance treads, and recks not his own rede."

She rolls her right hand like a wheel and yells, "You are denouncing Laertes's hypocrisy. He lectures her about things he refuses to do himself. Also, you're a woman in a man's world. More passion. More authenticity!"

"Authenticity?" I'm exasperated. "I'm finding my voice. I'm acting!"

Apparently, I'm not funny. The teacher flashes disapproving pupils and says, "Stop acting. You need to *feel!*"

"Okay ..." I regroup to deliver the line again.

This time, I don't try to act. I think of the hypocrisies we endure, and the lies we accept, the abuse. How Grandma beats Mom down. I think of baseballs and antique lamps and the authenticity of a bowl of mole.

How we fail to look inward, how it's easier to blame others for our failures and disappointments than to speak our own truth. I'm furious and indignant and oddly … vulnerable. For a second, I forget where I am and wonder if I even got my lines right.

Mrs. Basure cuts into my daydream by saying, "Perfect! Next scene!" I scurry off.

In my auditorium seat, I'm surrounded by a mess of backpacks, strewn sweatshirts, a few loose library books, and a rampant pair of gym shoes. I survey the scene and twitch a little. But this time, it's not the disorganized room that's making me feel so vulnerable. I'm still reeling from delivering my lines. Who knew that acting was so *real*?

Just before dismissal, Mrs. Basure gathers us to rehearse the last song of the performance. We stand around her piano on the theater floor as she begins to play. Our version of *Hamlet* is intense and heady. It's a tragicomedy, as I suspect most everything would be if we were really being honest. But, there's nothing heady or dark or overthought about us coming together in song.

Our collective voices vibrate the room and transcend the here and now. Waves undulate. My fingertips tingle. We are nothing but energy and light and never so much as when Mrs. Basure switches over to her acoustic guitar. That wooden gourd, seemingly still attached by roots and trunk to the earth that sustains us. The material of the wood and the transcendence of the spirit meet somewhere in the vibration of our song and strum to the very core of me.

I walk this afternoon through seagull cries, under gray skies. I'm flanked by a charcoal sea. Whatever winter we experience in Southern California, this is it. The Pacific is darker now, the sky crisper. The lighthearted sunshine has taken a back seat to this melancholy, and the beach is desolate. It rests. Without the peer pressure to party, the frenzy, and the mania, without the noise and the crowds and the sensory overload, I rest.

Twenty-five minutes into my walk, I push open our front door and climb the stairs to the second-floor kitchen, glancing out at the windswept beach. Footsteps in the sand have been filled in and retextured into zebra stripes by the breeze.

I hear Mom in conversation. "The lease should be assignable, Mom. It says it is."

I step farther into the room to see her sitting at the kitchen island and doodling on her yellow legal pad. For about a minute, Mom swirls her black pen, making dark shadows on leaves and flowers of her own design. This is an activity reserved for only one occasion. She's on the phone with Grandma. The doodling is her distraction and escape. The boys and I know never to move this notepad. It shall remain on the telephone stand where the wall jack meets the plug, where Mom sits captive, plugged into conversations in which she holds back the things she'd like to say for fear of the wrath they will bring. The pad is marked over and over in black ballpoint pen; swirly vines and leaves and flowers run six pages down like deep veins of unspoken truth.

"But she won't buy the shop from me unless you assign her the lease, Mom. Why wouldn't you just assign her the lease, so I can sell the business?"

Mom's quiet for about a minute, then starts talking really fast. "I want to do other things now, and I can sell the business and the merchandise and make money! Why would you make me close down in economic failure when you can just renew the lease?"

Mom darkens a leaf, swirls a vine. She holds the receiver in her left hand. She's silent for another minute.

"What do you plan to do with the space after the lease expires in January? You don't know yet?"

After another minute or two of silence: "Mom, I'll call you later." She hangs up, exhales, and turns my way. "Hi, Kate!" The chirp in her voice doesn't match the defeated expression on her face.

"Hey, Mom." I open the refrigerator.

"So, how was drama class? Finding your voice, faking it till you make it big?"

Her words hit a nerve with me, and I grimace. "Actually, Mom, you can't fake it till you make it. I mean, I guess it depends on what you're trying to accomplish, but you can't fake your truth."

Mom laughs a nervous, little laugh, as if she's raised a monster. I imagine she's mapping out the way to grab a knife from the block on the counter, but instead, in a big Broadway voice she says, "'To be, or not to be!'" I wonder if she's lost her mind.

I don't know why, maybe hormones, but I grimace again. "What kind of question is that, Mom? Really?"

I don't think this is the direction she wanted to go. I don't care. I go on, know-it-all me. Ironically, I know I'm being a know-it-all. I just can't help it. "Don't you think the question should be more like, 'Since we are in fact here, what are we doing with our lives?'" Mom looks out the window as though she sees a ghost.

"Hey, who's your best friend?" Now she's fake-smiling, and it's weirding me out.

"Uh … what?"

"Who's your best friend?"

"I don't know. You?"

"No!"

I feel a pit develop in my stomach because I know what's coming. Mom's ramping up, heading my way and swaying from side to side. She does this sing-song cabaret thing, like Liza Minelli on Broadway. Now, she's becoming a loud-talking, grand-gesturing broad in bright red lipstick. Mom's brash and ballsy Broadway demeanor clashes fiercely with today's laid-back androgyny in plaid. Sure, her jean jacket with shoulder pads is embarrassing, but it's not just that. My heart aches for her because I know this self-expression, the power and the joy she portrays is merely a façade.

Mom was taught to please other people at the expense of herself. And just like on Broadway, much of what she expresses to the outside world is an act.

After a particularly tense cocktail hour, the boys and I walked home down the boardwalk, forced to link arms with Mom and sing songs from *Bye Bye Birdie,* forced to "put on a happy face." My brothers and I sang out loud through gritted teeth, just hoping nobody we knew was out to see it. But we did it like soldiers, building a scaffolding of happiness for Mom.

Her song and dance is still a go-to, but I can feel her searching for her authentic voice. The façade is slowly falling away, and ever so subtly, she's trying to stand up to Grandma.

"So, who is it? Whose your best friend?" Mom demands in an over-the-top stage voice.

I surrender. "Me! Me," I repeat softly. "I'm my best friend."

I walk up to Mom and give her a big hug. She kisses my forehead, her own flesh. Though she seems distracted, I realize she's been watching me from the wings, and it's because of her careful and deliberate guidance that I'm so comfortable in my own shoes.

Once I've turned on the faucet to wash my hands, she begins singing Whitney. She gets louder as she continues along—pointing a toe, popping a hip. This is awkward. Oh, there they go, jazz hands.

I spin around, flicking droplets in her direction, and we sing "The Greatest Love of All" together.

We conclude Whitney's 1985 ballad, and Mom's over the top lesson on self-love by singing the last line together. And I realize, too, that Mom intends to build me a fortress of self-love that will get me through my darkest days.

"Nobody can hurt you unless you let them," she says.

"Yeah," I say. "Cool. Got it ... so, you're selling Fancy This?"

"I want to. I found a buyer who will pay top dollar. But they won't buy it without an extension of the lease from Grandma."

"And she won't agree to that?"

"Well ... you know Grandma. She's silly."

Yeah, I think to myself. "And a total bitch," I say out loud. Mom blinks twice and says nothing, but I'm no debutante.

The metal door knocker startles me. I run downstairs to let Quinn in. She bolts ahead, up the stairs and past the kitchen toward my room.

"Hi, Mrs. Brewer!"

"Hello, Quinnie," Mom calls after her. Mom is sweet, humble, and egalitarian. Our thirty-year age gap is nothing but the passage of time. She treats Quinn like a peer, and I think this is intentional, as it's the farthest thing from Grandma's domineering matriarchy.

In my room, we lie on our backs with our socked feet up on the wall. "You know who's a beast?" Quinn asks me.

"Uh, no ..."

"Knock, knock. Come with me to get Brian, or stay here with Maria?" Mom leaves without hearing my answer. Neither one of us moves.

"Anyways," Quinn resumes, "the beast is that guy whose locker is in the sixties hall, second one to the end."

I have no idea who she's talking about. "So, what exactly is it about him, though?"

As far as the laws of attraction go, our science class curriculum dulls compared with our own theories. We agree that for some unexplained reason, some objectively unattractive males are the most crush-worthy of all. Hence, there's a certain *je ne sais quoi* about certain people that has nothing to do with their looks. We've labeled these subjects "beasts," in homage to the Rolling Stone's song, *Beast of Burden,* and, of course, after Mick Jagger. We're prepared to spend our four years of high school exploring this concept.

"He's that guy who's been playing drums with Matt and Ross in Ross's basement lately. Remember?" I don't. "I think it's that he doesn't care, you know?"

"Can't be that. There are plenty of assholes who don't care." I still don't know who she's talking about.

"You owe me a quarter."

"Fine. Put it on my tab."

"Eric. His name is Eric, and he just seems like he's very real and completely committed to his music, you know? Like he's one hundred percent doing what he was meant to do. He's not hot, but he's a total fucking beast."

"Quarter."

"Yeah. Yeah …"

"Well, if he isn't Mick Jagger, I might not be impressed."

"Fair enough," agrees Quinn. "But I'd be his 'beast of burden' anytime."

⟡

When Mom and Brian are back in the kitchen, we emerge into the smoky fragrance. Maria passes through quietly, a bushel of green leafy something in one hand and a steak knife in the other. A pot of mole sauce bubbles on the stovetop.

Maria's mother was the village medicine woman. In the evenings, Maria tends to the narrow sand patch on the west side of our house with this passed-down knowledge. I like to imagine that she performs secret rituals out there with her plants. Inside, she makes teas from her herbs when we're sick; she dries them and crumbles them into our stew for dinner.

"Huehuetenango, Huehuetenango," I say audibly but hushed because it's really just for me. I like its softness, the way it rolls off my tongue and how it changes me into my Spanish-speaking alter ego. "Huehuetenango," I whisper, feeling like my authentic self.

Quinn slaps me on the arm. "You sound insane."

Most nights, while Maria cooks and tends to her garden, Mom is out in stop-and-go traffic, heading to the mall and Target between the to and fro of soccer practice. Mom rushes past me with her Louis Vuitton over her shoulder, a busy and important lady about town. Passing on the self-soothing domestic tasks here at home, passing on the grounding and nesting, the fluffing, folding, and cooking, she doesn't make herself at home in our home. Instead, she grabs her car keys and a Diet Coke and rushes through another door.

Quinn's hovering over the stovetop. "Smells awesome!" I follow her to the threshold of the laundry room, where Maria's folding laundry. "Smells tan bueno!" Quinn tells Maria in Spanglish, making Maria laugh.

I rarely see Mom eat. She doesn't have time for food or other little joys. When she does have time, she's busy "being busy." We know this is Grandma's influence. We see Grandma gesture a flippant wave, stirring meaning into these words, conjuring up some upper-class mojo as the words are uttered. It suggests, "Nonsense, I'll do what I damn well please. Housework is beneath me."

So, throughout our toddlerhoods, we kids ran to Maria. We ran to her with scraped knees. We ran to her bedroom at night when the winds animated the magnolia tree and it rapped on our windows. We ran to Maria, who folded and ironed and scrubbed, who tended to steaming pots. And she still does, whistling as she works, laughing freely, and being totally present for us kids.

But increasingly often now, Mom sits at the kitchen counter, waiting on one of us for a chat. She's awkward, expectant. She applies lipstick, as if she awaits her lunch date. The boys and I don't know what to make of this or whom to run to now.

It's Thursday, the official night off for Southern California's domestic help. The changing of the guard happens at 5:00 p.m. On the dot, Mom has emerged from her room with fresh lipstick and freshly combed hair. She sits upright at the kitchen counter with arms and ankles crossed as if she awaits some sort of consultation.

Maria passes through, one last time, to turn off the burner. She opens the freezer and surreptitiously holds up a Stouffer's creamed spinach with Salisbury steak—"TV dinner," as Mom calls them. She sticks her tongue out at me and makes a face as though she's been poisoned. I laugh. She throws it back into the freezer and leaves the kitchen, but first she points to the stovetop and winks.

At exactly 5:30 p.m., Quinn looks at the time on the microwave. She stands up and says, "Well, it's the witching hour." She says nothing else and takes off down the stairs for home.

Mom's still at the kitchen counter. I take the seat next to her. "Do you think you'll miss the shop, Mom?"

"Nope. I'd rather be here with you kids."

I get up and serve myself a plate of mole. "But, what would you do all day? Are you gonna start cooking and ironing and stuff?" I hold back my hair and take a sniff of the white heat from my dish. Maria returns and sparks up the burner before Mom can answer. I hear the sizzle of a frying pan behind me and smell the starchy sweetness of a plantain. We seem to have lost our place in this conversation. The questions seem already answered now, so Mom sits quietly with her chin in the palm of her hand. Her long skirt drapes over crossed knees at the kitchen counter.

"Comé" (Eat), says Maria. She serves Mom a hot plate of mole. We eat our mole together. It tastes like herbs and earth, like chocolate, and a bit like love. I stare down at my homework. I look over at Mom.

She's got dark, Snow White hair and perfect, olive-toned skin. She's delicate and pretty. Not me. I'm sort of pink and freckled and athletic, with quintessential beach hair that comes from a combination of year-round swim team damage and the use of hydrogen peroxide in the sun. It's still wet from today's workout and crunchy like straw from all the chlorine. Mom uses her hairdryer each morning and curls the ends of her cleanly trimmed bob under with a big, round brush. She tells me it's rude to show up with wet hair in polite company. Mom educates. She's careful not to criticize, and she compliments me often for my quirky differences.

I push my homework binder aside. "So, what exactly did you do today, Mom?"

"Actually, I started writing that book for teenage girls I told you about."

"Really? That's awesome!" I had expected a bargain hunt at Grandma's whim or an obsessive search for exactly the right napkin rings. I didn't expect this.

I have considered Mom a consumer. She inhales. She drives. She buys, buys, buys. She consumes gasoline and all categories of consumer goods. And though the sweetness of life should be celebrated from time to time, and the little joys should be consumed, I think it's the expenditure that really matters, that bitter work of giving back.

"Yeah, I really believe in this project, and I'm having a lot of fun!" Mom's voice is emphatic, so I study her face for signs of fakeness or cabaret.

I have a bad habit of studying faces. Sometimes, I see more than I'd like to see, a disingenuous smile or an unsure assurance. However, I don't see Liza Minelli or any forced song and dance right now. I blink twice and see she really means it.

"I'm doing research about body image over the ages. That's where I'll start." Mom grabs a binder from the telephone table and shows me her research. There's a drawing of a very curvy woman with elongated earlobes and another of a waif with a really long neck. "Then, I'll go on to talk about the basics of aesthetics and proportion and skin tones and different body types and feature shapes."

"This is exciting! So, it's all about positive body image and self-esteem, right?" I flip through the pages. "Then, what about the psychological part? You know, like how to help people like themselves, regardless of body image?"

Mom pauses. "Well, I think it has to start with a strong and positive female role model, right? That's a whole other book, I think." She scratches her head. She looks stumped.

I flip another page. There's the Apple, the Pear, the H, and the Hour Glass. The Spring skin tone, the Autumn, and Winter. I'm not into makeup or hair products, but I know my body is H-shaped and my clothes need to balance my shoulders with my hips. I know the only red that will ever look good on me has warm, orange undertones because I'm a Spring-Flow-Autumn. Being the daughter of a fashionista has unusual consequences for a beach girl who couldn't care less about the latest trends. I appreciate myself for my differences, even if they aren't ideal *Cosmopolitan* magazine cover body parts. I can confidently dress them and make the most of what I've got, if I really care to. They're just tools for my toolbox, Mom says, and she carries on accepting me in my brother's board shorts, with my stick-straight hair parted dowdily down the middle.

Mom, on the other hand, is an immaculate and skilled dresser. That part is easy for her. As she sits next to me, thinking of ways to teach self-esteem, I think about her own self-worth. She certainly wasn't gifted any validation from Grandma. It hasn't come from keeping up with the Joneses or by chasing the latest fashion trends. But I get this feeling that maybe it's still to come.

Mom smiles and grips my hand in hers. "I hope this book will help girls like you have a better future and more confidence." I look out toward the pier because a breeze has ruffled my papers, and it seems that the window is wide open.

On the first day of the new semester, I met Nicole. In one fell swoop, she flipped down the auditorium seat next to me, crashed down, and put up her feet. Without looking my way, she started talking like we were old friends. "So, how did you end up in here? Are you afraid of cutting off a finger in shop or becoming a sexist stereotype in home ec too?" Nicole is small and undeveloped and looks about twelve, but when she speaks, her age comes out in multiples, like dog years. I do that quick glance, and she's iridescent and powerful, like a garden pixie. If I were Auntie Anne, I'd for sure call her "an old soul."

It's the other cast's turn to rehearse, so Nicole and I sit in our cushy auditorium seats with our feet up on the chairs in front of us. We doodle in spiral notebooks with her sparkle gel pens.

After the bell, I go to my locker and start gathering my things. Nicole's pointy chin juts around my locker door. "What, no magnets for your locker wall? No decorations? What are you up to?" Her confident blue eyes demand an answer. I didn't even hear her fairy wings flap as she approached.

"Uh ... I don't like clutter. I'm going home now because the bell has denoted that the school day is officially over. You might consider doing that too."

"Yeah, yeah, yeah. Come to my house. It's close."

Instead of walking west through the eucalyptus grove and down the slopes to my affluent boardwalk enclave, we walk east. At her little wooden house off Artesia, she stealthily retrieves a key from under the doormat. After the fact, she looks around to see if anyone on the street was looking. When she turns the key and pushes the door open, a waft of stagnant air that smells of mildewed laundry, day-old trash, and musty house renders me speechless.

"That's my mom's boyfriend," Nicole says as we enter the tiny entry hall and pass a wooden side table with a framed photograph of a slightly heavy, bearded man in a red cap.

"Cool. Do you like him?" I ask solely for the purpose of seeming comfortable with this whole scene.

"Mm, not really." Nicole is neutral, unattached. "This is my room." I take another step inside the tiny room. I move my body slowly to deemphasize the tightness of the space, but on second thought, I'm probably the only one who finds the close quarters awkward.

"Where is everybody?"

"Work."

"Right," I say, cool and with Fonzie-like subtlety.

"It's just us. My mom's boyfriend used to live here, but he started drinking again, so my mom put her foot down. He comes around when he's on the wagon." Nicole starts rifling through a cabinet for a bag of chips. She talks and talks. Nicole's mom has a new desk job she's excited about since it pays better. Only thing is that she gets home after 8:00 p.m. because of the long commute. My heart sinks when I hear this news. But, Nicole looks utterly content. I don't dare tell her that my Mom wants to sell her trinket shop in order to be home for my brothers and me, let alone that Maria is there, too, keeping the air moving and the laundry fresh; she takes the trash out twice a day.

⸺ ⁂ ⸺

A few weeks in, we've got our routine down. As fourth-period drama begins, Nicole hands me her sparkly blue, green, and pink gel pens. We cozy into our auditorium chairs, pull down hinged, wooden tabletops, and hunker down.

"I love how you're not a robot," she says to me.

"Huh?" I laugh because I sort of already know what she means. "Nope ... it's a curse."

"I'm serious. I can probably actually talk to you."

"Yes, absolutely." I nod. I look down at her paper and see she's drawn a 3D robot and named her in block, gangster letters, "Botty the Quadie."

This high school is the breeding ground for the beach bots that flock to the sand outside my windows, so it shouldn't surprise me that my peers exhibit the same superficial qualities. What does surprise me is that Nicole has taken this concept right from my own imaginings.

Throughout our rehearsals, we talk about our lives, our hurt, our disappointments, and our dreams. Nicole is direct and confident. She knows who she is. Surprisingly, she also seems to know who I am. My heart is warmed, thinking there are two kinds of friends: those who know everything about you because they've been there, and those who might as well have been. As we chat, Nicole doodles flowers and vines and wizards with thunderbolts. But mostly, she draws robots. By the time the bell rings and the auditorium lights come back up, we find ourselves surrounded by them.

We follow the auditorium steps up toward the open door and out into the haze and the salt spray of day. It's bright, but somehow gloomy, as the light sopped brine of the coast can be. I hear a seagull cry as it flies by, and I wonder if it, too, finds the monotony of these afternoons tiresome. Nicole's holding the door open for me when I glimpse the black outline of a rain cloud on the inside of her wrist.

"What's up with the cloud and the rain?"

She answers me in the form of a question. "What if you had to draw your ultimate belief system, and it would be tattooed on your body forever? What would it be?"

"Uh?" I roll my eyes. "Tattoos are for 'the other girls,' Nicole. Whatever would *they* think?"

"Oh, right. *Them*. The fancy, insecure, society people who rule your grandma's thoughts. Oh, for sure, your mom and grandma would *kill* you for ruining their blue-blood image, but what about you? What do you think?"

"Okay ... if I *had* to pick, it would be a sun."

"Yeah, and? That's your message? That's weak."

"What?" I spit. "Is this rain cloud your ultimate belief?" I flick her wrist with my pen.

"Sort of," Nicole says steadily. "It's just a reminder, you know ... that sadness is a part of happiness. That balance is motivating to me."

On the sunny boardwalk at home, I'm stewing over Nicole's words. I get out my notebook and my black Sharpie and draw my sun. When its rays come full circle, I give her Egyptian eyes and outline them in black. I perfect her voluptuous lips in red. Her rays undulate like the dancing arms of a many-armed god. She is so full of light and joy. And somehow, she's so utterly incomplete.

I stare at her for a few minutes. Before I realize it, I'm drawing a tiny circle within her plume of rays. It's bifurcated by a curve and makes two opposing paisleys. In the head of the paisley on the left side, I draw a small, black dot. On the right, I draw a tiny, hollow circle and color black all around it. I see the interdependence and balance of yin and yang. I see clearly that Nicole's right—without darkness, there can be no light.

It's the 3:20 p.m. ode to joy. Quinn waits with me until Nicole pulls up to the corner of Ardmore and Peck in the passenger seat of her neighbor's VW Thing. I realize there's no way Nicole was in sixth period if she's already back here with her neighbor. Before they come to a stop at the curb, Quinn's already walking away. She mumbles back at me, "Don't get hepatitis or AIDS. If you do, I won't feel bad for you."

I duck into the back seat of the yellow Thing. Nicole slides the front passenger seat forward, gets back in, and pulls the door closed. Before she's buckled, we're rolling.

"Hi! I'm Sam." So this is Nicole's cool, nineteen-year-old neighbor. She's got purple hair, eighteen-hole Dr. Martens, and her yellow car spews sooty exhaust from the tailpipe. Nicole and I giggle as the vehicle jerks north onto Pacific Coast Highway toward Venice Beach. Nicole's laughter is full of fun; mine is just full of nerves.

"Are you sure he'll do it?" I don't take my eyes off the car we're tailgating.

"Pretty sure. He's done a few tattoos for me," Nicole yells over the whirring engine. I think I look a bit older than she does, so I'm reassured—or less assured, as now I'm questioning whether I really want to do this. We stop fast because, apparently, the car in front of us actually stops for stop signs. I wonder if this girl even has a driver's license.

At Abbot Kinney, we park and walk a few blocks. Depending on which way the wind blows, I smell either patchouli incense or trash.

"I'll see you guys back here around six?" Sam asks cavalierly and walks away toward the boardwalk before we answer.

The sidewalks are made of an obsidian and concrete mixture that sparkles in the sun. A few miles northeast of us is the Hollywood Walk of Fame. I imagine every star who's stuck a hand in that concrete sludge was greeted by a flashbulb and a sidewalk that sparkles like this. These are the streets of LA—gilded, mineral, and slightly trashy.

"In here." Nicole opens a screen door, and I follow her up a step into a dilapidated parlor. There sits an old-timey biker dude reading a magazine. I wonder if he's done any work since the 1970s. But I'm underage, and I hear this place isn't too concerned with legal identification, so I approach him sheepishly.

"What can I do you for?" He snuffs out his cigarette in a glass ashtray on the counter.

"I'd like a tattoo," I manage to say. He just stares. I'm sure I've offended him somehow.

"Right. Of what?"

I fumble through the back pocket of my vintage 501s for my sketch and place it on the counter. He looks at it blankly. "I'll tell you what," he finally utters. He leans in, and I smell cigarette on his beard. "You draw what you want." He slams a piece of carbon paper and a pencil back down onto the counter and takes off toward the back of the shop.

By the time he's back, I've doodled a crude version of my ultimate belief system, my tattoo to end all tattoos. He studies it for a moment. "Okey dokey. Hop up."

I'm face down on the table with the waistband of my jeans rolled over. I make awkward small talk. "What's your name?" Shouldn't I try to get to know this artist who is about to connect my body to my ultimate beliefs?

"Jack. Where?" he snorts and rubs his nose. He dabs some Vaseline where I point, and he slaps the carbon paper over it. Peeling from the bottom corner, he reveals the transference of my clumsy efforts in carbon soot. Surely, he will now reimagine her and perfect her for me.

I wait anxiously for his revisions, for charcoal pencil to meet flesh. But he just readies his equipment. I glance down at her, shocked to see my bright, confident sun so insecure. Won't Jack infuse her with my confidence and color her with my conviction? I say nothing as the needle cuts two layers down, infusing permanent ink into my flesh.

As it turns out, having a voice is one thing, but learning to use it will take practice. While Jack tattoos, there's a burning below the surface.

This is my truth.

I'll Follow the Sun

Mr. Heiser's in his room with the door closed. Quinn has resorted to calling him John. It's easy to pull his strings. He reacts. He snaps. The thrill is almost gone. Almost …

"John! Are you sulking?" Quinn gives a few quick knocks at the door.

"Stop it, Quinn."

She giggles. I thumb through a photo album of Mrs. Heiser on her 1965 "World Tour." She and Quinn's aunts are standing at the foot of a fallen column in Rome. Margaret's full skirt is cinched at the waist. She's youthful and thin. Her short hair with bangs makes her look distinctively French, though I don't think she was.

"So, are you a psychologist yet?" Quinn mocks the fact that I attend a zero-period class for peer-counselor training. "Because I'm thinking I might need a new one."

"Nope. Not yet. Anyway, you need a psychiatrist. A counselor can't help with your epilepsy. But I might get to leave class soon to assist peers in emotional crisis, so that's a bonus."

"Sweet. I'll spring you when I have my nineteenth nervous breakdown."

"Deal. How's your dad doing?" I'm *really* asking, "How are you, really?"

Quinn's demeanor is matter-of-fact, sarcastic. "John's still in his midlife crisis, but we'll get through it."

"Right."

Margaret Heiser died last Tuesday at the university research hospital after a routine change of her antidepressant. It's hard to believe this little house is still standing. Even stranger, it feels entirely appropriate right now to carry on as we always have, experimenting with Red Vines in the microwave.

Quinn hops onto the countertop and grabs a bag of licorice from the cabinet. She tosses them in and hits "30 sec." We watch through the glass as the shiny, red ropes melt and seem to breathe out. We grit our teeth in suspense, then race to hit cancel. We laugh and sink our teeth into warm, soft sugar.

"This is the best idea we've had in a long time," I tell Quinn. Then we spot a bag of Jet-Puffed marshmallows on the top shelf of the open cabinet and squeal because this might be the best idea ever. She slams the microwave shut, and within seconds, our marshmallows overtake the machine and smother the window glass. "Turn it off! Turn it off!" I plead through my laughter as the sweet, white cloud suffocates the window. We're absurd like that, ridiculous, and nothing seems to matter so long as we're having fun.

Flashes and Sparks 89

○○

Fridays feel like butterflies. My mind wanders in and out of Mr. LaRon's net of ramblings. He, too, has given up the structure of a week's work.

"This is chemistry, right?" Aaron sits next to me in chem. He's got his pencil stuck behind his left ear and is whispering in my right.

"I'm not sure anymore."

"A butterfly flaps its wings in Tibet and snow falls in India …" Mr. LaRon's still talking. He's sitting on his desk. Now, apparently, a tsunami in Japan is causing a landslide somewhere in Malibu. Meanwhile, the butterflies of South Coast High School are emerging. The class across the hall has been let out early. They're swarming into the sunny corridor and out toward the chaos of homecoming weekend.

"So … Halloween is three weeks away. What are you all being for Halloween, you freaky ghosts and ghouls?" He's watching the clock just as we are. Nobody says a word. "Speaking of …" Mr. LaRon continues. "Who here believes in ghosts?" I look over at Aaron, who trembles a little and opens his eyes really big as if he's just seen one. Still, nobody says a word.

"Science has found a link between the paranormal and electromagnetic fields. Actually, most paranormal activity involves teenagers with fluctuating hormone levels. So, you freaks might be the closest I get to a real ghost sighting this Halloween." Nobody laughs.

"Nobody here believes in ghosts?" Mr. LaRon chuckles and smooths his mustache. He drums his fingers on the desktop.

Just for a moment, I think of life everlasting. Maybe the spirit is real and transcendental. Maybe the people and places I have come to love don't ever truly disappear. They are the spirit that passes through me on the breeze, tingles my fingertips, drives my intuition. I think and hope, just for a second, that ghosts are real. They might be the answer to all my fears.

"Some studies also show a correlation between paranormal experiences and epilepsy or with those people who have experienced episodes of significant grief." My jaw drops. I look at Quinn, who's a deer in headlights. "Your brains are more powerful than you think, people. Let's be sure to use them over the weekend. Be safe out there! Class is dismissed."

We file out to the tree-lined corridor, into a buzz of talk and joyous outbursts. "Woo-hoo!" Jenny and Kelly appear from the burgeoning swarm.

Kelly has this huge grin on her face. I feel it's a trap. She's direct and stern and if we weren't becoming fast friends, I'd find her intimidating. Kelly has a tendency to seek out fun, which is totally contrary to my own serious nature. She lives with her aunt, has light red hair and a fair complexion full of soft freckles. When she stands next to someone with any other skin tone at all, it looks like one of those Benetton ads from the 1980s. "So, what are you doing next Saturday?"

"Um, very important relaxation activities, the details of which I will reveal when that day has actually arrived."

Kelly stares at me, waiting a second for effect. "Right. No. You aren't! Beatlefest is coming!"

"So, is this a group extermination party or some Volkswagen fetishist meeting? Because I don't have any pests ... or a car."

"Nope. This is the world's biggest Beatles convention, and it's coming back to the LAX Sheraton! I got us tickets, so you can't say no."

"Okay, fine. But if you want me to go to a *Star Trek* convention, I might have to put my foot down."

Quinn and I head down the locker hall. She's talking in a low monotone. "Mr. LaRon was reading my aura or something in class. Freaked me out. Does he know about my mom or about my epilepsy?"

"I don't think so."

"That was messed up."

"It was just coincidental. Go drop your stuff. I'll wait at my locker."

෩

At the corner of the seventies hall, Nathan stops me in my tracks. My eyes are locked with his, and I can't unlock them. The ambient noise of dismissal, the clamor of metal locker doors slamming shut—everything is silenced. It's like some emotional déjà vu on repeat, and I'm stuck here. I'm queasy. After a second, I manage to zoom out of his eyes and realize once again that he's wearing thick, corrective glasses, and he just grabbed his band uniform from his locker. No matter—it's personal and it's real.

"Ready?" Quinn appears over my shoulder and scares the hell out of me. "What's wrong with you? You seem really ... frazzled."

"Nothing ... just ST."

In addition to our constant search for beasts, Quinn and I are connoisseurs of sexual tension (ST). Unlike beholding a beast, which can be somewhat generic in nature, ST is random, individualized, and unexpected. The less seemly the object of desire, the better. We think this is art at its most authentic and unscripted best.

"Ah! Awesome! With who?"

"None ya."

"You have to tell me!"

"Okay, fine. Nathan."

"That skinny guy in the marching band?" Quinn doubles over laughing.

I was expecting her to mock me. "I don't want to talk about it."

"Then go talk to him!"

"I shouldn't have talked to you. You know ST is private. Plus, can words really ever do justice after that feeling of meiosis?"

"Wait ... you think your cells are dividing when you have ST?"

"It's just a theory, but don't you think it's possible that my body knows something that my brain doesn't?"

"You're a dork."

We're lighthearted as we leave school. I look back to see that the buildings look less important now that we're on the outside. The grounds are somehow shabbier and covered in more weeds. Just ahead, a dandelion has pushed its way through a crack in the sidewalk. We, too, break free.

In the parking lot, Jenny catches us just in time. She's laughing and pulling us off the curb by our backpack straps. Quinn and I get tangled. A lock of my hair gets pulled in the mix. "Ouch, Jenny!" But, before I know it, the three of us wind up in a huddle on the floor of Matt's van. Through her hysterical laughter, Jenny manages to slide the door shut, and the VW lurches out of its parking space and onto Pacific Coast Highway.

"So, where are we headed?" I ask, though I don't really care.

"Shut up, Patty Hearst!" Jenny giggles. Matt is silent at the wheel. He smiles at us in the rearview mirror. With his shoulder-length hair and his kind eyes, he sort of looks like Jesus.

Kelly's in shotgun. She turns to look at us in the back seat. "Quinn, how are you doing?"

"What did Kafka say? 'The meaning of life is that it ends.'"

"Yeah ... but are you okay?"

"I'll let you know before I fly over the cuckoo's nest."

"Good girl!" says Kelly. "I'm so glad you're a reacher-outer." She unbuckles. In a flash of freckles and strawberry blonde, she hops into the back seat with us and hooks Quinn's little neck in the crook of her elbow. Kelly's right; Quinn is a reacher-outer. She makes phone calls just to say hi and goes out of her way to introduce her friends to one another. She connects us like glue and creates a network of support for us all. Reaching out doesn't come naturally to me, and I wonder what implications this has for my life.

On the corner of Fulton and Aviation, the Salvation Army Thrift Store is lit from above with huge fluorescent lights. A bell chimes as we push open the door, and a waft of dingy must greets us, warm and funky like a wet puppy.

Matt holds up a pearl, snap-button shirt and looks at himself in the mirror. Meanwhile, Ross is eyeing a pair of denim, OshKosh B'gosh overalls.

"Kate, what do you think?"

"They make you look not so bright, sort of Lennie-esque."

"Wow. Well, just don't let me near any bunny rabbits. And, that's messed up to say." He fake-cries. "I'm getting them anyway." He throws them in his basket.

We come here to fill our closets for twenty dollars. We come here because this place doesn't limit our self-expression or turn us into trendy, mass-produced, factory freaks as the mall stores do. Plus, these clothes speak to each of us in unforeseen ways.

I also come here to reaffirm my dedication to the Earth. I'm renewed by the renewable, the subtle suggestion in the thread, the nostalgia, and the nuance. I touch the upcycled material with my eyes and my fingers. There's a spirit in these thrift store clothes that elevates my own.

Today, the men's attire is instantly more appealing to me than the women's. I touch a khaki, tie-waist, safari jacket on the men's rack and feel adventurous. A pair of wool—well, they can only be described as "trousers"—

grabs my attention. They're the perfect ironic plaid. The cuffs fall just to the sole of my Saucony running shoes, so I recite a line from "The Love Song of J. Alfred Prufrock."

"I grow old ... I grow old ... I shall wear the bottoms of my trousers rolled."

Jenny looks at me sideways. "Dork," she whispers jokingly.

Then, I'm suddenly girly, so I head for the women's department. A sheer, cream-colored, button-down blouse draws me in. It's a garden of dainty, blue flowers and delicate green vines. The Elizabethan collar ties drape softly from the neck. From across the room, I imagine it smells like tea rose and can teach me to sew and cook and tend to an herb garden, a soft and gentle grandmother. I adopt her and take her to the shoe department, where Jenny and Quinn are cracking themselves up over "pimp shoes."

Jenny's strutting back and forth in front of the mirror in flared bell-bottom pants, big circular glasses, and a hat with a really wide brim. I think she looks like Stevie Nicks, so I sing "Landslide" with a super raspy voice that makes Jenny laugh and stumble on her wedge sandal. Quinn and I fall to the floor in hysterics.

For eleven dollars and forty-five cents, I leave with a skirt from the seventies, a blouse from the forties, a pair of T.S. Eliot trousers, and a safari jacket that transcends time.

Matt drops Quinn, Jenny, Kelly, and me off at Quinn's. Jenny yells to her brother as the van pulls away, "See you at the football game! Tell Mom I'm here." Matt nods through his smile. Silently he waves. His shoulder-length hair frames his soft-spoken demeanor perfectly.

"Your brother totally looks like Jesus," says Quinn. We laugh because it's true.

※

I'm slumped in the corner of Quinn's room next to my thrift store trash bag. I still have my backpack on. Quinn shows Kelly her photos from Paris and flips the radio dial to 102.7 Kiss FM.

"I love this song," says Quinn, quietly. We nod. I reach out without moving my body, just far enough to grab the latest issue of *Rolling Stone*. We're exhausted from the week. We listen to "Runaway Train" on the radio, feeling appropriately jaded.

"So … anyway …" Kelly glares at me for cutting the silence. "Anyway," I repeat. "We got an invite to Amelia Demeraux's party tonight." I assess interest.

"Wow. Serious. I'll be sure to pack my needle and a spoon." Kelly laughs so hard she snorts. I give Quinn this one because Amelia wears her cheer uniform like a character from the "Smells Like Teen Spirit" video. She stared me down with cat eyes this morning, grabbed my wrist in what I can only describe as a dominant but loving way, and told me I should come over after the game. This was at 9:00 a.m., when her bleach-blonde hair with dark roots was knotted and tousled and her black eyeliner was smoky, like second-day coal from a campfire.

In the kitchen, Quinn opens a small cupboard door and takes out a glass bottle full of some brown alcohol. I'd had a few sips of beer at a party recently. This certainly seems like an escalation. "Quinn, good Lord! What are we, juvenile delinquents, now?" Quinn fills a few sport bottles halfway. I take a sip. "Oh, crap! Holy hell. What is this?"

"I don't know …" Quinn leans the bottle over to read the label. "Cognac?"

"Nasty!"

"Hold on." She opens the fridge and scans the shelves for something to improve the taste, then pours the bottles to the top with apple juice and snaps on the lids. "Okay, let's go!"

"Where?" I grab my backpack with my 35mm camera off the counter before Quinn locks the door behind me. The four of us walk down 28th Street, past the Mighty Mart, the neighborhood bar, and El Gringo restaurant. "Indeed," I say. Quinn knows what I mean. Only gringos eat there.

"Yeah, yeah, you're the whitest Guatemalan I've ever met."

We make it to the boardwalk and jump over the wall to the sand. I take off my shoes. Jenny and Kelly flop down into the cool grains and take off their shoes. Quinn wears her Birkenstocks as we head to the lifeguard tower at 26th Street. She walks abstractly for our amusement, like a "tourist," and kicks sand from her open-toed sandals with each step. We ignore her antics. We take pictures of ourselves on the lifeguard tower as the sun sets. The buzz from our brown drink makes everything just a little funnier, the sunset a little more stunning. The film in my 35mm captures this spirit in physical form, making it, somehow, more real.

When the wind gusts, salt exfoliates our skin. The sand pricks at our ankles. The breeze blows even our words down the coast. I can't hear what anyone's saying, but the squeals and the laughter bounce off the breeze and become meaningful utterances nonetheless. Through the numbing chill, I feel my cheek muscles start to ache from smiling.

The twilight sets in, that time between time, daylight's ambiguous, gradual decline. When the light is creepy in the best way and our shadows disappear into the dark, we turn our backs on the ocean and head home.

Mr. Heiser's standing at the apartment-sized machines, tossing the damp and wrung clothes in to dry. Electric lightbulbs and home appliances warm the air. The beach chill on my face evaporates into the aroma of laundry detergent and the cozy heat. My skin stings in the thaw. When he turns to clean the lint filter, we empty our sport cups into the kitchen sink and try to conceal our laughter when the nasty, brown alcohol stinks up the kitchen. Mr. Heiser seems not to notice. We shuffle past him and into Quinn's room and put on cherry ChapStick and brush our hair and head back out the door.

"Quinn! Be home by ten!" Mr. Heiser's calls are faint because we're already halfway down the alley.

"Yeah, yeah, John. I'll call you."

Amelia Deveraux isn't cheering when the game starts, but halfway through, she's sitting on the rear deck of a Corvette and circling the track. I hear a jumble of words over the loudspeaker, and all six homecoming princesses and princes take their places on the fifty-yard line. Amelia is pronounced homecoming queen. The grandmother of another princess is sitting in the stands next to me and says, "I was afraid that bad news cheerleader was going to win." I chuckle and head up the bleachers after a girl in my Spanish class who keeps stumbling on the steps. I help her to the top of the bleachers and up the blacktop path to the bathroom. It seems like a simple courtesy, so I wait outside her stall while she vomits.

Back at the bleachers, I look to the scoreboard for some clue as to what's going on in the game. Just then, it seems to come to an abrupt end. At least, it is abrupt to me, as I can never find the ball on the field or understand exactly what they're doing down there. But what's going on up here I get. Everyone around me stands and puts on jackets and starts calling to friends across the bleachers. It's party time.

Quinn grabs my arm. "Okay, I have a sick fascination. Let's go!" Jenny and Kelly shake their heads, no, so Quinn and I leave them behind and head to Amelia's.

At the corner of 4th Street, Amelia's chateaux-style house sits like a haunted mansion. A large swimming pool is sunken into stone pavers on the front terrace. It's lit from the bottom, and beer cans make their slow journey in currents across the top. We follow the yelling and the music up the stone path to a huge but tastefully distressed door.

"It looks like this party started hours ago," Quinn says, right as a slumped-over blonde girl throws the door open. I can't see her face because her hair is stuck to her left cheek. Quinn gives me an amused grin and we step inside.

We walk down the front hall to Pink Floyd's "The Happiest Days of Our Lives." I follow Quinn up the grand staircase, but a group of boys throwing beer cans comes thundering down the hallway between us, and I lose her to a room on the second floor. The music keeps getting louder, so I follow it. Maniacal laughter and helicopter sounds beckon me to a room at the end of the hall. I open the door and stand in the smoky obscurity.

"Hey, bitch!" someone calls to me, presumably.

Oh, good—girl drama.

I step inside. Sarah Chen is sitting on the floor at the foot of a queen-size bed. She's the leader of the mean girls I just ran against for freshman class president. I won. Sarah's throwing daggers at me with her eyes, meanwhile passing the joint to her left and tapping the knee of her stoned friend, who fails to notice it's her turn. I sit next to her in the circle.

"What are you doing?" Her glare repels me.

"I wanted to say hi," I say, convinced that my acting is convincing.

"Don't you know I hate you?" Sarah's circle of frenemies from the high school quad laugh on cue.

"I figured." They stare. After some awkward seconds, Sarah's enforcer, Briana, breaks the standoff by passing me the joint from across the circle. I take it from her, and holding on to the roach clip, I pretend to take a huge hit from her offering of friendship.

When I think the drama's subsided, I crawl around the circle like a puppy and tell Sarah, "I'm glad I ran into you." Wary of overstaying my welcome, I get up like a sprite and disappear down the hall, looking for Quinn.

Twenty minutes later, I'm still looking for Quinn. I just keep moving. I'm a traveling nurse and a mediator for drunk emotional girls in fights over boys or general jealously issues. I'm the concierge for vaguely coherent people wandering through the house looking to pee in the bathroom or the backyard. I make it to the kitchen and pour a splash of Boone's Strawberry Hill into a red Solo cup. I make circles through the house. I apply a Band-Aid to the leg of a junior who tripped over the retaining wall in the driveway. I nurse my Strawberry Hill. I'm entertained for a little while.

"Pigs. Pigs!" someone yells in the stairwell. Half the occupants of the house run through the kitchen and out the back door. The lights come on, but still a police officer shines his lamp in my eyes.

"Do you live here?"

"No, sir." He points out the door and I go. On the sidewalk, I find Quinn. "Let's go home?"

"Yes, please!" she says, looking up through the marine layer, through the smog and the streetlights to the stars. Palm fronds dance on the breeze. We walk through downtown. It smells like candles, a fireplace, or warm paraffin wax. It always smells like this on Beach Avenue in the fall. This mystery hearth mixes with the cool brininess of the sea air and the slight flora of cultivated grasses. I'm relieved to walk away from the drama and into the night.

"Sleep at your house?" Quinn asks, as if it's a statement.

"Sure." I look west toward the coast. A wave downhill booms on the shore. It cascades and fizzes and breaks south toward the Palos Verdes Peninsula. I see sparks of white froth through the black.

October is my favorite month. We walk quietly under the harvest moon. It pulls on my bloodstream. It stirs my currents. I'm starting to feel patterns of the seasons in my endocrine system and energy. I recognize the fluidity of emotion that swells in me like the tide. Once, over a candle flame on her Dia de los Muertos altar, Maria told me that at this time of year, the barrier between the living and the dead is the thinnest. It's these October nights, under the harvest moon, that I feel the most alive.

We stop on Manhattan Avenue to use the payphone. "Staying at Kate's. Nope. I'm good. I took it this morning. Okay. Cool. See you tomorrow." Quinn looks at me assuredly. "We good."

The open door of the Hungry Mind coffee shop calls us from across the street. We stumble into the light of open mic night. I get a black coffee. "John Wayne-style,"

I say at the counter. Quinn gets a black tea. Just as we sit down with our drinks, we hear, "We're going to take a little break now. Go order some coffee, and we'll start up again in ten."

"You should read a poem one of these nights." Quinn clutches her tea in both hands.

"Maybe," I say, meaning no. "I'd prefer to be underrated. So, did I ever tell you about my mom's peace pipe thing?"

"No. What?" Quinn's only half-interested. She's checking out the double plaid and the steel-toe Docs on the grunge couple behind me.

"Well, when my mom was in high school, she was picked to be the head cheerleader and this other mom was super-pissed that it wasn't her daughter." Quinn looks at me as if this story has already outrun its course. "My mom didn't know what to do because both this girl and her mother were physically and verbally abusive toward my mom. Like, once, the mom grabbed my mom's hair and pulled her across the stands at a football game."

Quinn perks up with this description of depravity. "That's insane. I hate pageant moms."

"Well, anyway, Mom finally brought a Native American peace pipe to a football game and smoked it with the other cheerleader and her mom after the game." Quinn just stares at me. "I sort of did that tonight."

"Wait, what?" Quinn laughs and puts down her tea.

"Let's just say that Sarah Chen and I smoked the peace pipe."

"Okay, so she's cool with you now?"

"I think so."

"Hmmm ... she'll find someone else to hate. Drama is the spice of her life."

"Yeah, maybe so. Why are people like that? I mean, isn't life crazy enough without creating drama for no reason?"

"Kate, not everyone is an isolationist, nature-loving hippie like you. Wouldn't the world be boring if they were?" Quinn looks up to see I'm not persuaded. "Maybe it's that ... maybe drama gives meaning to life, you know? Maybe it gives people something to do. Otherwise, what's the point?" She takes a sip of her tea and slams her mug down. "Plus, honestly, it's sort of fun."

The lights turn back down, and a goth woman in her twenties stands up from a table for two where she's been sitting by herself. She approaches the mic.

"Fuck you," she says. Then there's a long, awkward pause. Quinn whispers, "This is going to be a highbrow piece of work." I chuckle.

When the goth girl takes her seat, we bus our mugs and head out into the night. "That poem was fucking beautiful," I say with a mob-style New Jersey accent.

Quinn throws an arm at me. "Oh, shut up and quarter."

"Fine." I exhale as if I've got runner's high. "I love that place, though."

"Me too."

"There's nothing like leaving a party and heading straight to the morose poetry of a lonely stranger." I'm joking but not really. I prefer uppers to downers, loneliness to a crowd, and brutal honesty over saving face. That goth girl's fears and desires spoken into the night were pathetic, full of doubt and the fear that we're all just spinning our wheels in some pointless, nihilistic endeavor. Her words are the realest words I've heard in a long time.

It's always when I'm sullen and stone-cold sober in the face of this emptiness that I feel it—the flame, that spark that seems to come out of nowhere. It burns. It agitates me to act and inspires me to believe. It calls for me to create something out of this nothing, just like that girl's poem. And I think everything good just might come from this explosive nothingness within.

The breeze blows a desolate rustle through the palm fronds on Ardmore Avenue. I get a chill and shiver and I love it. We walk as far west as Continental US roads go, then we turn south, down the boardwalk in the fog.

〰️

In the morning, Quinn's in a sleeping bag on my floor. At 9:30 a.m., she pops up, "Gotta go. Brunch with my aunt!" She says aunt like "ont." I hear her shimmy into her sweatshirt and fumble on one leg with her Chuck Taylors. Then, she gently closes my bedroom door.

The house is quiet, so I venture into the kitchen for some cereal. I take my bowl down to the living room and open the bottom drawer and grab that audio tape. I tiptoe back into my room and, with the door closed, pop it into the player where Joshua Tree had resided for weeks on end. I hit play.

"Hmm ... ahem ..." A scratchy woman's voice comes over the speakers. "Today is March 3rd, 1987, the psychic reading of Linda Brewer." I was ten years old then. My heart pumps, and I'm drenched in a cold sweat. I check that my door is closed and listen on. A few minutes into some basics about Mom—where she was born, her birthday—the woman pauses. "You are challenged by a controlling figure. Who is this?"

"Uh, like a person? My mother."

"Thank you. Yes. How will you break free from this control and find your own path? Your challenge is to find your own voice and choose for yourself."

"Yes," Mom says, sounding mesmerized.

The woman pauses for ten seconds or so, then sounds hesitant. "Oh, no. I see a dark cloud in your spirit board. You see, if you don't take charge of your own life, the darkness will overtake you."

"Oh," says Mom, and I hear in her voice that she shares this ice water feeling coursing through my veins. I feel it rush to my heart, and I gasp for air. The woman pauses another moment. "It says you will come down with an illness. Let me see your right hand. Yes. See here, this line. Are you ill?"

I hear Mom's nervous laugh. "I don't think so." The woman moves on. She talks about Brian's need for affection, Doug's athleticism, Dad's pressures at work. I zone out for maybe thirty seconds.

And just when I choose to hear no evil, see no evil, speak no evil, just when I'm about to hit stop on the tape player, she starts talking about me.

"Your daughter, she's ten?"

Mom answers in what sounds like a daze. "Yes."

"Hmm ... she must be careful not to fall in love with someone that she feels sorry for."

"Okay," says Mom. I hit stop on the recorder because I hear voices in the kitchen.

I shuffle out and rinse my bowl and put it in the dishwasher. "Are you still in your PJs?" Brian accuses. "I'm going surfing. Later!"

"Sweet. Have fun." I wave him off and tiptoe back to my room. I pass Maria's door and see that she's watching Univision *News out of Central America*. It's graphic, like no news I've seen on the English channels. A man is thrown and gored by a bull. The screen flickers to several bloody scenes of chaos and excited sports fans. "Hijole!" I hear Maria say excitedly. "Ay-yai-yai!" she laughs. I keep walking, thinking, *Spice of life.*

"Hello?" I've just closed my door when I hear it. "Anybody here?" Grandma stops by every once in a while. Now that we're three doors down, she walks right in. It's always for some purpose, and it always seems urgent. I reluctantly open my door so I don't have to hear her nasal call again.

"Hi, Grandma."

"Hi. Where's your mom?"

Just then, out of the master, Mom emerges in her bathrobe. "Hi, Mom. What's up?"

"I don't like your side yard. Get rid of that broken patio chair!"

"Which one, Mom?" I hope Mom will shut this conversation down. Instead, she dutifully follows Grandma out into the public space of the boardwalk to examine one of our patio chairs in her bathrobe. I watch their conversation from my bedroom window. Mom's being lectured like she's been busted, like a naughty child.

Back inside, I hear Grandma talking, but I don't hear Mom. "My new neighbors are loaded, you know. The mortgage broker on Main Street told me they're all paying cash now." *They*, I think, and I try not to laugh out loud out of fear that Grandma and Mom might hear me. "All" comes out like "owall." "Cash" is slow and drawn out; it hisses through her dental implants.

A few minutes later: "Oh, I think he'll cheat. Too many interesting young bodies in bikinis out here for her to keep his interest." "Young" sounds like "Yonge." There is something scathing in every word she utters, even the benign ones. I hide in my room, watching the oil tankers make their way north through the South Bay, thinking, *Ay-yai-yai ... spice of life.*

༒

After about twenty minutes, the coast is clear, and I come out of hiding. "Hi, Kate, don't you look cute!" Mom looks up at me from a stack of papers. She's got her reading glasses on and it looks serious.

"What are you doing?"

"Refinancing. It's boring. How are you? Look at this cute outfit! Did you go shopping?"

I don't dare tell her about the Salvation Army Thrift Store, let alone my hidden, lower-back tattoo. That's all for "the fast girls." And good Lord, what would Grandma think?

"Really charming," she says, looking down at my blouse. I smile and sort of shudder and step back because it might just smell used.

I feel a light tug on my armpit and realize she's inspecting a price tag I left under my arm. "Where did you get this?" I hear a tone I only hear when Grandma, or rather, *they,* are conjured up in the ether. Mom is panicked.

"Where it says, Mom. The Salvation Army Thrift Store. Don't worry, I won't tell Grandma. How was your week? What'd you do?"

"Well, Grandmama is looking for a new fur coat, so we went to Barney's in Beverly Hills."

"Right, but what did *you* do?"

"I just told you, Kate." Mom seems to not understand my question. "Oh, and I got a few things." On the glass coffee table between the family of crystal elephants and what I think is a polar bear, I see a few paper shopping bags.

"You would have been better off writing your book, Mom." She knows this, I can tell by her expression, but she's not cured of her Stockholm Syndrome, not in the least. She has no control over how she spends her time.

Mom changes the subject. "What's new with you? How's school?"

"Good. I've been hanging out a bit with that new friend, Nicole."

"Oh, how nice!"

"Yeah, she's awesome. She has all these little, meaningful tattoos that she designed herself. We made hummus after school the other day with fava beans and lemons. She lives in this sweet little house on Artesia with her mom ... and when her mom's at work, she does lots of cooking and stuff."

"That's sad." Mom makes a fake frowny face.

"What? How?"

"She lives in a little house near the highway with her single mom?"

"I think you're missing the point, Mom. They are authentic and self-sufficient, and they make awesome food and create tattoo art, and they aren't putting on a show for anyone. Plus, they have realistic expectations about life, and they have a voice, and when her mom's boyfriend is drinking, they tell him to leave. They put their foot down!"

"And the boyfriend is an alcoholic?" Frowny face.

"Mom, that's no worse than a codependent. I'm starting to think that you can't be happy just by living on a sunny beach and faking it till you make it. What was on that audio tape, again? What was that all about? Your choice? When is it going to be too late?"

Mom freezes in position. She knows exactly what I'm talking about. For a moment, she appears overtaken by acknowledgment and stares out toward the pier. But within seconds, she's ignoring me, back to her papers, and refinancing our façade of a perfect life.

Our crystal zoo animals collect light on the coffee table. I find myself wishing we lived in a small, musty house. I wish Mom commuted long hours for "better pay" and would see Grandma on her own terms, as Nicole's mom does. There were no shiny crystal zoo animals on their table. Nothing was very shiny at all. But I get the distinct impression that Nicole and her mom are just themselves, and there is tremendous freedom in that.

⌒◎

At 6:00 p.m., the garage door below shakes the house just a tad and sets off my internal earthquake sensor. Like always, I think to duck and cover, but it's just Dad coming home to change for the gym. Maria's plating dinner for Brian and me when the phone rings.

"I'll get it!" Brian pops up. "It's Quinn," he says to me with a serious look on his face.

"Hey, Quinn!"

"Kate ..." She's crying on the other end of the line. She sounds terrified. "Kate!"

"What?" Goose bumps run down my arms.

"I hear her."

"What? Who?"

"My mom. In the house. Her voice." Quinn's voice cracks. "I need to get out of here."

"Meet me at the Sandcastle." I hang up and run for a sweatshirt. "I'll be right back!" I say to Brian. He nods.

I don't see her at the corner of 19th Street, so I keep running up the boardwalk. I run into the streetlights at each corner and back out into gradients of obscurity like moon cycles. At 21st Street, I see her. She looks small and vulnerable. I feel like a giant with a huge, swollen heart. I hug my best friend and bring her home.

At the top of the stairwell, we reach the living room. Mom calls from the couch. "Hi, Quinn! Brian told me you were on your way."

"Hi, Aunt Linda."

"Quinn heard her mom's voice in her house, Mom. She was alone. She's really scared."

Mom doesn't look surprised. Instead, she looks purposeful. "Come here, Quinn." We sit on chairs in the lamplight and face Mom on the couch.

"Quinn, honey, your mom loved you more than life itself. It wouldn't surprise me if she's still here in a way, guiding you."

A single tear falls from Quinn's eye. *Oh, no,* I think. This was not my plan. I'm racking my brain to say something hilarious and snarky. But then I look over at my friend and see her face has gone from white to pink. Her eyes have gone from glazed to focused. She looks … consoled.

At 7:45 p.m., Dad gets home from the gym, and we drive Quinn home. We wait in the driveway until Mr. Heiser waves to us through the front window.

༺༻

"So, what's your favorite Beatles song?" Mr. Heiser makes conversation with the four of us as he watches the red light. He turns on the wipers because the morning mist has obscured his view. This is Southern California rain.

"That's not the right question, John," Quinn says to her dad. "Each album is a story. You can't separate the beginning from the middle from the end."

"Ah," he says. He's done with the attitude and this conversation.

"Yeah, it's really about which incarnation of the Beatles you prefer." Kelly dorks out for a few minutes about the metamorphosis of the Beatles and the sociopolitical implications of their music. I'm painfully aware that we analyze a time Mr. Heiser clearly recalls and during which we weren't even born. He seems happy to let us out at the curb when we see the big marquee at El Segundo Boulevard and Sepulveda flash "Beatlefest!"

Kelly hands each of us a ticket. "We can go to the ATM so you can pay me back," she says sternly. She grabs Jenny's arm and pulls her out of the back seat and onto the sidewalk in front of the hotel convention center, right in front of a long-haired woman in a fringed, suede vest.

A papier-mâché yellow submarine on six legs passes us on the sidewalk. It's a bit literal for my taste. Before Mr. Heiser can make his escape, three shaggy-haired, twenty-something men in black, skinny suits step off the curb to cross the street in front of him. A big Blue Meany stumbles up dramatically, blowing his whistle and gesturing at others to stop. With a cartoon-style, white-gloved hand, he ushers us into the building like a traffic cop.

Inside, a heavyset woman in a Beatles T-shirt rips off our ticket stubs. "Have a Beatific time!"

I roll my eyes at Kelly. "What have you done?"

"Why are you so serious all the time? Life is about fun!"

We head down the convention hall to a swap meet of Beatles paraphernalia vendors. Into the vortex of a white lava lamp I slide. I float around for a minute with the purple shimmer goo. It's slow, like tai chi, and I start to understand why people like these things. I touch it with both hands and feel I'm harnassing it's energy.

"No touching!" the vendor barks, and Quinn pulls me away. We giggle-run down the aisle.

Kelly's mesmerized by a glass display case full of "original" pin-back photo buttons. She negotiates with the friendly hippy on the other side of the glass and selects her favorite five for six dollars. We contribute greatly to her choices, but at the last minute, she switches out Paul for George.

"He's edgier," she explains.

"More of a beast," agrees Quinn.

Down the hall, speakers boom high-pitched British voices. The lights flicker muted shadows of a midcentury movie. Heeding the call, we walk mesmerized into a ten-foot-tall screening of *Yellow Submarine*. For a few minutes, we rest on folding chairs, then Jenny taps Kelly on the shoulder, and the four of us spring out into the hallway to see what else there is to see.

Past a few conference rooms marked with poster board, "Poetry in Beatles Lyrics" and "The Beatles and the Avant-Garde," we get to a space called "Impromptu Song." Inside, a few patrons sit in the audience with guitars. A woman holds a tambourine in her lap. A mop-headed man in a mandarin collar shirt sits alone at front-center with a guitar. He starts to strum and sing.

As we file in, I'm an instant devotee, a believer. The room joins in singing like prayer. From my chair, I see out to the hallway and El Segundo Boulevard. The sky opens up and the sun creeps in. Just then, a rainbow bridges the street. It's fleeting, we know; we don't dare blink. Together, we sing as one—"I'll follow the sun."

༺ ༻

Monday, after school, I stroll down the boardwalk. The crows squawk their ugly cry that pulls on my heartstrings and makes me feel incredibly lonely. The salted mist gives me a chill and, the hum of passing cars makes me think the brine is contaminated with carbon emissions. So, I turn my face west and look out to the uninhabited expanse of the Pacific.

At home, the dry air cures my bones. Mom is in the living room, looking out at the pier. "Hi, honey!" Mom's voice is faint and she looks tired, but she smiles, and I feel her delight in seeing me.

I take a seat near her, just as a car door slams in the driveway. Brian's carpool has arrived from the Country Day School. Maria drops a pan that clangs loudly in the sink. She laughs. "Lo siento" (Sorry), she says and rushes down the stairs to greet him. "Como se fue el dia?" I hear her ask from the foyer.

"Bien, bien," says my brother, and they make their way to the kitchen.

"Kate, how's Quinn?" Mom asks.

"I don't know. She didn't come to school today. Visiting her aunt, I think."

"I want you to promise me something, Kate. If I ever come to you after I die ... I don't want you to be afraid."

I'm stunned. I cannot imagine these circumstances. I don't know what to say. But I take a leap of faith and look Mom in the eyes.

I declare, "I promise." And I mean it.

Solar Eclipse

Sunlight is either blocked or reflected by lunar activity. It's no wonder women are also regulated by the moon; channels, we are, of its life-giving force and regulators of darkness and light.

༄

Quinn's face down in her sleeping bag on my floor. Her dark-blonde hair is splayed over her pillow like straw. I flip onto my side and the bed creaks. My blanket rustles.

"Argh! What the hell?" She rises and squints. "Is your sunshine butt tattoo lighting up the room? It's going to give me a seizure." She huffs and puffs and stands abruptly to close the blinds, then burrows back into her nylon sleeping bag. "Uh!" She flips abstractly onto her side, like a fish flopping on a deck, demonstrating just how annoyed she is that I woke her up.

"Shh!"

"I'm hungry!" Quinn and I are, perhaps, too comfortable with one another. We're whiny and sarcastic like quippy sisters. She stretches both arms to the sky and groans again. It's no use trying to sleep through this, so I roll over the edge of my bed onto two feet.

We head to the kitchen where Brian's reading the back of the Cheerios box. Quinn grabs it from him. "Hey!" he says. She just glares.

At ten o'clock, Quinn leaves with her little backpack of stuff, heading up the boardwalk toward home.

Brian is super into this episode of *Knight Rider*. With bright eyes, he looks my way. "I love this one!" When Doug is home from boarding school, he gets into *Knight Rider* with Brian, but there's only so much enthusiasm for Kit and Michael I have to share this morning.

"Uh-huh," I mumble and sit on the couch next to him and zone out. Mom and Dad come in together. Dad heads straight for the remote and turns off the TV.

"Hey!" squeals Brian.

"Let's go for a family walk."

"Doug's not here, so technically, it's not a family walk." Brian has learned a new word, but technically, Dad is humorless.

"It doesn't matter. Let's go." I think this is a bit odd. We're not really a walk-on-the-beach-together kind of family.

Mom and Dad are quick out the door and over the boardwalk. Brian and I run toward the ocean to catch up. Where the sea meets the land, we reach them and turn south along the shore. We find that sweet spot in the grade, where we can walk straight and the crust crumbles underfoot with the sand giving way to the sea. The Pacific in winter lacks some of its effervescence.

Soft, undulating ripples and white water full of light have given way to waves that crash with intention and strong, dark currents.

A few minutes into our pilgrimage south, Mom speaks. "Dad and I have to tell you two something very serious." Brian stops to grab a seashell, drops it, and reaches out again. "I have lung cancer." Brian freezes in place. I lose feeling in my fingers. My sea-drenched feet are even colder after her words wash over me. "But don't worry," she says, "I'm going to fight this."

I try to imagine what it means to fight cancer. I think Brian imagines she's joined a cage-fighting league. He reaches out with a little pink hand that Mom grabs. "I'm very sick," she says. Brian looks comatose and Dad's green eyes are rimmed in red.

We walk in silence until we fall under the shadow of the pier, where Brian takes off running. He runs for the break wall ahead at the marina. I jog toward him and kick some seafoam around like a fierce ballet dancer in *West Side Story*. I have this third-person view of myself I watch in black and white, an old movie reel of me playing by the shore. It's pitiful and dramatic, and I don't quite know what to make of it. As the closing credits roll, Brian rescues a sand dollar right before it's dragged back to sea.

○○

After school, Quinn and I part ways at 28th Street. I reach the boardwalk where a few people pass me on bikes. A very slow jogger breathes heavily down my back for an entire block. I try to speed up and lose her, but figure I might trigger her prey drive if I run. So I just put up with it, that noisy threat of her heavy breath chasing me down. At 16th Street, I take shelter behind our gate. Here, I shudder and let her zombie on by.

Mom's at the kitchen counter. Her hair is thinning. Her eyes are swollen. I walk up with my arms outstretched. She swipes the shoulder-length locks from her collarbone in anticipation of my embrace, and we watch in horror as some of her hair floats to the ground.

It's come right out from the roots. Neither one of us says a word about it.

In my room, I close the door. I can feel the all-consuming pull of my own changing chemistry. I've become a self-absorbed teenager. In a strange twist, I'm acutely aware of my own self-centeredness. My teenage self contemplates the teenage condition—that these years should feel full of infinite possibilities. I should believe in eternity and feel larger than life. In this ironic clash of worlds, I'm beginning to mother myself, all too aware that this is the time to be carefree.

But, of course, mortality looms. I replay the little moments in my head. I take my dinner plate from Mom's delicate hand. It's ridden with cancer. I see her cough into her napkin, and I shirk away because it's tainted with cancer.

Mom has always believed she could never be too rich or too thin. But now, she's thinner than she would ever want to be. Her pectoral is marked by a surgically-installed port—this white, android-looking body part that allows for easy and frequent access to her bloodstream. Our fridge is full of aloe vera juice. A few times a day, she takes swigs of this cloudy, green drink. It's thick and bitter.

At 5:30 p.m., there's a knock downstairs. "Kate, please get the door." Mom coughs through her words. That signature cough is how I find her in the aisles of Target or the country club locker room. I open the front door for a sterile-looking woman in a white tunic and pants. She's got a folding table under her arm.

"Hi, I'm here for Linda." The woman speaks apologetically.

"It's my massage," Mom says, though it's faint, so I let the woman in.

By dark, Brian's watching Roadrunner cartoons. I make some chicken scratch on my math homework. I think it looks like a valiant effort, but it's the bare minimum with some embellishment.

"Hey, Brian, let's go outside."

"Why?" he grumbles.

"Dunno. Let's just go." I walk outside to the boardwalk in my bare feet. "Come on," I gesture. He throws down his skateboard and follows me. Every few feet, he does an ollie or a kick flip. When a pedestrian passes, he glares, as if somehow that person is responsible for all his pain and disappointment. A little old woman lets her Yorkie nose up to a wheel of his board and he scowls.

At Pier Avenue, we make a left onto the wide walk-street toward a few bars and T-shirt shops and into a courtyard with a manzanita tree. I look up at a neon sign over the storefront, kitty-corner from what was once Fancy This. It's a coffee shop called Yesterdays.

"Hey, Gwak, do you have any money?"

He flinches at his babyhood nickname. We've never bothered to ask Mom why she calls him this or whether she regrets that momentary inspiration of a grunt sound that could possibly follow him for the rest of his life. "Uh." He turns the pockets of his gray corduroys inside out. A few quarters fall to the ground, and a five-dollar bill seems to appear out of nowhere.

"Did you rob a bank or something?" I take his money and buy a coffee for here and a root beer. We sit under the manzanita at a table for two.

"How's everything going with you, Brian?"

His eyes well up, but he remains tough. "Uh. Bad." He shakes his head and looks down at his soft drink.

"Yeah." I don't try to argue.

"How do you think Preppy Prepster's doing in Massachusetts?" We like to make fun of Doug. He's out of place here in this beach-bum land of surfers and skaters, but he looks so appropriate in his preppy attire. It's as if he's caught the fancy gene or something.

"Dunno. Rockin' the pleated khakis, probably," I say. "Playing lacrosse and generally just dorking out." Brian laughs and his face softens. I remember he's only ten.

"Hey, Kate, we should hang more."

"Yeah, it seems so obvious. I'm not sure why we forget that."

When we get back home, Mom and Dad are talking on the phone with Doug. It's late in Massachusetts. "It's wicked late," I say to Brain. He grins in acknowledgment of the overused colloquialism that Doug's picked up since he's been "back" there.

Hoping for the best and preparing for the worst is having different effects on all of us. Brian and I stand in the stairwell and eavesdrop on our parents talking to Doug. "You should stay at school," Mom says. She might think she's protecting him from her reality by keeping him away. But I can feel him here anyway, as if a part of him has traveled through the fiber optics of the telephone lines, traversed the valleys and mountains and state lines to be here with us. Mom persists, "Stay there at school. We'll let you know if anything changes."

We jump when Maria startles us in the stairwell. She reaches out like a spider biting my arm. "Te pica!" (It bites you!), she says quietly, so as not to give away our position. A minute later, she comes back with a stack of laundry balanced on her head. We share a glance and I see it. She thinks Doug should be here. She doesn't understand why my parents would deny him the togetherness he seeks.

Maria worked for years to bring her own daughters here from Guatemala. Their togetherness was her reason for this American life, the reason why she worked and saved and worked. We WASPs carry on working for the sake of work itself. With our Protestant work ethic and our faith in science, we wait for things to change as we just carry on.

But back in my room, I see that things are changing, all right. I look out my window to the tide. The waves crest and crash. Sea creatures hatch and die and leave a shell or a sand dollar on the beach, a little bit of joy or tangible beauty. There's an order to the world, if not any actual meaning or purpose. I hear the rustle of the whitewater rushing backward into the rapture of the sea. In these small moments, that order is everything to me.

I pull Jenny's cheesy trucker hat down low. Quinn squeals something about lice. "Jenny! Did you wash that hat yet?"

I round the corner to Jenny's bathroom, passing a framed photo of Mr. Cipriani fishing with his brother. It must be 1975. They must be in their twenties. They wear side mesh, vented trucker hats almost identical to this Salvation-Army find. In the bathroom mirror, I look at myself in this hat and think I look awesome—and maybe I have lice.

"Bye girls! Be good!" Jenny's dad's holding a guitar case. Her parents are wearing western boots and button-down flannel shirts. They peek into the kitchen from the foyer, looking giddy, and wave to us. Then they're gone.

"How do you know when the spaghetti's done?" Quinn yells to Jenny from the stovetop.

"Hold on!" Jenny props open a door in the hallway. I hear her thump from plank to plank as she descends the basement stairs. She comes back after a few minutes, holding a bottle of red wine. "Ta da! It's Italian! You just see if the noodles will stick to the wall. That's what my mom does." The cork looks red from years of contact and seepage. Jenny turns the bottle around and around on the countertop and pulls the corkscrew from the bottle until it pops.

"Won't your parents notice?" I pull down on the brim of my hat. Strands of hair have fallen from my messy pony and I swipe them away from my eyes.

"Nope. All the wine down there actually belongs to our landlords. I'm pretty sure they don't even know they left it. My dad's gigs go on all night, anyways. We're good."

"Cool." I hop onto the kitchen counter and tug at my trucker hat again. I make sure it carries the proper ironic effect. A noodle flies over my left shoulder and sticks to the tile behind me on the wall.

In the living room, Jenny lights a match and throws it into the fire. She touches the needle to an LP of *The White Album*. We eat from our heaping plates of noodles and tomato sauce. She hands us each an oversized fork and a glass full of red wine. Jenny's a doer. She's skilled at working with the elements. None of the Ciprianis are waiting for a servant to come through and handle the living for them. Mr. Cipriani makes his own beer and music. Mrs. Cipriani paints. I think this engagement with the art of living makes them a happy family.

Halfway through my bowl of spaghetti, I realize my fingers are warm and my thoughts are fuzzy. The music seems to be getting louder. We take turns in the large, wooden rocker in front of the fire. We sit cross-legged around the rustic coffee table, lounging back onto our hands on the 1970s river rock floor. It imprints our palms and sort of hurts but feels rustic and right. We're surrounded by crocheted, afghan blankets in bright tattered patterns and beaten-up flotaki rugs that were most likely inherited a generation ago.

"Have you noticed that our favorite stuff is from the seventies?" I say.

Nobody answers, but we all look around.

"Ah, so true! The Beatles, the Allman Brothers Band, the Rolling Stones. Even modern grunge came from Neil Young and seventies rock." Quinn looks down at her floral button-down shirt. "Our clothes too."

"Why *is* that?" Nobody bothers to answer me. I roll my wine around in its glass. A little sloshes over the edge onto the floor. "Oops. Maybe it's this place?"

"What place?" Jenny looks at me sideways. "My super cheesy, outdated rental house?" For a second, I think she's offended, but then she puts her wine down and dances around the coffee table before draping an afghan over her shoulders and squatting before the fire. The Ciprianis' home isn't fancy; it's full of creature comforts and meant for living.

"It's not this *house*, at all," I say. "It's the opposite! It's LA, you know? Everything is torn down and built new. There is no time for the spirits to dwell. Maybe our fascination with our birth decade is as simple as our quest for ancestral memory, like, our need to look for clues about how we got here from the relics of the past."

Quinn and Jenny look wide-eyed at each other across our gathering on the floor. They're mocking me. Jenny laughs and spits out a little wine. To my amazement, she's totally unconcerned with the carpet.

At some point, the room begins to spin. I make my way to the bathroom, past the trucker hat photo. There's another one of Matt and Mr. Cipriani side by side in Birkenstocks and sunglasses, like young and old Jesus in shades. I tag it with my right hand as I pass. I brace myself on the walls and have a confrontation with the doorjamb on my way in. Kneeling in front of the toilet, I do a double take at the wooden toilet seat. I am completely out of my element here. It's refreshing, except that I have to grab on with two hands as I vomit.

From the bathroom floor, I see the light fixture is made of jute and wooden beads. Quinn and Jenny come in cackling. I lift my head to berate them. "Shut up, you witches!"

Quinn plops down and strokes my hair. "How are you, baby bear?"

"Uh ... dunno. Not good. But I *love* this wallpaper!"

"You like the old lady flowers, baby bear?"

I reach out and touch the antiquated floral wallpaper. I imagine that an old woman picked it out some thirty years ago and paid attention to every nook and cranny of this cozy home, so it was just so. The bathroom spins. In my peripheral vision, I swear I can see the love in this house. Then, I catch a glimpse of Jenny standing in the doorway, looking in on us, frazzled and sort of ... pissed.

"I think the seventies are awesome," says Quinn, emphatically. "Because it's the love-child era, and we're sort of earth-loving hippies." Then she vomits all over the wall.

"Uh-oh! Hold on!" Jenny bolts down the hall to the left toward the kitchen. I hear her pick up the phone. "Can you leave him a message? Yes, this is Jenny." The phone clicks. A few minutes later, I hear her on the phone with Kelly. "Yeah. I just called him there and left a message. No, he's out on a delivery. Okay. Thanks."

The phone clamors back down onto its plastic receiver. Jenny comes back through the doorway and just stares at us for a few. "Okay," she says, opening the bathroom drawer and grabbing some elastic ponytail holders. I feel her little hands pulling at my scalp and moving my hair into position. "This will be okay," Jenny says. I hear her exhale.

"I can feel the rotation of the earth," I mumble to Quinn.

"I'm the Leaning Tower of Pisa," she says.

After a while, I hear the whir of an old car. A loud knock at the door is answered simultaneously.

"Matt's on a delivery out in Redondo, so you get me. Okay, where are they?" Ross and Jenny are in the doorway, looking us over. "I've got two deliveries in the car, so we have to hurry." He taps me on the back and helps me up. "You're a mess, huh?" He walks me to Jenny's room and zips a sleeping bag around me.

"See, you're like Jesus, too. Not just Matt. So nice!"

"Oh-kay. Lie down. Go to sleep."

Jenny hands me a coverless pillow. It's old and yellowed and full of comforts past. "Sweet, comfy pillow," I tell it.

"I can do it myself," Quinn argues from the bathroom. Then she's on a mat next to me. The world spins and the lights go out.

∽

"Knock-knock!" Jenny's standing behind her mom. She's peering in at us apologetically. "So, what happened here, ladies?" Mrs. Cipriani is chipper. She's talking really loud. "Do we have a roof leak?" She points to the metal cooking pots on the floor all around us. "Are we expecting a flood?"

"They have the flu," says Jenny.

"Ah ... I'll tell you what, let's go look for winter formal dresses. You're all going, right? Breakfast in ten—then we'll head out!" We watch her leave with our mouths open.

At the mall, Mrs. Cipriani speed walks from store to store. We trail behind, miserable. At each store, she's overcome by some fashion frenzy and pushes one of us back by a dress on a hanger, saying, "Try it on! I think this is the one!" We head dutifully to the fluorescent hell of the dressing room, pretending to be just as excited as she is.

Now, she's backing me into a corner with a black and white dress. I take a few steps back before I grab it and pretend to admire the polka dot material. I pull Jenny in with me. "Your mom's trying to kill us!"

By the third store, I just take Mrs. Cipriani's dresses and hang them on the hook inside the dressing room stall. I sit on the little bench inside for a few minutes with my eyes closed.

After an hour and a half, Mrs. Cipriani seems to be taking mercy on us. We stop at Hot Dog on a Stick, where she buys corn dogs and three small lemonades. The Willy Wonka-looking workers bounce up and down behind the counter, pressing on a circus-spectacle machine to pump out our drinks. Their little pinwheel hats spin and make everything worse.

There's some orange chicken from Panda Express smeared onto the tabletop. I watch as Jenny drags her elbow right through it. Quinn speaks very slowly, very intentionally. "So ... your Mom is totally trying to kill us, right?"

"Possibly," says Jenny. "Probably, yes. Yes."

༄

It's Saturday, December 7. First thing in the morning, there's a note on the kitchen counter. "Went to Kenneth Norris with Mom for observation." Mom had her monthly dose of chemo yesterday. They plug her into a bunch of tubes, and she sits around in a huge, white chair in the outpatient center for several hours. She comes home exhausted and sleeps for two weeks. Sometimes, she stays overnight, and they watch her during the subsequent days of flu-like symptoms that Mom calls "The Crud."

I head out to the balcony and watch a few sweatpants-clad joggers hustle by. Seagulls squawk, and the sound drops off in a dull, Doppler aftermath. Brian's standing on the beach wall below, sizing up the surf. "So? How does it look?" A jogger shuffles right through our conversation, oblivious because she's wearing headphones. The desolate feel in the air is intensified by the fact that this woman seems not to notice us at all.

"Surf Line says no good." Brian shakes his head. Each morning is like Groundhog Day for the South Bay surfer. It starts with an early morning call to "Surf Line." If the surf report is bad, there might be a few hours of extra sleep. If the waves are at least three to four feet, a crowd will gather at the beach wall in hoodies and jeans and check out the break for themselves. It might warrant a closer look. They will come in droves and trudge across the sand toward the water in their flip flops and Uggs.

"Let me check out the pier break." He hops onto the wall like a tightrope walker and looks for his dream swell that's still glassy from the night, for a "left" or a "right." He walks along the wall toward the pier to check microclimates as the sea floor changes to the south. I watch him walk back. I listen for the verdict, though I think I know. "Nah. Wheesh!" He jumps backward onto the boardwalk and lands on his feet like a cat.

At 11:20 a.m., Dad comes home. I'm watching *Little House on the Prairie*. "Where's your brother?"

"Sleeping?"

"You louse. Stop watching the boob tube and get off the couch! Tell your brother to get dressed. We're going to visit your mother."

After forty-five minutes in the car, up the 405 to the 110 and east over the Los Angeles river basin, into graffitied streets and through whole neighborhoods of barred windows, we arrive. Brian and I glare out past our own reflections at the oil-stained concrete and blacktop intersection, at the gas station and a convenience store. Dad is a born-and-raised Los Angelino and a frequent motorist through her urban streets. He maneuvers the car into a driveway and up a ramp. He spins the car around to the top floor and parks. We beach kids exit the car with sea legs, feeling seasick and stumble into the building.

We exit the elevator on the fifteenth floor and walk through fluorescent lights and linoleum flooring to room 1532. I expect a nurse to appear in a 1950s pillbox hat and fluff Mom's pillows, perform shock therapy, or drug her against her will. Instead, nobody's here but us.

We see Mom's sleeping, so we file in quietly. I head for the window. Outside is a Mr. Roger's neighborhood of white concrete buildings, railway yards, and truck depots. I see the dry bed of the Los Angeles River in the distance. Outside is a tiny, sun-splashed empire, so ordered and manageable compared to what's going on in here. I feel the heat radiating through the glass. But inside, the air conditioner blows cold, and the curtains enshroud the room in darkness.

"Hi!" Mom says sweetly, raising her head for a moment to greet us.

"Hi, Mom."

"Kate, Brian, do you know you two make me happy every day?"

Subconsciously, I must be weaning off of any reliance on Mom. And I'd been doing so well. Now, my heart muscle cramps, and I fear a full-blown relapse.

∽

I ended up finding a dress for the winter formal at a vintage shop right next to the Salvation Army Thrift Store on Artesia Boulevard. It's pink satin coupled with burgundy velvet. I think it looks like a candy cane or a valentine. It's not even close to "in-style," and that's what I like about it. I took in the waist and added a belt. Jenny and Kelly bought a rainbow of men's bowties at the Goodwill Store, and they are just hoping one of the boys knows how to tie them.

In the kitchen, Quinn and Mr. Heiser are ironing Quinn's dress. I creep around the corner and watch them. He's doing a great job as a single dad. He holds the iron in his right hand. He turns around to rinse a dish with his left. Quinn gives him instructions on how to iron the pleats of her skirt. "Iron over it, over it!" The two of them seem like a team. They are slowed down to take on the challenge of this new reality together. This is *life in a different gear,* I think. My dad doesn't touch the home appliances, except for the coffee percolator.

Mr. Heiser looks to the doorway where I've been creeping. "Hey, Kate ... how's your dad doing?"

"Uh, I don't know. He's working or at the hospital."

"Yeah. Well, please give him my regards."

"I will."

It's a special occasion, so Quinn's wearing lipstick and face powder. She looks beautiful, but I say, "You look like a hussy."

"I know, right? Did you use a blow dryer? You bimbo."

Quinn stuffs her ATM card and a house key in the pocket of her J.Crew barn jacket, and I pull on my black velvet blazer. When we hear the whir of Matt's van, we're out the door.

"Bye, John!" Quinn calls from the stoop in her defiant, little way. He waves through the open door, shaking a shirt that's just come out of the dryer.

At Ross's, a bunch of moms are hanging out as the boys tie their bowties. Quinn and I didn't expect that.

Ross's mom heads our way. Ross told her he has a pizza delivery job, so he can stay out late on weeknights. At her request, he's brought home pizzas, but they're from various different venues. I guess she's sort of an idiot because she still believes him. "Oh, hello, ladies. Is this the fashion these days? I haven't been to the mall in a while to look at the trendy fashions for girls." She's wearing lots of diamonds—stud earrings, a tennis bracelet, and a huge engagement ring. Her brown hair is dyed blonde and curled under—the bangs too.

Quinn pulls on my arm and whispers in my ear, "I feel like we're not getting the mothers' stamp of approval here. She's making me feel like a tramp." Within our group of friends, our dates are chosen by a preschool rubric of who gets along best with whom, and who's left. We're prepared to wait in the photo line together and contribute toward the eighteen dollars for the prints.

"This is just for fun, just like the boys' clothes," I assure Ross's fashionably concerned mother. I point across the living room at our dates in their powder blue tuxedos and ruffled shirts. The six boys in our group are wearing Stetson hats. My date, Dane, wears Adidas with a straw hillbilly hat. His long locks hang underneath like a scarecrow's.

"I see. I assume all the other girls will be wearing new fashions. Won't you look silly?"

"Yes. Probably." She stares at me. She doesn't understand my answer.

Jenny floats over at just the right time. She's wearing a full-length, cream-colored lace gown that I didn't get a good look at on the ride over. It's mock neck with an empire waist, and she has a ring of pink roses on her head like a crown. I think she looks like a fairy princess. Ross's mom looks her up and down. "Oh, you're doing it too … how cute."

"Quinn, Kate, come with me." Ross's mom calls us into the kitchen with a wag of her finger. "Kate, you look so pretty. Dane is a lucky boy." I feel like a hussy for sure now because it's not like that. But my concerns are alleviated when I step into the kitchen and I see them, real-life women in cocktail dresses with cleavage and four-inch heels. "Do you girls know Alma and Soliel? Would you like a Perrier?"

"Hi!" the first girl says sweetly. She walks over without swaying or dragging her ankles even one bit. I look down to check out her strappy sandals. "I'm Alma."

"Hi. Kate."

The crowd gets loud and starts to mobilize. Kelly's aunt drops her off on the curb in the nick of time. She's dressed like a red-headed extra at the Brady Bunch junior prom. The twelve of us file into a blue limo in the driveway. Out the window, I catch a glimpse of Stireman retrieving a bottle of Wild Turkey from the trunk of his VW Bug. He jumps into the limo with us, and before I realize it, we're off.

"You look awesome! This is for you." Dane slips a Gerber daisy corsage over my arm. I wish he hadn't. This makes it seem more like a date than a group hangout. Quinn flashes crossed crucifix fingers at Jackson to repel any similar gifting. He raises his hands in surrender and shows he has no such plan. She turns toward the window and swigs off her PBR.

"Three cheers for Dane!" says Matt. "This is a pretty sweet ride." Dane's dad is a television producer. He lent us his personal limosine for the night. Dane introduces us to the driver, Ron, then gestures like Vanna White all around the inside of the vehicle.

"So cool," I say. "So, who are they?" I point quasi-discreetly with a wave of my index finger across the back seat to the grown women who are going to our high school formal with us.

"Right," Dane laughs. "Ross's neighbor and her friend. They've known Ross and Stireman forever."

"Well played."

"For sure."

"Bye, Mrs. Ross," Alma calls from the window as the limo leaves the driveway, and I remember that Ross is just his last name. For the life of me, I can't remember his first.

In the high school gym, Matt and Kelly dance to C+C Music Factory's "Everybody Dance Now!" And almost everyone does. When the song's over, Matt turns for the bleachers until the DJ fades in EMF's "Unbelievable." He spins enthusiastically around and pulls Kelly back to the dance floor.

"More Than Words" starts up and it's awkwardly romantic. I drag Dane off the floor because I don't want to give him the wrong idea. I look over at Ross, who's staring at the punch bowl. Alma grabs his arm with her utter womanly confidence and pulls him out there. Soliel beelines for Stireman, who's been a deer in headlights since the first chord.

Dane and I sit on the bleachers and sway and watch the four of them dance a slow dance. I follow the strobe light on slow mode across the floor, until it blasts my junior-class buddies and their lady friends. I see a light of confidence in Ross and Stireman that wasn't there before, and I think that whoever these ladies are, they are good people.

After the slow dance, Dane looks at me. "Should we get out of here?"

"Sure. And go where?"

"Wherever!" Dane yells over the music as he starts rounding up the troops.

Within five minutes, the twelve of us bound happily into the mist of the December night, toward Ron, who is waiting at the curb. "So, where to?" Dane shrugs absentmindedly. "Never mind, kids. I'll show you a good time." Ron laughs and closes the partition.

As the car starts to roll, Alma starts rolling a joint. I put out my hand to her friend. "I'm Kate."

"Soliel," she says, shaking my hand. I nod because she looks like a Soliel. I take them in. They're like fortune-tellers, tanned with high cheekbones. Alma's dress is made of purple velvet and Soliel's wearing a printed chiffon, three-quarter bell sleeve dress. It actually looks good on her.

"So how do you know Ross and Stireman?" Soliel's straight, brown hair is parted down the middle. She has a hoop nose ring that makes her look exotic and magical.

"I grew up with them. Our parents are friends." She takes a hit off Alma's joint, then shakes her head as if she's surprised and says, "Sorry. I didn't offer you one—do you want a hit?"

"No, thanks." I take a sip of my Boone's Farm Strawberry Hill. Soliel exhales a dense, white cloud that fills the back seat of the limo. "So are you in school?"

"Yes," Soliel answers warmly. "I go to the junior college, and Alma goes to Chico State. She's home for Christmas."

"Welcome home," I say to Alma, and the limo breaks into a round of cheers.

The doors fly open and we file out. "Welcome to Dockweiler Beach," Ron says in a cheesy, official way. He takes my hand to help me out.

"Thank you!" I smile and hug him. "I love this beach. You can bring your dog here, and it's one of the only places in LA you can have a bonfire! I have always been the girl driving past, looking out at other people lost in a moment in time, their bonfires breathing life into the wind!"

"Well! Then I did good. Tonight's your moment, dear." Ron's eyes twinkle.

I hold onto Quinn, who's steadying herself on the side of the limo. We take off our heels and run barefoot into the elements.

A golden retriever runs up to greet us by rubbing its back on my leg and licking Jenny's hand. Her date, Mark, does his job and takes the brunt of it when the pup goes primate to lick her face on hind legs. Ron stumbles out onto the sand, drops a stack of firewood into an empty firepit, and lights our hearth. I sift through the cool sand with my feet. I look up to the highway, thinking that in one of those passing cars, a little girl might see us and want to be out here herself one day.

Quinn takes out Dane's Polaroid camera and snaps a photo of our group around the bonfire.

"Doesn't it feel good to take photos?" says Alma. "It's such a life-affirming act, creating art, connecting souls." She takes the photo from Quinn. "Look—no matter where our minds were in that second, this photo brings us together in a moment." She shakes the picture in the breeze.

"Yeah, love is art," says Soliel. "It's committing to an ideal." For a second, I think she's the smartest person I've ever met. Then, she dives into the sand and starts swimming freestyle. "I'm so stoned!"

When the fire reaches full height, Alma stands up. I expect her to sing "Circle in the Sand." Instead, she proclaims, "Okay, guys, we're playing I Never! I never go to class high." She takes a swig from her bottle of Wild Turkey. She elbows Ross.

"Uh, I never filled up my dad's whiskey with a cheap replacement." He drinks. We all stare at him. It's Jenny's turn.

"I never took a rotten hundred-year-old bottle of wine from my basement cellar and almost killed my friends with it." Jenny drinks. Then, Quinn and I drink because we survived.

※

The fire smolders. I look through the flames at Alma and Soliel, who are huddled together sweetly. Just when we're all staring, the two jump onto their bare feet, grab their shoes, and run hand in hand to the car. Their chiffon and velvet dresses bounce behind them like a spell.

Ron rolls down the partition, looks at me, and asks, "Well, princess ... did you create your moment?" I smile and show him the picture. He nods. His eyes twinkle. "How about the views from the hills?"

"Sounds good!" says Dane. He pops in a CD and hits play. "Hello, I love you ..."

We head north on the highway until we get to Marina Del Rey. We pull onto Lincoln Boulevard in Venice Beach. I knock on the partition.

"Let's go see Jim!" I say, and amazingly, Ron knows exactly what I'm talking about.

"Sure thing, princess. Wavecrest Avenue?"

"Love me two times ..." I look across the limo at Matt. He wears his Stetson low over his brow and takes a swig from his beer.

The car stops, and Ron jumps out to open the door. I'm the first one out. I look up at the wall and get a chill. "Oh!" I utter out loud and startle myself because I sound just like Grandma. I rub the goose bumps on my arm and it's her arm. I stand here, looking at this rendering of *Starry Night* that's as large as the building, and think that this postimpressionist madness, the bold colors and dramatic impulsive brushwork, is more full of life than a composed piece could ever be.

"Wait! Abort!" yells Ron. "Wrong street, wrong mural. Sorry! We need to go a few more blocks."

"Kate! Get in!" I hear from behind me. I don't care. I stand here another minute under the *Starry Night*. I allow myself to float away in the emotion of this madman's swirly sky of teal, yellow, and black. It's always the passionate mad ones who speak to me—the Van Goghs, the Munches. I get goose bumps again and I think of Grandma.

After a few more blocks, we file out of the back seat and I see him. Jim towers above us, twenty feet high, life-like, bare-chested, and beaded in leather pants. The waves crack and reverberate between the buildings in the back alley of the Venice boardwalk. Dane hands Ron the camera, and he snaps a shot of the twelve of us leaning against the Jim wall in dresses, the boys in cowboy boots and Stetson hats. We look like a gang of outlaws.

Back in the limo, we ascend the hills of the Palisades. Streetlights dim as we wind through residential streets. Matt messes with the CD player until he gets to "L.A. Woman," then he turns it up. Alma opens the window and lets in the smell of eucalyptus. As we climb away from the sea, warm vegetation overtakes the smell of salt. The even tempo of cymbals builds until the empty spaces crash into themselves. Bright peaks of energy fall back into deep lows where my desire resides. These waves reach a crescendo, and my fingertips tingle with life.

"This song is so orgasmic!" yells Soliel above the music.

Alma nods. The two of them close their eyes and roll their heads back and forth to the song. The very waves that infuse my fingers seem to choreograph their dance. "So tantric!" yells Alma. I breathe in and out and tingle with wide-eyed revelation.

"Last stop," says Ron through the cracked partition. We file out of the back seat and shuffle through gravel and dirt to a clearing where he says, "Voilà!" The back door of the limo is open, and we hear Jim Morrison through the speakers not twenty feet away. "L.A. woman … L.A. woman …"

Are you lucky, he asks me. Gazing past dark arroyos to the jewels of the city below, I get goosebumps. A flash of gratitude runs through me. I am, this is—lucky, indeed.

༄

It's Monday. I woke up to a scratchy throat and Dad knocking at my door.

"Just a second!"

"Uh, Kate … Brian just got picked up for school. I can drive you, but you are going to have to go early, okay?" This isn't a question. He's telling me. I'm thinking of rushing through my breakfast to take him up on his offer, but then I vomit on the floor.

"Oh, crap!" Dad spits. He's more angry than empathetic. "Okay, stay home. I'll call you in an hour."

I grab some paper towels from the kitchen and start cleaning the floor.

An hour into my solitary morning, the phone rings. "Mrs. Reznick is going to pick you up. She picked Ami up from school; I guess she's sick too. You can stay home together."

The Reznicks live down the boardwalk. I've known Ami my whole life, but still, none of this makes sense.

"I'm fine here alone, Dad," I say, but the phone just clicks, so I grab my backpack and sit miserably at the bottom of the steps and wait for my ride.

Their minivan pulls up, and I hear spritely footsteps leading up to the door. Ami knocks once and is startled when I immediately answer.

"Hi," she hugs me. Ami was named after a nurse at the hospital where she was born, one who shared in the excitement as her parents waited for her birth mother to deliver. By all accounts, her biological mother was a pale, Scandinavian blonde. Going off this premise, Ami's own cocoa skin and soft curls don't provide many clues to her paternity, but she and I have speculated that her father was Caribbean or Croatian. For a while, we fantasized he was a basketball star, and when we found an old newspaper clipping on the floor of the Reznick home office of a player in full dunk, we were certain this was the fantastic secret they had been keeping all along.

Ami and I are devious together, little menaces. And knowing her as I do, I look into her sea-green eyes for a clue about what's really going on.

"You don't seem sick."

"Uh, yeah, I am," she says. Then she does a fake little cough, and we hop into the back of their champagne-colored Astro van and close the sliding door.

"Hi, Kate! We have movies and cough drops, and I made the playroom up for you guys to lounge around."

"Okay." I'm suspicious of them, but happy for whatever this is.

⁕

We're halfway through *Thelma and Louise* for the second time when I cough, and then Ami coughs. I reach out for a Ricola, and then she reaches for the same one. I swear she's just copying me. I look her in the eye up close but from the side, like a sandpiper. We have this sideways stare-down thing that makes us laugh. She freezes because she's been caught. Something is definitely up.

The phone rings, and I hear Mrs. Reznick traipse across the wooden floor in the kitchen above us. A few minutes later, she's rambling down the stairs in full conversation. "Kate, get your street clothes on. Your dad is coming to pick you up."

A car in the alley screeches to a stop. Mrs. Reznick heads out, and I hear a shrill, nasal voice. It's not Dad, it's Grandma.

I straighten my sweatshirt and cinch my ponytail in the hope I can pass without ridicule. Mrs. Reznick and Grandma share a quick and businesslike conversation, then it's silent. I get into the back seat of her white Mercedes. Ami and her mom wave slowly as we pull away.

Grandma doesn't speak to me. She drives her stop-and-go New York City driving. As we pull onto the 405, she finally says, "Your dad will meet us there."

Forty-five minutes later, I'm seasick from the stop-and-go. I'm defenseless against the seriousness of Grandma's mood, and nobody is here to get my mind off her terrifyingly quick stops or her lead-footed acceleration. We stop, every time, just a few feet from the bumper of the car in front of us.

It's funny when Doug and Brian are here. We make wide-eyed faces and throw our bodies forward from fake inertia. We toss a callous arm across the back seat from time to time to simulate Grandma's half-hearted attempts at preventing passenger injury. I think of all the gestures I'd make if my brothers were here, but it's no fun being Grandma's passenger alone.

In the parking lot of the Kenneth Norris Research Hospital, Grandma comes to a quick stop. "Get out!"

Through the lobby door, I see Dad and Doug standing under fluorescent lights. I make a little eye contact with Doug to let him know that my ride was less than pleasant. He does a whiplash type of headbanger move, raises his brow in acknowledgment, and within an instant, his face is solemn again.

I nod. Yes, exactly.

On the sixth floor, Grandma pushes Dad aside as she exits the elevator and heads for the reception desk. Several nurses are there to greet us, but none really look at us. It's a polite, noses-to-the-grindstone act they're performing. Grandma is given four sticker ID badges that she holds in her hands. She storms down the hall.

"Come on!" she barks. The nurses behind the desk finally look up as we turn to walk away. I look to their faces and see everything I was afraid to ask.

They know. We have come to say good-bye. Now I know.

"How did you get here?" It's been two months since Doug left for the winter term at school in Massachusetts. He looks windburned, and his hair color is flat from lack of sunlight.

"I took the red-eye. My RA woke me up at midnight and drove me to the airport. Dad just picked me up. Where's Brian?"

"School, I guess."

Outside room 632, we stop under the fluorescent light fixture. Grandma grabs me by the shoulder. I watch as her fingernails clamp down on Doug's arm like talons. "Go!" she says, pushing us into the room. I stumble on Doug's foot as we enter. I would have preferred being pulled in by the earlobe.

A nurse inside puts her head down. She changes a bag of fluid hanging on a metal rack and says quietly, "She can't move or talk, but she can hear you."

Doug and I stare down at Mom. I want to reach out and hold her hand. But I'm not sure she'd feel it, and I'm afraid of the power we might generate by connecting my life with her death. So, I reach out to touch her, but I retract before I do. I fear sparks or electricity or even worse, nothing.

A few minutes later, Grandma comes in. She's followed by Dad, who lurks in the corner. Grandma asks the nurse something about the fluid bag filling up quicker now and barks, "Well, change it, then!"

When the nurse is finished, Grandma walks over and touches Mom's arm. The nurse stands, stunned, and looks on as Mom's right hand starts to rise, ever so slowly. Finally, her arm is suspended in air. All of us look on as Mom points her index finger right at Grandma.

"You … need … help," Mom says breathlessly and determinately. Then, she shuts her eyes and lays her arm back down on the bed.

Grandma gasps, "Oh, that's the morphine talking!"

"No, ma'am," says the nurse, from behind the headboard. "We took her off the morphine yesterday. She wanted to have a clear mind."

"Come on!" Grandma demands and brushes Doug and me out the door.

In the hall, Grandma turns to the elevator bank and leaves. Dad glows like a zombie under the hospital lights. His eyes are glassy and swollen and even greener now that the rims are so red.

A middle-aged man in a lab coat approaches us. "Hi. Are you Doug? Kate? I'm Dr. Neibaum. Please, come with me." We follow him to a small waiting room with brown pleather chairs. He gestures for us to sit.

"Your mom is actively dying." He pauses and looks at us. "She is not in pain. We will give her medication to keep her comfortable." He pauses again. He looks down at the ground, then at his hands and asks, "Do you have any questions?"

There is no question I could ask that I want the answer to. We shake our heads. Dr. Neibaum pats each of us on the shoulder, picks up his clipboard, and leaves us in the little room under the fluorescent lights on our pleather chairs.

On the forty-five-minute drive home, nobody speaks. I watch a man at the gas station in his business suit. He glances at his watch hurriedly. He can't pump his gas fast enough. The bus stop is brimful of captives waiting in line to clock in. There's a lack of inspiration out here that has nothing to do with our hospital visit. It makes me eager to create something, to make a little piece of my soul tangible and earthy while I'm still here. In the world of forty-five-minute drives, this one is gritty and has an aftertaste of time passing too quickly.

Dad's Baltic Blue BMW careens up the apron of our driveway and then comes to a jolt and a stop. "Okay, I'm going to work. I'll see you tonight."

Inside, the vacuum cleaner is running, and the sound is like a thousand angels singing. It's normalcy in a life where removing dust and pet hair from our home still matters. Maria turns the vacuum cleaner off as we enter.

"Mijo! Mi reina!" (My son! My queen!) she calls to us with arms outstretched. We hug her, and then we lock ourselves in our rooms.

After ten o'clock, I burrow in my bed, just lying in the dark and listening to the waves crash. It's not until the first crack of dawn, when I'm assured the light will make good on its promise to return, that I surrender to sleep. Dad knocks around 6:30 a.m., telling me I can stay home from school today, so I sleep some more. Around 10:15 a.m., Doug comes barging in with a basketball that he throws at my feet.

"Get up!"

"Why?"

"I don't know. Just get up."

I roll over and pull the covers over my head. "Ugh, Doug, I just want to sleep."

"Dad's at work or something. Brian's at school. I don't want to hang out alone."

Dad must've sent Brian to school in the hope that the normalcy and structure of being in school would shelter him from the pain here on the outside. "Fine," I moan. "Give me five minutes." Doug takes his basketball and leaves.

I stumble out to the kitchen in my sweats, and Doug says, "Let's go outside."

"Fine." I follow him down the slate steps in my bare feet. We cross the boardwalk and hop the beach wall. We're halfway to the water when Doug sits down in the warm sand. I lie on my stomach, letting sand into my shirt and up my pantlegs.

Doug takes a driftwood twig that's dry and dusty and starts writing his name. It's bright, and my pupils have shrunk as much as they can to save my vision. But still, I look up, and Doug's head hovers over me in a dark shadow.

A wave booms. A seagull shrieks past. Thump, thump, thump—a skateboarder hurries down the boardwalk, and then he's gone.

All of a sudden, the cloudless sky flashes purple, like when a rain cloud passes before the sun. I look up for a rogue cloud or the world's largest flock of seagulls, but there's nothing.

"Did you see that?" Doug asks. "Mom just died. Let's go inside." At home, we close the front door. My eyes struggle to adjust to the dark. Before we can make it up the front stairs, the phone rings. Doug runs for the receiver and I listen.

All he says is "Okay." He puts the phone down. "Yup," he says, looking at me with blank eyes. We wait in the living room for Dad to come home, wondering how we're going to tell Brian.

Doug sits across from me in his chair. He palms the upholstered arms. Both his feet are flat on the floor. I think, *He could return a pretty mean tennis serve like this*. I see the wheels spinning in his head.

"Dude, pretty amazing, right?" I just look at him. His words barely rouse my mind from its numb state. I have no idea what he's talking about. "The purple flash. You saw it, right? When Mom died. We knew."

"Yes."

"And how Mom woke up from her coma and finally told off Grandma?"

"Yeah," I say in a daze. "I guess it's the last thing she ever did."

Falling from Orbit

I see red currents in the surf. I think I'm losing my mind. My gaze falls on the boardwalk below, onto a group of girls walking toward my house. For a moment, they're ugly strangers, nobodies. Then I realize it's Quinn and Ami. I think about hiding, but as they approach, their visit becomes inevitable, so I cover up in a sweatshirt and cut them off in the yard.

We move quickly through condolences to topics like how the quaddies are all starting to look alike because the ringleader cut her hair and started a trend, and how none of the guys on the football team are actually very cute.

It's the cheerleader effect but for boys, I guess. We move inside and the phone rings.

"Hello."

"Kate … it's Mrs. Reznick. Your mother was so dear to all of us. The girls and I want you to know that we are here for you. Please, tell Ami to be home by six."

I listen to her voice over the line and realize what a meddlesome and wonderful woman Ami's mother is. Grandma calls her a "bleeding-heart liberal" because she has apparently burned her bra and other unladylike things, like performing social work and serving as a nurse in Vietnam. Unlike Grandma, Mrs. Reznick isn't lost in abstraction, those little, reckless fragments of hurt and jealousy that fuel one's ego. She seems to see the big picture of our connectedness.

By orchestrating this visit, and our *Thelma and Louise* movie day, she has become truly meaningful to me. All I say over the telephone is, "Thank you," but I hope she understands the full breadth of my gratitude.

When the girls leave, the house is dark and I'm alone. There really is no reason to stay here, so I put on my sweats and zip up my hoodie and run out the door to the ocean. I turn south, but see a bulldozer off in the distance. Its steely claws and soulless body dump sand in a heap by the pier, so I turn north and flee.

A safe distance from the John Deere, I run up the berm until the sky reflects in puddles on the sand, and the earth is spinning a little. My lungs burn from inhalation of the December sea. I run until I can barely see straight, and my cheeks are frozen in the cold, salt air.

I have no idea how long I run, but I finally come to a stop under the Manhattan Beach pier. I sit between pillars on the sand and watch the waves as they careen toward me from ten pilings out.

I think about nothing.

I feel nothing.

I sit here until it's dark. It's not until I get hungry and cold and start to lose feeling in my toes that I stand up, brush the sand from my sweatpants, and start walking south again toward home.

I roll slowly over the ball of each foot. Little puddles of quicksand jiggle under my weight. In the last light of dusk, I leap over a bed of kelp and notice a boogie board is obscured in a tangle of waxy seaweed. Some sand crabs scurry from the receding tide and burrow into holes that have appeared and disappeared before my eyes.

I trip a little and kick up some wet sand, and when I do, a spark shoots out on impact. I look back to see my footprints have left glowing, green pools. I twist my foot deeper into the sludge and make a tiny pond. The water warms when I agitate it and answers back in a phosphorescent glow.

The whole way home, my mortal feet connect with this celestial light. In front of my home lifeguard tower at 16th Street, I stand to face the waves. White seafoam rustles over the red tide. A wave forms and crests and cascades over itself. I watch it crash. The entire coastline lights up in an intermittent turquoise flash.

There's not a soul out here but me and the tiny plankton that have lit my way. I think, *Spirits come in so many forms.*

⁓

I haven't seen or heard from my grandparents in months. Before I talk myself out of it, I walk four doors down the boardwalk. I rationalize along the way that casual visits with grandparents are normal. In the four-foot breezeway separating Grandma from her neighbor, I ring their bell. The sound incites chaos within, and I get chills just listening to the shuffle. Pico and the poodles, Daphne and Delilah, bark to alert the occupants of my presence. Grandma yells to Grandpa, "Robert! The door!"

They answer as a team and look down at me on the stoop. Their faces are distant as they wait for me to explain the intrusion. I feel like a Jehovah's Witness, and in order to gain access to their home, I tell them my intentions.

"I just came by for a visit."

"Oh?" Grandma looks me up and down. "Okay," she says coolly and steps aside to let me in.

On the inside, I am offered a place on the couch and a Coke. In return, I offer some companionship. When I object to her characterization of my outfit as "homely," Grandma punishes me by acting as if I'm not here. She passsive-aggressively peruses a stack of papers on her desk and returns phone calls from frenemies with whom she likes to gossip. I'm more or less ignored. I stare at the floor, down at her cheetah-print carpet. It's interesting and intimidating all at the same time. It's very her, and I'm convinced this is the hottest thing in home fashions right now.

After about ten minutes, Grandpa comes in from his workshop in the garage and wrangles up the poodles for a walk. This is a good opportunity to drag myself out of here. "Hey, Grandpa! I'll walk with you." Despite his PhD in astrophysics and the fact that his patents are invaluable to our national security, Grandpa never says much. He is my step-grandpa, after all, so he stays out of it, letting "Mama" do all the talking.

"Good-bye," she says to me, dispassionately. I tag along awkwardly with Grandpa and Daphne and Delilah to the corner, where my empty house has never looked so inviting.

"Good-bye, Grandpapa."

"So long, now," he grumbles. He waves good-bye without looking, or even turning his head my way.

༺ ༻

At ten to one each Saturday, I arrive at Café Strada. "How's my favorite barista?" calls Chip.

"Hey! I thought I was your favorite." Shelby slaps him in the back of the head. This is my work family. They're dependable and give me the togetherness and structure I seek, without any of the emotional baggage. Plus, the smell in here is awesome.

Over the past year, I've worked here on the weekends. Dad, of course, thinks this is a great display of the Protestant work ethic. I hear from Brian how mortified Grandma is that I'm working as a waitress on Pier Avenue. *They,* of course, will have a field day with this one.

Grandma plants ideas she hopes will sprout and grow until we can no longer contain and keep them to ourselves. Brian tells me it's good that I've chosen to start working now, as Grandma doesn't plan on giving me anything when she dies. Maybe, if Brian is good to her, he will deserve her money instead. This is how she tries to drive us apart. This is little Brian playing right into her hands.

Her message is also a provocation for us to do more to please her. It's brilliantly executed, with the dual purpose of causing strife between us. By uniting, we stand; by dividing, we fall. She swings. She plays us against one another and keeps us from forming alliances.

But, somehow, my brothers and I are united by humor. "When I die …" we joke to one another. We fall over laughing. But it's not funny, not really.

Grandma seems to believe her value to us will become apparent in the form of a lump sum after she's dead—or not—and that's the carrot she dangles. But we laugh because her comments are shocking and unexpected of a grandmother. We emulate her nasal voice, a few decibels too loud. We startle each other from around corners and through open doorways, when the other believes they are alone. "When I die!" We shock one another as she shocks us, and our laughter is fantastic therapy.

What Grandma will never understand is that I like work. It's real and honest. It's a constant practice in perseverance and grit and a study in the pitfalls of human psychology. There is no time for drama at work; we just move on, doing what we do, and we do it as a team. I think coffee shops are like churches, so full of hope and energy and communal connection.

I tie on my apron and take my place behind the register just as Creepy Guy walks in. Like usual, he flirts and asks his inappropriate questions: "So where's your boyfriend, again?"

Not today. I flash Chip a look and make a swift U-turn to the back. He takes over at the register just like that.

"Where's Kate?"

"Uh, dunno, maybe unpacking boxes in the back."

When he's gone, we switch back, just as seamlessly as before.

The next guy sashays forward. "Do you remember my name?"

"John? Bob? Joe?" He's not amused. "No, sir, I don't. But, I know you come in often."

"I come in here all the time! Why can't you remember? Do you think you'll even be able to get my order right?" His eyes are distant, as if he looks through murky layers of condescension. He rubs his little boy's hair and puts him on alert. Watch and learn, son. "Half-caf, nonfat, doppio Americano, with just one inch of whip cream."

And maybe a side of self-esteem, I think.

I smile at the little boy. I hand his dad the fussy drink. I think of the irony. This man seems to feel so powerless in the world that he tries to belittle others. He feels this small, and yet he's narcissistic and seems to not believe in anything greater than himself.

At work, I practice the art of spreading positive energy and dealing with difficult people. I think about Grandma and her cycle of emotional abuse, the gaslighting, how Mom was starting to put her foot down with the gift shop and how she came out of a coma to tell her off while she still could. But, no matter, it took its toll.

Here at work, I shake off the superficial, the needy, and the ego. With my negative ions coated in grace, I dole out coffee and community. Customer service is an ugly, beautiful thing. Still, it's easier than dealing with family.

After work, I head for the boardwalk. I sit on the lawn at the little, beachfront park for a few minutes, ruffling blades of grass with my palms. Thank God for this grass. It's green and lush, and it absorbs my despair. Thank God for this earth. It lives and dies and endures. After some minutes of silence in the breeze and the sun on these fresh blades of grass, I stand and head for home.

⁂

At home, Grandma's on the stairwell with her arms full of clothes. Though she lives on the next block, I've seen her only a few times in the months since Mom died. There's a cardboard box on the landing full of silk jewelry bags and a few Louis Vuitton purses. The oriental carpet in the living room is rolled up on the far side of the room. "Hi," she says to me with a good-bye tone. She's here merely to collect what's hers.

At 7:00 p.m., the phone rings. Doug's voice on the line is like a distant memory. "Hey, Kate, is Dad home?"

"No."

"I'm coming home on Monday for spring break. Can you write my flight information down? What are you guys up to?"

I don't know how I can answer for the group. "Uh, well ... I haven't seen Dad in a while. I think Brian's home. Do you want me to check?"

"Really?" Doug sounds surprised, as if he expected the three of us to be enjoying a family dinner. "No, that's fine."

"It'll be cool to have you home."

"Yeah, wicked awesome," he replies all Massachusetts-like. I write his flight details on a yellow sticky note and stick it to the cabinet above the telephone console. We hang up, and I sit silently, hoping the inertia of our family's past is enough to keep us moving forward together.

⁓

Monday after school, my instant oatmeal bowl's still in the sink. A few beach towels grace the living room floor where Brian left them after surfing this morning. Maria's been spending weekends with her daughter in Inglewood. I think she must not have come in today. I think maybe the bus schedule is off because of spring break. Then I realize that's not even a thing for bus drivers or bus schedules. I knock on Brian's door.

"What?"

"Hey, have you seen Maria?"

"No. Dad fired her. He said we need someone who drives."

"What!" I open the door. Brian's still in bed. "Dude, did you go to school today?"

"Nope."

"Well … Doug's coming home tonight. That news is exciting enough that Brian follows me into the living room, where I turn on HBO. I pick up the phone to call Domino's, and we wait for our pizza. A half hour into *Bill and Ted's Excellent Adventure* and twenty minutes into our large pepperoni with olives, we hear the garage door.

Doug looks even taller now, more grown-up. But he has the aura of someone coming back from war. He walks right in, drops his backpack on the chair, abandons his rolling suitcase in the corner of the room by the rolled-up rug, and sinks into the couch between us. Without a word, he swoops down over the coffee table and grabs the half pizza that's left in the box, folds it, and puts it down in ten bites. "Doug!" yells Brian. "You're such a dufus. You big gorilla!"

"You know it," he says, all Bostonian-like. He ruffles Brian's hair and puts his size 12 shoes up on the coffee table. The three of us are together for the first time in a long time, and it feels we're right where we should be.

༺༻

"So, your brother's home? Party at your place?" I assume she means his presence is one big party.

"Yes, Christi, it's a constant party these days. He's pretty funny."

"So, it's true?" Christi grabs my locker door just as I slam it shut.

"Dude, that's super ungratifying, to slam the door and not have it slam!" She's holding me hostage for an answer. "I'm late for Spanish." She tilts her forehead toward me and gives me "Really?" eyes because she's late for something too. Only, I actually care. "I'll talk to you later." I run off.

By lunch, after numerous passes through the locker hall to retrieve different coursebooks and my customary bag of mini-carrots that I eat for lunch, I have this sinking feeling. Doug's up to something, and it's not good.

After school, he's lazily strumming his guitar on the couch. His grown-out, prep school hair splays out from his white baseball cap and just covers his ears.

"Hey, Kate, what's up?"

I drop my backpack at my feet. "I don't know. You tell me. There's a rumor going around that there's a party here tonight." He looks unconcerned. He picks up his Styrofoam ramen cup and turns it upside down over his gullet. He chews once and swallows.

"Dude, Doug, this isn't boarding school! These kids won't just politely leave when you ask them to."

"I just invited some people from your school and Redondo and told them to bring some friends."

"What? You invited both schools?"

"It's not a big deal, Kate. Don't be such a Goodie Two-shoes." He turns on the TV and diverts his attention away from me.

⁂

Just after dark, there's a knock at the door. Brian turns down the TV and the house lights and looks out the window like a paranoid shut-in. "You weirdo," I say.

"Dude, go get the door!" Doug orders.

"We're here!" Quinn announces sarcastically, like, "Surprise!" Ami, Quinn, Kelly, and Jenny appear in the living room. I see on Doug's face that this is not the reception he had hoped for. Quinn puts down her grocery bag full of wine coolers. I see the other girls surveying the scene. They are seasoned partygoers and good friends. They are here to hold down the fort.

Ami grabs a few of the crystal zoo animals from the edge of the coffee table and moves them to higher ground. Quinn plops herself on the couch between Doug and Brian and throws her white Chuck Taylors up on the table.

I hear Kelly singing in the kitchen. "Plastic, plastic, where are you?" Kelly can turn anything into a song. I stand in the doorway and watch Jenny grab some Scotch tape from the telephone table drawer and tape the cabinets closed.

By nine o'clock, Doug's local friends from both high schools arrive. By ten, it's everyone else. A senior from Redondo named "Roach" is, by all accounts, on the roof. And, by all accounts, he's wasted and preparing to jump from the roof, over the boardwalk, down to the sand below. I find my big brother doing a keg stand in the basement.

"Doug, there's a super drunk guy on the roof!"

"Sweet."

"No, not sweet. I'm unsure how to impress upon you the seriousness of server liability for Dad or of the imminent bodily injury to this Roach guy. Not okay!"

Doug pauses for a second, then just laughs. He gets the attention of his momentary entourage, who join in laughing. He turns to a group of girls balancing pool cues on their foreheads and spinning in circles. They fall in a heap, but Doug's attention has migrated elsewhere, and he fails to notice.

I make my way to Brian's room, but he's nowhere to be found. Instead, Ami's in there with Nicole. My little pixie friend looks up, smiles her little pixie smile, and utters something I don't understand about the fairies in the air. Ami pulls her mouth away from a clear vacuum cleaner tube they've named "Bob." She coughs and exhales and says, "Cherry tobacky."

"Right," I answer. Quinn and Jenny find me in the doorway.

"Is Ami in there with Bob?"

"Yes … with Bob."

"The excitement level has reached nine," says Quinn, very matter-of-fact. "It's time to call the cops." She closes Brian's door and dials the nonemergency police station number she gets from the big telephone book in the hallway console. "Hi. There are lots of people in my house who won't leave."

At 1:00 a.m., the house is empty, except for my soldiers and the spoils of war. I saw Doug file out with the crowd to the next house party. I haven't seen Brian all night, but as I sweep up broken Waterford crystal from the slate in the kitchen, he comes up the stairs with his skateboard.

"Um, hello!" says Ami in her most maternal voice. "Where have you been?"

"Why do you care?" he sneers.

"Anger much?" she retorts.

"At the pier, skating."

"All night?" I ask him, but he just walks away.

⁓

At 8:00 a.m., Quinn's throwing the last of the wet towels into the dryer. "So, is your Dad ever coming home?"

I watch a soap bubble burst in the sink as I scrub a dish. "I don't know."

Just after ten, Quinn leaves and my brothers come trudging up the stairs. They grab cereal and bowls that I've just put away in the cabinet, and with a canine sort of consciousness, they pour the milk in and eat.

Doug tilts his head like a dog hearing an approaching car. "Hey! Let's go for a walk."

On the boardwalk, the three of us pass Grandma's house quickly. At the next corner, Doug cracks the cap off of a beer bottle inside a brown paper bag and takes a swig.

"Dude, it's ten in the morning and this isn't boarding school."

"Stop overreacting, Kate." He takes another swig. Brian sides with his big bro. He sneers, rolling his eyes and mumbling, "Sheesh."

⁓

At 30th Street, Doug turns east. Brian and I take a few corrective shuffles and catch up. We make our way across Hermosa Avenue and up the hill under old-timey lampposts.

"Why are we going this way?" Brian asks. "I mean, I know, but why?"

"Chill out, Brian!" Doug takes another swig. "I just wanna see our old house."

We pass charmingly tucked houses and discreet garden sanctuaries. Life on this walk-street is simple, quaint, and lived apart from prying eyes. At least, that's how we remember it.

At the top of the little hill, we stand outside of house number 353. We look on and reminisce. The magnolia tree lives on in the yard with the white picket fence. Doug's basketball hoop is still there on the brick retaining wall. I feel the hollow vibrations of his basketball on the pavement and hear Brian's shrieks as he and his little friends run around in the yard with water guns. It looks as if our very own sand is still in the sandbox.

The door opens, and a woman comes out, followed by two little, curly-haired girls. She sees us standing, gawking. "Hello?" she calls and lets us know that she sees us. She pulls her girls tight to her hip.

I'm feeling outwardly motherless in front of this young family—the abject, derelict, and dangerous. The mother legitimizes. Now, we're illegitimate vagrants threatening this curly-haired family. I look to Doug as our spokesman. He sets his brown-bagged beer on their brick wall and says, "Hey, we used to live here. Is it okay if we come in and look?"

"Doug! That's totally not necessary." I laugh, mortified. "He's kidding. I'm Kate."

The woman looks closely at the three of us. "I remember you. I'm so sorry to hear about your mom. Yes. Come in."

Brian and I follow Doug up the patio steps into the yard where we were once a sweet, young family ourselves. The woman opens the front door, and I see the foyer hardwood has been stained pink and the borders are stenciled with country-home motifs. I'm immediately offended by ribbon-adorned baskets and cutesy hearts stenciled in white paint. It might have been better to let this place live unscathed in my mind.

The woman and her girls walk us through the house. It's awkward enough that we're here at all, but there's just no good reaction to the changes they've made to the décor or any meaningful way to describe what this space has meant to us.

Doug is wide-eyed and emotional. But in an instant, I feel him turn envious of the bond between these little girls and their mom. Brian points to a photo on the wall of the two little girls on the swing set we left behind. "Little brats," he says and looks to his big bro for approval. "Yeah, dude," says Doug, and they high-five.

I can tell Brian doesn't really remember this place. I touch the walls he scuffed with his Tonka trucks. I walk the kitchen floor where he army-crawled and dragged his tiny body. We pass the laundry chute where Doug and I threw toys down to surprise Maria below. Brian doesn't remember sledding down the carpeted staircase in nylon sleeping bags or making forts out of the open cabinetry with blankets. He doesn't really remember these wooden doors Mom picked out with our contractor eight years ago, which she had stained to match the bannister—these doorways to our past. I can never forget.

I'm surprised everything looks so small. I label it "Childhood Joy," and as we leave the house, I'm relieved it hadn't grown larger and more important to me in our absence.

But on our way down the concrete steps and through the backyard, back down from an idealized past we know we won't visit again, Doug says, "Hey, remember Petra?" Mrs. Hornton lived across the walk-street, a warm and loving retired schoolteacher with a thick Greek accent. She was often visited by her two grown children.

"Of course!" I exclaim. I look at our magnolia tree adjacent to her yard and hear the wind and the birds whisper, "Petra." It's that synonymous. I take a step down toward the walk-street and hear a voice from across the way. A little old lady comes to the fence, aided by a man in his forties. "Oh my God!" whispers Doug, like a child who's spotted Santa at the mall. "It's Petra!"

His eyes well up with tears. He calls out loud, "Petra! Remember me?" He's embarrassing, a toddler calling out from a six-foot-five man body. The little old woman squints and says something to her companion. Then she says, "Dougie?"

"Hi, Doug," the man next to her says. "It's me, Don." And the three of us rush across the walk-street to their yard for a happy reunion with the Horntons.

Inside their unchanged home, Doug sounds like a ten-year-old; he talks and talks. "Remember when our dog got into your yard? My friend Scott and I climbed your fence to get her, but we got stuck inside. Then, you came home and gave us pie. Did you ever see my dad playing basketball out there in his business suit?" Doug slaps his knee and laughs like a little boy. He goes on and on about our young family, comparing his recollections of the past with Petra's view of things from across the walk-street. He sounds as if he's listening for answers to questions he's forgotten to ask.

Petra, ever the retired schoolteacher, has kindly asked her son to get out the photo albums. Now, we're recounting the history of the wide sidewalk between our yards, the space that connects us and bridges our generations. After half an hour, I say to my brothers, "We better go." We give the Horntons hugs and leave, taking a bit of their warmth with us.

However, our walk home is silent and cold. Doug starts to cry. Brian looks over at his big brother and sheds a tear. "Dude, that was intense," he sniffles, but I think he's reacting more to Doug's tears than anything else. I begin to feel tremendous jealousy having seen Petra and Don together, twenty years into our future that will never be.

We get home to a note on the counter. "On a date. See you tomorrow."

"That's weird," says Doug. "So, he's not coming home?"

"Probably not," Brian answers. He goes to open the fridge and ends up just standing there and staring at the light. I order another pizza.

༼ ༽

The lady with the scissors gently combs my hair with her fingertips. She asks where I part it. "Here?" She sounds vaguely Guatemalan. I recall Maria's fingers on my scalp, on my fine baby hair, when she combed it into tangle-free strands. I admit to myself that I'm lonely. I let this woman care for me and melt under her touch.

"Gracias," I say, when she's combed my wet hair straight.

"Como hablas español?" (How do I know Spanish?) I tell her about Maria, about my upbringing, that I ate mole and plantains and speak in Guatemalan slang. "Que shuka" (How gross), we agree when a dog pees on the sidewalk outside the window, and we laugh. But after a minute, I feel like a fraud. I can't claim this culture as my own. I come from an upper middle-class Caucasian American family. I've never experienced guerilla warfare. I'm no survivor, no refugee.

When my haircut is over, she shows me the simple straight line of my cut. I smile at her, this woman who has welcomed me home for just a little while. I stand up and she unbuttons my smock and pulls on my strings. She says softly in Spanish, "Your heart is Guatemalan."

It's painful and cathartic. I leave the salon with my frayed ends snipped away and a little sense of belonging intact. But, like my childhood home, I know I won't come back here.

There are three weeks left of my sophomore year. Doug will go back to Massachusetts in the fall for a post-grad year, but he's already home for summer. Dad and his new wife, Patty, picked him up at the airport this morning and dropped him in the driveway of our new rental house off Pacific Coast Highway. I hear the car door slam and go out in bare feet to help him inside with his trunk full of linens, his duffle bag, and his suitcase.

"What's up, bro?" I drag the trunk over the concrete, horrified to see that I'm leaving a black mark.

"So, this is where we live now?"

"Yup. This house will grow on you. It's quiet, and we have a few trees out front and an El Pollo Loco restaurant on the corner of the block. Mean bean and cheese burritos for two dollars and six cents. You'll never go hungry." My room has a funny box window like a terrarium. It's pushed out into the trees of the front yard. I like to sit in the windowsill and listen to the rustle of the leaves.

What Dad likes about this house is that it is acceptable to Patty, as she refused to live in the house we shared with Mom. Plus, Patty is skilled at overseeing budgets, as that's what she does at her job. The rent here is relatively cheap compared to what we're making by renting out the boardwalk property. And, as an additional cost-saving measure, she sold the used car I've been driving to school the past year since I got my driver's license. On the downside, I have to walk in the dark to zero-period swimming. On the upside, the walk from our rental is no longer uphill.

Patty's a producer at Warner Brothers, a professional—worldly and cool. In the few conversations we've had, she's already taught me about the Beat Poets, the Free Speech Movement, and 1970 punk rock bands like The Kinks and X. At their wedding, I wore a ring of white roses on my head that she ordered from her florist especially for me. That little kindness was all it really took to win me over.

"But there is some weirdness," I warn Doug as we get inside the house. I point to an inoperable Alexander Graham Bell-style telephone that's mounted to the kitchen wall. We live with this odd kitch left behind by the landlord. We also live with Patty's one-year-old baby from her first marriage. "Oh, and that's a babysitter," I say quietly, gesturing to the living room. The babysitter often wears sweatpants and thumbs through her *US Weekly* Magazines. She watches me coolly, as if I'm intruding, every time I pass through the room.

Doug's eyes widen in shock. "Wow. Can't we just kick the renters out of our old place on the boardwalk and move back there?" He laughs nervously. "So, where's my room?"

"Holy crap ... I don't actually know." It's a four-bedroom house, which is all we've needed since Maria moved out. It occurs to me that the master is occupied, and Brian and I each have our rooms. The only room left is occupied by a baby crib and might as well be cordoned off with caution tape. We're forbidden to enter or make even a peep outside the door. "You could get a blow-up mattress and sleep in Brian's room." Doug lowers his head, like, "Don't be stupid." "Well, out in the yard is sort of a room. Wanna go look?"

Through the brambles and over a small, muddy lawn, we make our way to investigate the structure in the yard. It's the size of a large shed and packed floor to ceiling with the landlord's furniture: stacked chairs, upside down tables on top of a beat-up old couch, and an old Lazy Boy recliner. Doug flips the light switch and we see spiders scatter for safety.

"There is a bed," I say happily, pointing to the corner. "But no bathroom," I say, sadly. "Are you good?" I ask my brother, knowing he probably isn't. "I told Quinn I'd be there by six, so I better start walking."

After twenty minutes, I arrive at the Heiser's little beach cottage. Quinn's rifling through her closet in search of just the right jacket. "So, Quinn, what's going on with you and Jackson?" I don't wait for her answer. Since Mr. Heiser isn't here, I sashay past the washer and dryer into their little kitchen space and grab a handful of Red Vines from the cabinet. I hop onto the kitchen counter where I sit chewing on a bunch of them like they're cud.

Quinn joins me in the kitchen, all ready to go in jeans, a white T-shirt, her J. Crew barn jacket, and white tennis shoes. "Jackson?" she finally responds "Nothing. It's really all about the Mustang. Plus, I feel like, you know, what if ST is as good as it gets?"

"No. I don't know. Explain."

"It would be a huge letdown to have a scene with him, just to find out that the tension itself is really what it's all about."

"That empty feeling of desire, that explosive nothingness within?"

"Um, yeah, something like that." Quinn grabs the bunch of Red Vines that are hanging from my mouth. "Don't be gross."

A little after five, I hear the muffled imperfection of Jackson's car pull up in the driveway. His navy blue 1964 Mustang growls and purrs in all its beautiful antiquity. I push a polished chrome button and pop the metal door open and sink into the leather of the back seat. Jackson hits a switch on the eight track and the sound of the Beatles comes over the speakers. Cradled in terse leather and enveloped in the spirit and history of Detroit's Americana, we pull onto Pacific Coast Highway.

Quinn's riding shotgun. Jackson looks over coyly. "So, what's up, ladies?" Jackson isn't necessarily attractive. He's skinny and pale and frizzy-haired with a sharp nose. But he's not one for conventions. His turn of phrase and his passion for art and mechanics make him attractive. He might actually be the quintessential beast.

Outside of Dane's, Stireman is shooting hoops. Matt and Ross are sitting on the hood of Stireman's Volkswagen Bug. The sky's turning pink and teal. Quinn and I get out and lean against the car and watch the drama of the marine sunset.

Jackson slides up the front of his car and onto the hood. "Hop up!" In my vintage Levi's, I climb, careful not to scratch his paint with the metal grommets. Flat on my back, I tug the strings of my Rip Curl hoodie tight around my chin.

The three of us lie on the hood and look up at the sunset. Someone in the driveway turns up the Allman Brothers Band in Stireman's Bug. It's loud and rattles the metal of the open door like a percussion instrument. I watch as the pinks and blues above smudge like watercolors on a brush of breeze. Blinking planes fly in and out of view.

Stireman and Dane come out of the house with more beers that they pass out like communion wafers.

"Jackson," says Quinn, "you know we're parked in the middle of the street, right?"

"Yeah, yeah, Unabombers, hang tight." He slides off the hood and into the driver's seat. Unlike Quinn, I remove my hood as a consequence of Jackson's description. Quinn and I brace ourselves, and the car roars to life. Jackson pulls the brake, and the car inches slowly downhill. I make a valiant effort to save my beer before grasping the antenna with my right hand. But before I can grab hold, I'm sliding slowly toward the pavement. I slide right off the hood, onto the blacktop, and roll down the street like an action movie hero.

"I'm good. I'm okay!" Everyone's gathered around and staring down at me.

"Are you sure you're okay?" Quinn asks, but she's laughing. She pulls on the cord of her sweatshirt and turns her head to laugh into the hood.

"Yeah, well, I'm good. I can't feel my wrist, really, but I'm good." She looks down at my wrist. It's starting to swell. She grabs my left hand and points out that my tiny gold and diamond ring is cracked.

"Wait!" she says and tries to pull the ring off my finger, but opts instead to just bend the broken ends away from one another. "Here. You can probably have it fixed. I don't know. Maybe not." She sticks it inside the front pocket of my jeans. Dane takes my hand and looks closely at the damage. "I think maybe you broke something."

"Nah! I'm good." I use my right hand to dig out my ring. "This, though. This is broken for sure."

Again, Dane takes my hand and leads me down the hallway. "I'm so sorry about your ring. Is it special?"

"If a ring can be special. Yeah, sort of. My mom gave it to me. It's like a circular token of her eternal love ... or something."

"Oh my God, I'm so sorry!"

"Nah! It's just a thing!" Dane looks really serious. Crap, make it stop, whatever I just did.

"No, I mean about losing your mom."

Like always, I'm not sure how to console him on this point, so instead I talk really fast. "Don't be. She was awesome! I feel bad for people who didn't have her as a mom. I'd take a few years with her over a lifetime with someone less awesome any day." Dane looks at me pitifully. "I'm good," I say, realizing that I really am.

"I love you," he blurts out.

"What?" I look to see if he's joking. Then, without thinking, I say, "I'm sorry."

It seems like an eternity when neither one of us says anything, so I bolt down the hallway and find Quinn, who's sitting in Dane's room, listening to the guys on drums and guitars. I go in with my arms only. I snatch her through the cigarette smoke like a zombie. "Excuse us," I say and slam the door. I stumble down the hall, dragging Quinn behind me.

"Have you finally lost your mind? What's wrong with you?"

"So ... Dane said he loves me, and I said I'm sorry."

"What?"

"Shh!" I clap my hands over her mouth.

"You said you're sorry?"

"Yeah, well … I'm not really about a relationship right now. He's cool and all, but no. I don't like him like that. Plus, maybe I feel sorry for him or something."

"What?"

"Ugh—there was this psychic one time who recorded a premonition for my mom, not on a CD but on an old-school audiotape, about me falling for someone I felt sorry for or something."

"Oh my God, what are you talking about?"

"I'm heeding the warning, I guess, just taking precautions."

"Okay … well, for future reference, maybe 'I'm sorry' isn't the correct response."

The two of us bolt out of the house to the driveway in our bare feet. Cool entryway pavers lead to driveway blacktop that's still warm from the day. With my index finger, I brush the chrome grill on my way around the car to the passenger seat. I pop the chrome button and we get in. The key's still in the ignition, and Quinn gives it a turn.

Eddie Vedder comes over the radio. "Yellow Ledbetter" riffs of spacey highs and deep, grounded lows arrest us until we're speechless. A tinny note is followed by just enough air so I can catch my breath. I grab the lever on the side of my seat and recline.

Up in the purple haze of the LA sky, blinking lights of 747s and Airbuses appear then disappear into the urbanity of nearby rooftops as they descend into LAX.

"I mean," Quinn says, "if someone rocked my world as much as this song, maybe I'd think ST for the sake of ST was overrated."

I'm sedated on wine cooler and a throbbing wrist. I nod my head in contemplation. "True dat," I answer, wishing I had a forty and a mouthful of gold teeth, just for effect.

༄

After three months, Dad and Patty get a divorce. The whole thing is so sudden and so outside the realm of our adolescent understanding that my brothers and I never see it coming. But by junior year, we're back in the boardwalk house. I'm in my room, studying the Ming Dynasty. And Doug is home. He flew in last night for Christmas break.

I hear the front door open and slam shut. I guess he's back from Grandma's now, where he's been for a curiously long time, and I don't imagine they've been baking cookies.

I turn down "Blue Train" on the jazz station because I hear some unusually tense conversation that seems to be escalating in the kitchen.

"Well, did you?" Doug shouts.

I toss my textbook upside down on the bed and storm out to shush them. "What are you guys yelling about?"

"This doesn't concern you, Kate." Doug glares at me. Dad stands over the countertop with white knuckles and a red face. I've never seen him angry. If I didn't know that before, I know it now.

"Grandmama said that the money Mom had from her dad was supposed to go directly to us."

"Doug, I've told you six times. Your mom and I shared our assets. There were no trust accounts. The money your mom had was and is mine to raise you and pay this mortgage and send you to college. I don't know where your grandmother gets these stories."

Dad walks to the master bedroom, passing me in the hallway. When we're shoulder to shoulder, he looks in my direction and says, "So, you and your grandmother are a team?"

I don't know what he's talking about. I haven't talked to Grandma in over a month, and rarely do I talk to him.

Doug follows Dad into his bedroom. "Well, did you?" he demands. I tiptoe to the threshold of Dad's room and lean into the doorframe, hiding half of my face behind the wall.

"Did he do what?" I whisper to Doug.

"Forge Mom's will when she was in a coma."

"What?" I say. "Doug, that's nuts, even for Grandma." I head toward my room, and Doug follows me into the hallway.

"You act so innocent, but I know what you're up to when I'm away at school, how you ruined Dad's marriage. He told me you're the reason they got divorced. And Grandma told me you're the reason Dad is using the money Mom left to us. You said you don't care if he uses our money to pay off his divorce from Patty. You're an evil bitch. I feel sorry for your husband," Doug says.

"You mean someone is going to be so stupid as to marry me one day?" I'm shocked. I back down the hallway toward the threshold to my room. I'm about to go inside and close the door. Instead, I turn to him.

"You know me—little hippie honors student who just loves to interfere in grown-ups' marriages. And are you seriously falling for the oldest trick in Grandma's book? I know that you guys are angry and disappointed about a lot of things and that you want someone to blame, but I'm not your problem." I back into my room and close the door. I pray he doesn't follow me inside. I've never seen him this angry before.

An hour later, I come out and find Brian sitting alone in the kitchen. The room has grown dark around him. "What's up, Gwak?" He just leers at me. I sit on the barstool next to him, and immediately, he stands and mumbles, "Later." He picks up his skateboard and takes off down the stairwell to the pier or wherever angry skater punks go.

When I'm alone in the kitchen, I wonder what's happened to my family. They're lost in abandonment and grief, suspicion and greed. And, for some reason, they seem to blame me.

Outside, the moon rises over the Pacific, casting a path of gold from the sand to the sky. Outside, the ocean is drawn, dark, and glassy in the cool of night. Its currents ebb and flow under the force of the moon. I, too, am subject to its pull. We women possess this power, to bring people together or pull them apart, to make or break a family.

When I'm stronger, I will spread the moon's energy. When I'm stronger, I will bring people together. When I am stronger, I'll be that boulder in the river. I will withstand the current. The water may chip away my edges, it may smooth my exterior, but I will remain, unmoved. I will do it when I'm stronger, but not now. Now, I'm threatened by external forces. They chisel me and nudge me downstream.

Outside, night has fallen. Earth spins and the moon pulls. With so many moving parts, I can depend only on myself.

⁓

By senior year, the thrill is gone. Our big group of guy friends graduated two years ago. Our exciting little beach town has grown dull and senioritis is consuming us. By late spring, Quinn and I are bickering old ladies. "Grab that table by the window. I'll get your nasty black coffee for here."

"Awesome. Thanks," I tell her.

This craftsman house converted to a coffee shop is one of the last holdouts in our latest and greatest bedroom community. It smells like mold and grit and has a great vibe. I feel the love of generations here, the souls who called this house their home. But what I really like is its mild state of decay. I like to imagine that, one day, the floorboards will give way to termites and roots and be reclaimed by the soil.

The boards creak under my feet. I follow the sound of the leaky faucet to the restroom with a small claw-foot tub, where I wash my hands in a clumsy stream of lukewarm water. I think of the devotion and hard work that has kept the hardware and the pipes working. Meanwhile, all around us, the real estate is scraped clear. On a ten-year rotation, the lots of our town are repopulated with shiny, new structures and shiny, new faucets.

I wait for Quinn at the table, gazing at local art all over the walls, at thoughtful strangers sipping their drinks. In the inorganic plat of LA, within gridded streets and concrete sidewalks, where everyone has a schedule and an agenda, we like to come here and do nothing.

"Here. Enjoy." Quinn returns and slams my mug down with not the slightest bit of polish. She hangs onto the handle of her teacup. "So, I got another fat envelope in the mail. Middlebury. I don't know. Maybe we should both stay here and go to USC, maybe get an apartment together."

"I love you, but no."

"Why not?"

"I need to get away, to escape the drama, you know? To just … be alone."

"You mean, like, what that freak lab that studied you said? That you need complete silence?"

"Do you seriously mock my paranormal babyhood and my old soul?"

"Of course I do. But, you know my theory. Your 'old soul,'" she actually makes air quotes, "is really just your inability to deal. I think running naked into the forest of Berkeley is probably not your answer."

"Okay. I get the running part, but why am I always naked?"

"It's just funnier."

"Right. So, you think my old soul is like some personal failure?"

"Sort of, yeah. You know how babies seem like they still remember wherever they came from, like with that super-spacey omniscient look in their eyes, and you always have to tiptoe around them so you don't wake them up or startle them or freak them out? Maybe you're just having a hard time adjusting to Earth and being a good human."

I don't necessarily disagree. But I say, "Did you just line up the corner of your napkin with the corner of the table and accuse me of having a hard time adapting to being human?"

"You're a fine person, Kate. You love nature and stuff, I get it. But maybe you can just not be so stubborn, lighten up, open up more to other people."

"I open up to you because you don't disturb my chi."

"That's exactly what I mean. Why is your chi so easily disturbed? If you want to escape, why don't you just move into the ashram or an abbey now? Go commit your life to God or whatever. But if you're committed to being a human among the other humans, maybe don't be so black and white. I just don't think you need to leave town to escape bad juju. It's everywhere."

"Maybe you're right, Quinn. I'll just stay here and let people tell me who I am, just fall into that box of what they expect of me. It's all about the herd mentality anyway, right? I'll make sure I get everyone's approval on my attire and hair before I decide what I actually like. Maybe I'll take up loud gum-chewing and super-clingy close-walking and one-upping and all those other mindless, idiotic things people do."

"Now, you're not making any sense. This snobbery used to protect you. I get that, but we're older now. Now, I think it's holding you back. And by the way, you have faults too. The most obvious one I see is your fear of relying on other people, like somehow you're going to lose yourself."

I want to be pissed at her, but I can't. "You're right. I'm just not strong enough to break the cycle of negativity around here right now. I need to be free to become a stronger version of me."

"Fair enough. But, I do think you're taking this whole misanthrope loner thing too far."

I touch Quinn's arm in breakup fashion. "It's not you. It's LA. There's just not enough moisture in the air here to house wise spirits." She glares at me. "Not enough old, musty house restaurants," I say, and she understands me completely.

PART II

1995
Alone

Only when I was truly alone, did I feel the god and the genius within.

~

"How's your car?" Dad kicks a tire and waits a second, as if maybe the hubcap will fall off. I think this is the extent of his automotive capabilities.

When nothing happens, he says, "Well, daughter, I'm proud of you. Call me when you get to the Casparis'." The starched collar of his white shirt pokes me in the cheek. He gives me an emotionally detached, WASPy hug and heads to work.

Brian trails behind me up the stairs. I turn to him and plead, "Come with me to Grandma's. I need to say bye."

"No way."

"Fine."

He helps me carry my camo-patterned camp trunk full of clothes and shoes into the back of my Jeep Cherokee. I make another trip for my clock radio/CD player and a few boxes of bed linens and CDs. I throw my backpack on and grab the duffle bag. I'm surprised by how little I actually need. After straightening the quilt on my bed, fluffing the pillows, and aligning the books on the shelf, I close the door on my childhood room.

Half a block down the alley, the poodles bark as I knock. Grandma claps and barks back at them. "Behave!" she says, but they don't. "Robert! The door!" They open as a team. "Well ... to what do we owe this surprise?" But she knows.

"I'm leaving for college."

"Yes ... I heard." I half expect her to tap her fingers together in evil praying formation while she mulls this one over. Her speech is slow and menacing. Her wheels spin. "You know ... when your mom and uncle were *yonge*, I took them up there, to San Francisco, to see the kids lying naked in the streets, on drugs."

"Oh." I fake inquisitive sweetness, playing dumb. "At Berkeley?" I move slowly into the foyer with a doe-eyed look of inquiry.

"Barb, it's a good school!" says Grandpa. This is all he says this morning, but it has some degree of effect on Grandma I don't expect.

"Well ... come in." She's huffy and resigned. "Do you want a Coke?"

"No, thank you." Grandma likes us to appear invested in our visits, so I lean against the center island and pretend I'm getting comfortable.

"Well ... you made your bed." She shrugs. Clearly, this is not a confidence-builder. "You're an idiot, you know ... not going to New York, to dressmaking school."

"Maybe I still will, Grandma, but I'm going to try a regular university for now."

"What are you going to do there? Wear a serious suit and become a sexless lawyer like your dad? Don't be cute!"

I hold in a laugh. I'm not sure if Dad is sexless or if lawyers are. But either way, that's not my plan.

"Look! Here!" *Cosmopolitan* magazine appears inches from my nose. I push it back and see a fashion editorial piece portraying scantily clad women with smudged lipstick luring their men around by their neckties. "See? You should be a fashion vixen. Go find a husband. Men want sexy, Kate, not studious! Go attract someone worth something while you're still *yonge*."

I look again at the fashion spread, at photos of women in power suits shot in a library. They're disheveled and vampy and wearing reading glasses. I think they're sexy and studious. "See? Women can be both, Grandma." She doesn't answer me, but I know already she's no champion of women.

"Well, Grandma, I have to get on the road." I stand slowly and stretch my arms to the sky in a disarming manner. I'm careful not to trigger her prey drive.

"Okay," she says, but her eyes widen and she starts to look anxious. "Wait a minute!" Her neon-green, ostrich-leather slides hustle up her cheetah carpet to the second floor. I glance over at Grandpa in his armchair. He's staring down at his hands. He twiddles his thumbs like a nervous captive, and I wonder if he knows what she's up to.

"Robert!" Grandma yells from the top of the stairs. "In my craft room, there's another box. Go grab it! On the floor. Upstairs!" Without a word, Grandpa plays fetch. He heads up, passing her on the stairs as she comes back down with a large cardboard box.

She drops it at my feet and tells me, "Stay." She heads back up and returns with a heap of clothes. With some dramatic flair, she opens the floodgates of her arms and dumps the remaining garments at my feet. "Here!" she declares. It has the effect of, "Take that!" Grandpa and I look wide-eyed at the strange and sudden pile. I see a twinkle in Grandpa's eyes and a suppressed smile … amazing! He loves that she's a crazy bitch. Never underestimate that spice of life.

"Robert! Put all this in Kate's trunk before she goes." Grandpa is obedient, complicit in her passive aggression. He nods, and I remember a bit of Grandma's advice, "Treat a man like a little *dowg*. They love that."

"But Grandma, I'll be living in a dorm room with a roommate. I don't think there will be space for any of this stuff. What is all of this, anyway?"

"Oh …" She turns her head away from me as she talks. She grins behind her huge cocktail rings and her Cruella Deville nails. She uses her hands like a maestro to demonstrate the plethora of nonsense she's dumping on me. "It's clothes, bags, some fabric so you can sew …"

"Hmm ... okay." This is a last-ditch effort to control me, my punishment for choosing independence and not following her orders to go to design school. This is her emotional baggage, her control issues. They're all packed and ready to go.

At home, I hug Brian and hop into my small SUV. I think to call Doug at his fraternity at USC, but then I realize it's moving day there too. I don't have time to dangle on the line of the hallway payphone while a fraternity brother searches for him in the house. I pull up the alley to Grandma's garage and let the two of them fill my back seat and trunk with junk. Grandma starts to look relieved, as if impregnating my space with her things has given her renewed purpose.

As the two of them shuffle about my vehicle, arguing over where to stuff a frayed roll of material, I think it's ironic that Grandma is so stuck in the material. Maybe it's sweet that she wants to leave me with a piece of her, as frayed and burdensome as her material world may be. When they're done quarreling and arranging, the two of them wave me through the alley. As I leave, I roll down the window and call out, "Bye!" I look past all the stuff in the back seat to the rear window. My view is obstructed by junk. It makes me feel weighed-down but also, in some odd way, loved.

Up Artesia Boulevard and past the high school, I stop at the Salvation Army Thrift Store. I dump Grandma's junk onto the donation step one item at a time. It's cathartic, and my spirit feels lighter with each item. In my back seat, under the piles of material, I find a framed print of a woman with big, sprayed hair. Her makeup is Eastern European or 1980s, I can never tell which. There's a caption on top that reads, "I create beauty because I must!" It makes me laugh because it's so cheesy, but it speaks to me for some odd reason, so I keep it.

Into the great unknown of fate and recycled retail, I let everything else go. Energy can't be created or destroyed, but, ideally, I think it's repurposed by the right person, in the right spirit, at the right time. For now, I clean the slate. I leave almost everything behind.

⁐

"I round the ramp onto the Harbor Freeway and pick the lane for 110 North. I'm barely out of town, but feel a thousand miles away. "Take It Easy," comes on the radio. As I head away from everything I've known, it seems like an attainable goal. Maybe I should have adopted this catharsis years ago. I grip the wheel tight and refocus my eyes on the road. I shed a cleansing tear and whisper to myself, "take it easy."

Just beyond the Westwood exit, I push my Aerosmith tape into the player. Polyester film feeds the reels just as "Dream On" ends. I grip nine and three o'clock tight. I smack my steering wheel with gusto and wait for the intro because I know what's coming next. Da da da da ... da da da da! I sing along to "Cryin'," an anomaly of classic rock, a song so expertly crafted by a classic rock icon that it passes on the classic rock station, though it's only two years old. I cry, and I sing out loud.

A couple of songs later, "Crazy" comes on. This video might be the inspiration for a hundred thousand tramp stamps and a thousand more belly rings. I embarrass myself to think it may have been mine. When it's over, I rewind the tape and listen to "Cryin'" all over again. I cry. I feel like a maniac. I sing at the top of my lungs. And it feels really good.

At the exit for Mulholland Drive, I turn the music off. I look up the hillside at the new Getty Museum, iron and glass, blank walls for adorning. I think this is one of those blank spaces in time when anything is possible.

I could go anywhere. I scare myself by imagining I've just veered off to the west, never to return. I could drive through the oaks of Santa Barbara County and on to San Simeon to see Hearst Castle.

"Rosebud," I whisper to myself. After all Kane had accomplished in life, after all he had amassed, the thing he valued most at the end was his childhood sled, the freedom it afforded him, the connection it gave him to nature. That mattered most. In his sunny Florida mansion, amid unimaginable treasures, Kane calls out for the dark, cold winters of his poverty-stricken youth and his rickety, old sled. "Rosebud …"

I think of the citation on the wall of our old house, how Mom called Dad from the San Simeon jail. "The guard told me to go for it!" He never imagined she would, but she did.

Mom was the first person to swim in Hearst's Roman Pool in over thirty years. The guards pulled her out at gunpoint and booked her. She framed her citation with a photo of herself in drenched attire, handcuffed, smiling a smile full of endless possibility, her childlike joy. Her Rosebud. We lost that citation and photo in the move. I wonder if Mom ever missed it in her castle on the sand.

What if I turn south toward Mexico? What if I actually do it? I can go anywhere. I can do anything.

A hot wind perks up at the gas station. It blows dust and leaves around the hem of my skirt. Inside, I hand over my credit card, but before I tell the clerk it's nozzle number four, he nods. He rings me up. I'm mute and that's okay. I'm not compelled to engage or explain myself, to defend my actions or those of others. There is no gaslighting at this gas station. Nobody wants anything from me. Alone with my thoughts, I'm free.

Back on I-5, I check in with myself. What do *I* want? I ask it again out loud. "What do *I* want?" Maybe the vibrations of my vocal cords will rouse some unspoken truth. Maybe the universe will answer back, tell me what it wants from me.

I think of the spark that night on the beach, those colonies of sea plankton that consoled me. They ignite in my gut sometimes when I'm really listening to myself. Those celestial sparks of conscience tell me where to go. I look to the road ahead and dare ask it out loud, "What makes me happy?"

My Jeep blows slightly to the right. I grab the wheel tight. I hear the whoosh of the wind over the windshield. What are my gifts? What should I do? What beauty or joy or truth will I draw from this life? What earthly material will I mold and render spiritual?

What do *I* want? And, why haven't I ever asked myself these things before?

The garden in bloom, the tide as it retreats, the triumphant heart as it beats; I want to capture these ephemeral joys and make them last forever. I say it out loud, "I create beauty because I must!" I barrel down the road. I'm adamant. I feel permed and pouty, like a femme fatale from a noir-era movie.

Somewhere past Coalinga, the classic rock station starts a tug-of-war with the ranchera channel. A BMW passes me on the left. Sunglasses protect the driver from the glare of this no man's land, the empty space between LA and San Francisco. There is nothing to see here.

But to me, out here is everything. Out here, beyond the rows of lettuce, feed lots, and concrete aqueducts are hills of splendor. Now, they're dry and brown, but I once saw a postcard: "Poppies in Bloom, Tehachapi, California." The grass was tender and green, and the flowers were a vibrant orange. I imagine the photographer was pleased to catch that ephemeral bloom on silver-coated film and to think that one day a stranger like me might be moved.

In the valley all around, the land is scraped and scarred and etched by hundreds of factory farms.

Conspicuous industrialized sprinklers spew water onto fertilized seed. Exposed aqueducts cut deep, blue lines into the landscape. But discreetly, they dive. They arrive in the city through underground conduits. Secretly, they drain the valley. Unseen rivers, mostly unconsidered, usher water out of the valley and into Los Angeles.

In Santa Monica, a woman on the fifth floor sings, "LA, LA, LA." She hits a high note in the twentieth minute of her shower. The neighbors can't hear it, but the echo cracks the valley floor a hundred miles away. Outside my car window, the dust rises and the heat scorches. The farmers struggle to feed the hungry economy. Meanwhile, the lady in the shower sings.

The radio wavers between ranchera and rock and roll. I let the sounds blend into an urban-agrarian mix.

When it turns to static, I turn the radio off. With the window open, I hear the calls of insects and doves flapping through the fields. The world rushes past, blurry blues and browns, the dried grasses and shrubs against a backdrop of sky. I breathe it in and start to sing. I sing anything with words I can recall and some songs where I just hum in place of lyrics I've never known. I hear the call of insects and doves, of Earth herself, and using my voice to protect her feels like a calling.

※

My SUV passes under a road sign for Tracy. I turn left toward the 680 Freeway, west toward manifest destiny and the setting sun. It hovers on the edge of the continent and shines over hills of brown and a slew of windmills with ten-story blades. They spin like murderous androids and seem to take aim at me. My little Jeep and I weave through the hills of the Altamont Pass. Here, my mind weaves through countless insecurities and irrational fears. Alone is awesome, but it kind of sucks too.

With the sun dropping down behind the Sibley Volcanic Range, I enter the Caldecott Tunnel and come out to bright light and coastal greenery. I remember this side of the mountain from childhood road trips. From the back seat of Dad's sedan, lodged between my brothers, I would imagine the freedom beyond. If we had only taken one of these wooded exits with names like Fish Ranch Road, Shakespeare Festival Lane, or Grizzly Peak Boulevard. If we had only deviated from the plan for a moment to frolic down a country road. At the Fish Ranch Road exit, I leave the highway.

Peeling my sweaty legs from pleather seats, I exit the Jeep. Warm air dries my sweaty skin and brown dust coats my white Adidas. On the far end of the parking lot, there's a path somewhat obscured by a canopy of bushes and vines. I'm halfway there when I think, *Maybe this is a bad idea*. Here in the canopy could be a rapist or killer, lying in wait.

But here in the canopy, the air is soft, and I hear the reassuring songs of birds and the gentle whisper of the wind. I hear the faintest landing of a crow and the scamper of a squirrel. I choose to trust my instincts. Out here, I let my irrational fears go. They don't serve me.

I breathe out and gone is my aversion to half-open drawers and leaky faucets. I shake off my grandmother's living room and my self-doubt, that paralyzing hesitation that was imprinted on us kids when we watched Mom squirm for so many years under Grandma's gaze and voice. I let go of Mom's illness and Dad's pain, and I embrace my own pain. Alone, I'm free to reinvent myself.

Back on the road, I veer to the right and follow the two-lane street that flanks the highway. It starts winding up to the top of Grizzly Peak. Up here, I've caught up again with the fierce stare of the setting sun. Around blind corners, the road drops off abruptly. I spot a sign for a scenic overlook and pull over.

The Bay Area Rapid Transit comes to a stop at a station below. It beeps and chimes with futuristic metallic tones. Its steely rails hum like a lightsaber, and I hear the archaic rumble of a freight train in the distance. I see where their tracks meet, and the freight line dips underground to make way for BART, bridging the past, present, and future.

Now, the occupants of my new world make their way on highways of red and white lights through rush hour, home to families and pets or to happy hour.

At the edge, I grab the guardrail. I have yet to dismiss my fear of heights. *But it's not heights for the sake of heights,* I think. It's a fear of my own impulsiveness in the face of high places.

This might be the work of *they*. I try not to surprise them or shatter their preconceived notions about who I am. I have been raised to fear *they*. But, below is a world of new people with new eyes. I won't let their gaze limit me.

At this scenic overlook, I vow not to limit myself with imaginary boundaries. But then, I think of the pool at

Hearst Castle, and I back up a foot, in case impulsiveness in the face of beauty is inherited. I take a step back from the cliff, just in case.

"Are you feeling the feng shui?"

"Jesus! What?" I spin around to see the man with the booming voice.

"Oh, man," he laughs. "Did I scare you?"

He's wearing black bicycle pants and clip-in shoes. He looks as though he rode his way up here. "It's no wonder they built the UC here, huh? After all that searching for the perfect academic energy." He's out of breath and sweaty, but he just keeps talking. "Did you read that article about the cultural geography of this place, about the cosmic force field that creates and shapes successful thoughts? How it all converges right down there on campus?" He points over the guardrail.

"Uh ... no. I didn't. But I believe it."

"Well, you have to believe it to live it, right?" The man exuberantly shakes out his legs. He grabs hold of the guardrail and stretches his calves, one at a time. He gets back on his street bike and clips in. He waves at me and rolls out of the scenic overlook just as quickly as he rolled in.

I stay here until the sun descends behind the white façade of San Francisco, until the glare on the water is tempered by the impending night. Behind the filter of dusk, I see Alcatraz Island and the rooftops and tree-lined streets of Oakland and Berkeley below. And, far to the west of it all, the Golden Gate spans the strait.

I feel the wind rush in from the Pacific. I let it play with my hair. It brings new energy from far away. I breathe it. I believe it, and my fingertips tingle.

⊙⊚

In the last moments of daylight, I roll into the town of Orinda. At 25 Lomita Road, I spot Mr. Caspari's red Mercedes out front. With my backpack draped lazily over one shoulder, I stroll up to hit the doorbell.

"Hello! I'm here!"

"Hello, dear!" Mr. Caspari takes my backpack. He's the friend of a friend Dad met at the Los Angeles Athletic Club in 1974. It's funny how people meet and hit it off, how dynasties of community can be built upon affections founded upon synchronized exercise schedules. When the Casparis returned to Northern California in 1982, their little town just east of San Francisco became our home away from home. Now, with their own sons grown and out of the house, they welcome me like the daughter they've never had.

I follow Mr. Caspari through the kitchen to the patio. Under a trellis, he pulls out a heavy iron chair. "Sit, my dear." I sit and pet their chow chows. I forget their names, so I call them Girl Chow and Boy Chow. "Hi, Chow," I coo and pet them in turn.

We're surrounded by happy, chirping birds. It's a stark contrast to the sad squawk of the seagull I'm used to back home. These little birds live with seasons and change. Their songs vary in pitch and duration. One particular bird sounds like a referee's whistle in a basketball gym. Tonight, they flap around us in the warmth of the waning summer and happily siphon the nectar from Mrs. Caspari's garden.

I look closely at her roses. I reach out to smell a yellow one, and a petal falls to the ground. "I pruned the roses a little late this year, dear. You can tell because they're usually more robust." Mrs. Caspari refills my lemonade. I don't know what she's talking about. Her roses smell like perfume, and their stems are green with life. They aren't like the tired, dusty variety back home in LA. Rather, they're born of the scorch and the fall and the rain, fresh from seasons that make all the difference.

"They're gorgeous!" And she's gorgeous; the roses reflect in her cheeks under porcelain skin, and her long, black hair shines in the sun. I see seasons of planning and optimism on her skin and the faith of rebirth in her eyes. The plants all around repay her for her dedication with color, texture, and scent.

"Tell me about your drive." Mr. Caspari pours himself a glass of lemonade and takes a seat.

"Oh, you know ... it was glorious—five and a half hours of music and meditation," I say sarcastically. Then I have a flashback of myself driving and crying, and I think maybe they can feel my vulnerability or see remnants of this tiny crisis on my face. I don't make eye contact.

"Yes!" says Mr. Caspari, just as if he's witnessed the winning goal of the World Cup. He's an exuberant, high-on-life man. "The best thing I ever did, Kate ... the best thing!" He's talking about his own move north. He touches his wife's back gently, and they smile at one another. I think it's nice to be in the presence of people who are truly happy with their choices.

"To find yourself, Kate, you must first find your place." He holds up his crystal juice glass full of lemonade.

"Well, then ... here's to this place!" I say, and we do a round of cheers.

After dinner, Mrs. Caspari serves a French press. "So, what is this scholarship you've received? And the brunch is tomorrow? Mr. C. can drive you there in the morning. He goes right by campus on his way to work."

"Alumni Scholarship for academics and leadership ... supposedly." I tilt my head in a self-deprecating way and rummage through my bag for the information. "Eleven, maybe?"

"Perfect!" says Mr. Caspari, with his trademark exuberance, and we're conversing at a sidewalk bistro somewhere in Italy.

The Casparis are Europhiles, disciples of old-world joys. They seem to have perfected that joie de vivre. Their way is so foreign to my serious Protestant upbringing, I imagine I'm a young American on holiday.

"And you move into your dormitory on Monday?" Mrs. C. asks.

"Yes. I hope I'm not imposing."

"Are you crazy? This is fantastic!" says Mr. C. "Tonight, we eat on the veranda!"

∽

It's been barking at me about five minutes. At least, that's as long as I've been awake to hear it. I sit up and see Girl Chow. I dangle a hand over the bed so she can take a whiff and so she won't bite me. Instead, she licks my arm.

The sun shines on Mrs. Caspari's roses outside the guest room window. Foreign birds sing in some romance language I don't understand. I shut off my mind and listen to the serenade. The smell of freshly ground coffee wafts in from the kitchen along with the morning chatter of a couple just enjoying their routine.

I slip into my leather Mephisto moccasins and put on an ivory eyelet, thrift-store dress and a brown corduroy, old man blazer. I wonder about its previous owner because I feel wiser when I wear it.

After some pastries, fruit, and coffee, Mr. Caspari and I hop into his immaculately detailed, late-model, ragtop Mercedes. He starts up the engine and we head west.

"Isn't it gorgeous out here, Kate? It's like Tuscany!" He rolls the ragtop down and our hair blows.

"Indeed, Uncle Cas!" I put on my sunglasses and tuck my hair behind my ears. We don't take the highway. Cas seeks out the side roads and rural routes. I wonder if this is because he's also from Los Angeles—he now seeks the wooded path. But he answers me before I can ask.

"I'm never in any hurry, Kate," he yells above the sound of the engine and the wind. "I love the road!" He veers off to the right and follows the fence line of some protected open space. I see a sign for Mt. Diablo State

Park and we cut through the gate. "Don't worry, dear. This will get us there." I'm totally unconcerned.

After ten minutes, we begin to wind up the backside of Sibley Regional Park and back up to Grizzly Peak. Cas looks over at me. I pull my hair away from my face so I can see him. It's just like a 1960s movie shot over the cliffs of the Italian Riviera. Mr. Caspari has that essence, anyway.

The car and the wind muffle my hearing, so I try to read his lips. "We'll drop right down by this sweet little lake, just above Berkeley," he says decadently. He says everything decadently. I nod and assure him I'm not concerned. He points to a sign, "Tilden Regional Park."

"You're gonna love it!" he says above the engine noise. I smell the plant life and the rolling hills of intrigue all around this winding road, and I really do.

We descend Grizzly Peak and drop into the sweet and musty suburban streets of Berkeley, right behind the Claremont Hotel. We make a right into a neighborhood full of historic-looking mansions. They're built surprisingly close to one another.

"This is the Claremont neighborhood, dear." Cas points excitedly. "It was built by wealthy whalers at the turn of the century. Look at the old mansions! Look at the history! Isn't it gorgeous?" I nod. It is.

We make a left and skirt a campus of whitewashed Spanish architecture with arched front porch awnings and red-tiled roofs. It sits serenely at the base of the hillside we've just come down. I think if a tiered water fountain could make sense anywhere, it makes sense here. And there it is, larger than life, right in the middle of the circle drive. Cas slows to admire it, and we roll on past.

"Oh my God! Do you feel it? Kate, these are some of the dorms. Can't you just feel the buzz of the hormones? It says, 'I want you.' Oh my God! It's just too much!" He laughs heartily.

I squirm. Then I read the sign, "Clark Kerr Campus." I don't dare tell him this is my dorm, my future home, the hormone-laden lair that says, "I want you."

We veer left through a roundabout to another road. We get to what looks like frat row. "Oh my God! Can you feel it? Buzz ..." Mr. C. says, laughing with wild joy.

At Bancroft and Telegraph, the light turns red. "Gimme a kiss, dear. Call the missus if you need a ride before 5:00 p.m. Otherwise, I'll see you right here on the dot." Mr. Caspari moves his face toward mine. I'm confused. The light has turned green, and I'm in a state of panic. I plant a peck right on his lips. As soon as I do it, I realize my mistake and jump out of the car.

"Thank you," I yell nonchalantly, trying to erase what I've just done. I venture north onto the UC Berkeley campus.

Uncle Cas! What the hell? This isn't Europe! This isn't a world of nuance and debate over two salutation kisses versus three. I was raised a cold WASP, taught to give handshakes and stiff hugs and to go in with my shoulders first. I've had no training for this Europhile cheek-pecking.

I pass through an open space that's flanked by commie-looking midcentury buildings. I imagine how Mr. Caspari will embellish the story when he tells it to

Mrs. C. I shiver midthought of the tales he will tell. My Lolita era has begun here in this place, the place that says, "I want you."

༶

The pavement opens up to another plaza of white stone façades and classical architecture. I pass under a green copper archway with a Beaux Arts motif, into the symmetry of large-scale buildings. Sun rays stream past stone walls and tree branches into the square. A creek flows under a bridge on the far end, where wise, old trees push forth around the watershed with all the weight of Mother Nature's glory.

I meander east along the creek and under redwoods, through romantic courtyards to a large, stone building called Phoebe Hearst Women's Gymnasium. A plaque on the door says this is a "clothing-optional area." Oh, would Quinn have a field day with this one. And Grandma. I recall her description of Berkeley like an absurd chant in a Greek chorus: "We took your mother there, to see the naked people lying in the streets on drugs." It's stuck on repeat in my mind. I assume this is exactly what she wants, to haunt my thoughts and make me question my own sanity.

I keep walking uphill toward the east edge of campus. With each step, I practice the art of amnesia. I take a step, and mothers are inconsequential. I take a step, and the material things of life don't matter. I find my voice and lose it again. I learn to follow the joy of the light, and then I forget which is better, the light or the shadows. But maybe my own thinking is the problem.

So I turn and start walking the opposite way. I take a step, and Mother Nature is everything. I take another step, and the material things of life might be all we can hope to master. I lose my voice and find it again. I learn to follow the darkness of the shadows. But then I forget which is better, the light or the dark.

I veer to the left, over Faculty Glade, past a grassy slope of studious people lounging around on the lawn. Some wear only shorts, some business suits, one girl has on what looks like a toga. Everyone seems happy. All of a sudden, I hear the tin clang of a drum and the dark boom of another. My heart beats with this rhythm. Over the grassy hill, I see a band of people marching in procession. A woman carries a banner, "The Explicit Players." They're naked except for their instruments. Nobody looks twice, and the group passes into the forest on the other side of the clearing toward the east edge of campus.

A Sikh in a perfect white turban carries a model building into the architecture hall. A duo of women speaking Mandarin meander out of the Julia Morgan building, carrying violins. From across Bancroft Avenue, the scent of espresso wafts my way, and a man on the park bench sips a doppio shot from a tiny paper cup.

Along the path, a university employee carefully prunes a wisteria bush. The vines bend over a trellis in a way that looks predestined. Looking at this fusion of earth and human devotion, I ask him, "How do you get it to bend like that?" He looks at me, shakes his head with his hands splayed to the sky as if to absorb my meaning. He laughs. I say it again in Spanish: "¿Cómo consigues que se doble así?"

"Con el amor de cada dia," he says with a smile. Then he points to a woman walking hand in hand down the path with a toddler and to a student who whistles for his obedient dog. He gestures at a professor talking with a student and points to his vines and smiles. He says it again in English, with a heavy Spanish accent, "With the love of each day." I think to ask if he means he tends to them lovingly each day or whether he loves each day because he tends to them, but I confuse myself and say nothing.

Upon second glance at the bent and twisted vines, I think it's both. We are that symbiotic, plants and humans, teachers and students, like that gardener and the garden itself. We tend to our own souls by our good works and our dedication to others. With the guidance of a gentle hand, we respect the will of the life within.

But what happens when our vision is clouded by the heavy-handedness of self-serving desires? That I exemplify the Becker wealth and Grandma's highbrow fashion sense, lest I end up naked on the streets on drugs. Grandma's purpose has become enshrouded in my willingness to bend to her desires and her worth in my compliance.

Her reverse psychology, henpecking, and fearmongering will never again work on me, not after sitting on these steps of Sproul Hall where the Free Speech Movement began, where freedom still rings. She must know this. She must fear she won't be able to bend or manipulate me anymore. What, then, is her purpose?

But each of us has our own purpose to fulfill, choices to make, and passions to discover. I walk aimlessly through the campus, toward the campanile tower and under gothic-looking trees with upstretched branches like thick, muscular arms. I pass the campanile just as the bells begin to ring. People buzz around me. They gather in huddles and walk in small groups. I'm left with my thoughts and my senses. I'm exhilaratingly alone.

Roots

Twelve years ago, I was six years old. It was late, and Grandma wasn't quite done with Mom. So Maria walked me home down the boardwalk, as she often did.

Digging my Mary Janes into the pavement, I tugged her toward the odd, little patio garden, toward the bush adorned in glass ornaments. Inside half-open enclosures, just wavering in the breeze, were the airplants.

"Dime otra vez" (Tell me again), I'd implore, wanting to hear for the umpteenth time about these marvelous plants. Free as the wind, as they were, I worried they'd die without leeching nutrients from the soil. I was pleased to learn, years later, that they use their roots just to connect and not for any of their vital necessities. These beautiful plants can thrive all alone.

A pool ball lands on my ceiling. That's the second one today. But the heavy clack of resin on plaster isn't half as annoying as the boisterous laughter. It rattles my walls and the roots of my teeth. I look over at my clock radio. It's just 7:29 a.m.

Classes start on Wednesday, and aside from the noise upstairs, the slam of a door, or an errant sneeze from a ghost resident in the hall, this dorm is quiet.

Shelby's note is still on my desk. "Hello new roommate! Most of the time I'll stay at my brother's house in in El Cerrito. Hopefully I'll see you sometime this week." It's signed, "Shelby." I have yet to meet her.

I get up before my alarm can sound. I put my sweats on and use Shelby's microwave to warm water for tea. Outside my first-floor window, the gentle cascade of a three-tiered fountain bubbles in the courtyard. I unlatch the window and throw it open. I sit here on the ledge and take in the morning fog.

I'm startled by a knock on the door. I hop down to answer. I'm abrupt, huffy. I don't hide my annoyance.

"Hi. Welcome! I'm Chaun, your RA." I look down at his feet; they're white socked and slippered in plastic, Adidas sandals. "I'm a junior. I'm in charge of the residents on this floor. I wanted to introduce myself and see if you have any questions about the dorm." I look over at the clock. It's 7:45 a.m. and this dude is ruining my chi.

"Uh ... no. I'm good."

"Um, okay ... well, this is a coed hall, as you may have noticed. There are two bathrooms, both with showers and restroom facilities."

"Yup, I saw."

"You may have also noticed that the students on our floor have taken it upon themselves to put up signs designating one for men and the other for women. Of course, it's your choice." He laughs. I don't react.

"I've just been using the woman one. Seems good enough."

"Okay, good. So, you may have also noticed it's quiet here. This is traditionally a 'jock' dorm to allow our athletes to rest." He actually makes air quotes and pops his hip and giggles. "Are you on any of our sports teams?"

"Nope."

"Okay, so, lots of non-team members actually end up joining the Greek system in order to meet other students. They move out because they find this place to be too quiet and too much like a country club." Chaun looks apologetic.

"Hmm. Okay. Well, thanks. I like the quiet." I start to close the door.

"Okay … good. Well, let me know if you need anything. I'm in room 110 at the end of the hall."

"Cool. Thanks for stopping by." Buh-bye. I walk away from the door and let it close quietly on its air pressure hinge.

Back on the window ledge, the birds start chirping just as the sun streams through the trees. I look up at the hills behind the campus to see the lifting fog. A cloud of white dissipates into the conifer bloom right before my eyes. It returns like a wisp of cotton and then evaporates into the light. I watch the trees do their morning stretch. I watch them breathe, the clouds appearing and disappearing with each breath.

In the facility marked "Girls," I take a shower. I walk back down the hall in my robe. I think I hear someone, but a door closes softly and again it's quiet. In my room, I sort a few hangers in my little wooden closet. To amuse myself I say, "No wire hangers!" Then I make my little wooden bed. If I had more stuff, I'd have stuff to do. I'd organize it and feel purposeful. But the stuff of the world can't help me now.

So I tie on my running shoes and head out the window into the Spanish-style courtyard, passing the tiered fountain and looking ahead to that breathing forest, a wall of evergreens and eucalyptus in the distance. At the edge of the property, I pace back and forth like a caged animal, just walking the perimeter and looking for a way through the brush and into those hills.

At the highest point of my containment, up several brick staircases with iron handrails, I find the edge. I duck to avoid a wall of branches and clamor through a thicket of ground ivy in search of a footpath. Instead, there's a crudely paved road. It's narrow and winding. It intrigues me, so I follow it and climb with my heart and arms pumping until I'm high above the city.

The road makes an abrupt turn at a yellow sign, "Sharp Curves Ahead." I swing my hip to the right and take it on the outside. I hold my hip bones with my index fingers and thumbs and continue to climb, rocking back and forth, breathing heavy into my belly and extremities. I'm powerful, as I imagine the Ohlone women were, who carried water in tightly woven baskets up these hills from the streams below. They carry me now, their spirit on the wind. I say out loud, between breaths, feeling my hip bones and the exhilaration of exertion, "Sharp curves, indeed."

A few turns later, I'm at the bottom of another staircase. This one's grounded by moss and concrete posts. They're odd, stately architectural accents in this untamed thicket. *A lost civilization,* I think, *overtaken by trees*. On a landing with a concrete bench, I sit for a minute. I look out at the city below. I root for the triumphant vegetation all around me, but I smile because someone had the vision and perseverance to build this stairwell I happened to stumble upon and this bench that invites me to sit amid all this beauty and just be.

Another ten yards into the canopy, I hear a voice. "Good morning!" In a long skirt, she wields a broom about her doorstep, which opens right onto the staircase. She and her hillside cottage seem to have appeared out of nowhere. The arch of her French-blue doorframe is all I can see through my dizzy peripheral vision, but I imagine she's an old recluse who's made herself way too comfortable in this hermitage.

"Hi! Good morning!" I say between heavy puffs. A cat walks in front of her broomstick. "Tesla ... Tesla!" the woman calls, then makes kissing sounds, and the cat rubs up against the ruffled hem of her skirt as I continue dizzily to the top.

Where the stairway ends, the road continues across the ridge to a barricade. Beyond it is dirt and a yellow sign with a fire truck outlined in black. "Fire Trail," it says. I continue toward it, even though my hamstrings and calves burn.

Into the soft canyon I run. The road bends to the right under a eucalyptus grove, and a bunny scurries across the path in front of me. "Bunny Bend," I say to myself, flying into a gully and jumping over a trickle that crosses my path on its way to the creek below. The road ascends now and bends a bit to the left. Another bunny scurries in front of me. "Bunny Bend Two." I mark my mental map. A warm breeze meets my sweat and with it comes the smell of eucalyptus, mud, and glory.

At the bottom of the wash, I stop. It's just me and the hills and the plant life. I listen to the desolate hush of wind through the trees. I double over, hold my hips, and feel that my waist is cinched in delicious hunger. When all my energy is spent, it's this very emptiness that fuels me. And when I've breathed in the life of the natural world, I'm ready to go home.

The blood slowly returns to my fingertips. I shake them and hum songs by Simon and Garfunkel. I sing out, "I am a rock!" I'm stoic, and impenetrable. Back past Bunny Bend One, I see the blacktop ahead and the world of civilization and people. I take a deep breath, and everything burns. I breathe out and I'm numb, untouchable, behind my own firewall, I return from the fire trail fortified and alone.

In the courtyard, I pry my window open and hop back into my room. Bolting into the hallway to the bathroom marked "Girl," I run right into Chaun.

"Oh, hi there! So ... a bunch of us are going down to Telegraph Avenue later to just hang out. Do you want to come with?"

"Uh ... nah. I'm good."

"Are you sure?" He gives me a sweet, sideways look and big, anticipatory eyes.

"Absolutely," I say a little too convincingly.

He giggles awkwardly. "Okaaay!"

I head into the girl bathroom and hide in a stall until I'm sure he's not coming in. It occurs to me that I'm hiding from the one person I've talked to in days, and I realize there's no glory in that.

⁂

It's late September, and I'm alone in the dorm room I share with a roommate I have yet to meet. I'm staring into my little wooden closet, looking for something attractive but unfussy. My roommate's phone rings and I jump. "Hello?"

"Hey, it's me."

"Quinn? Where did you get this number?"

"You gave it to me, remember?"

"Oh, yeah. It's my roommate's phone, though."

"She doesn't let you use it?"

"I still haven't met her. How's USC? Have you run into Doug and his derelict friends yet?"

"No, because I don't believe in the Greek system, remember? You haven't met her? That's odd … so, what are you doing?"

"I think I'm going to rush."

"You're serious?"

"Yup. My self-mothering sensor's going off. I think I'm getting too comfortable in this quiet dorm room all by myself. You know ... socialization. Oh, hey, actually, it starts in fifteen minutes. Can I call you later?"

"I don't know. Will your nonexistent roommate let you?"

"Right. Probably not."

"Fine. Call me later. I'll pray for your soul."

I brush my hair straight down the middle and apply ChapStick. I zip up a white, vintage housedress and grab my Birkenstocks before taking off down the hallway, slowing only to fumble on one leg and place my sandals on my feet. I stumble out the building and into the lukewarm drizzle of a San Francisco September.

At the corner of Channing Avenue, I catch up with a gaggle of girls in heels with curled hair and what looks like a shared lipstick. They're close-walking, the eight of them huddled under two umbrellas, and hanging onto each other for dear life as they teeter-totter over shaky ankles and cross the damp street. I get to Wheeler Theater way ahead of them, only to find that the rest of their tribe is already seated inside.

"Testing, testing, one, two, three. Um, okay ... hi! Quiet down, everyone! Um, welcome, prospective pledges! We are so excited to have you here!"

I think of running, but the doors are already closed. After several speakers and a bunch of information about "sisterhood" and "bonds" and "rah rah yay yay," we are set free on our routes. The girl next to me grabs my paper. "Where are you going first?" She gives it a once-over, makes a frowny face, and says nothing more to me. Next, she grabs a schedule out of the hands of a girl to our right and says, "Yay! Come with me to the first house!" They squeal and squeak and jump up and down together, and on account of matching rush schedules, they appear to be fast friends.

I follow my map to a cream-colored mansion. The occupants are on the front lawn in single-file rows along the entry pavers. They're all smiles and hellos as I pass, and it's weirding me out. A flash of that scene from *Annie* runs through my mind, the one where the Rockettes welcome her to Radio City Music Hall. I'm barely inside the house when someone says, "Hi. I'm Becca!" She shakes my hand.

Oh, wow. She is talking very close to my face. And she's making really *intense* eye contact. I try to return her energy with a handshake but realize this might be a staring contest. "Where are you from? Is this your first rush?" She never blinks.

"LA. Yes."

"Me too! I knew I liked you!"

She looks right at me. I try not to blink. She smiles and is clearly thinking of what to say next. Then she continues on with her intense agenda.

"So, like, LA, LA, or LA County?"

"Uh ... county. The South Bay."

"Oh my God! I knew it! Me too! The Palisades, though!"

"Cool." I'm exhausted already.

At the next house, a girl in a white button-down oxford and small, ivory pearls says cryptically, "I can tell right away how I feel about someone." Again with the eyes. She doesn't blink or take them off mine. There's a flicker in her focus, and she asks, "You know?" I blink to shake the grip of her glare. Yes, sadly, I do.

Another girl walks up just in the nick of time. She looks me up and down and does some sort of sorority-girl calculus before she puts on her stewardess face, shakes my hand, and starts with the intense eye contact. Subtlety is apparently not a Greek system virtue.

On my way out of the last house, the girls line the front steps in two, single-file lines. They sing me a serenade of archaic meaning and rote memorization. Nonetheless, they seem to be having fun. I can taste the freedom of the street beyond, and this is exactly when my captor says, "Your gift! Wait here!"

It's just me and them. They're still singing to me as I wait. It's getting really awkward. A few of the girls look to who I assume is their leader. After an optical conversation that I see bounce down the row, it's been decided. They will continue on singing like this until I leave.

By the fourth round, we're still waiting. Since I now know all the words, I step into line and clap and sing along. When the girl finally returns with a little bag of chocolates, I yell "Thanks!" and take off running.

Back at the dorm, I pick up Shelby's phone and dial Quinn. She answers on the first ring.

"Hi!"

"Hey ..."

"So, how did it go? Did you make a deal with the devil?"

"Not yet. Not explicitly, at least, but I did join them in song."

"Oh, you're screwed."

∽

"The individual has always had to struggle to keep from being overwhelmed by the tribe. If you try it, you will be lonely often, and sometimes frightened. But no price is too high to pay for the privilege of owning yourself."

This is the third time I've read this passage by Friedrich Nietzsche. A pool ball or a cackle from upstairs breaks my focus every time. I take a sip of tea and hear some scuffles outside the door, then a knock. I open the door and nobody's there. But there is an envelope with a red wax seal, all wrapped up in a bow, and it's addressed to me.

"Dear Kate, we cordially invite you to join the sisterhood of Pi Delta Pi." I toss the envelope on my desk and continue on with my philosophy reading.

I've lost circulation in my feet from sitting so long. Shelby's phone startles me out of my *Beyond Good and Evil* trance, and I run on pins and needles to answer it.

"Hey, Kate, it's Doug. What's up?" This is the first time we've talked in a long while. It's loud in the background because the pay phone is on the first floor of his fraternity house where, his housemates think it's appropriate to play football. "How was rush?"

I fumble for a second, trying to decide how to approach this conversation with my fraternity-brother brother. "Good, I guess. Rush is weird."

"Did you get any bids?"

"Uh, yeah. Actually, just a minute ago."

"Which house?" I think of quoting Nietzsche, but Doug blurts out, "So, dude, did you get a bid from Pi Delta Pi or what?"

"Yes, just a few minutes ago."

"Are you stoked?"

"Um … I'm just not sure, you know?"

"It's the best house on the West Coast, Kate. You should do it." I think of asking what constitutes "the best" in this circumstance, but I don't. "Hey, I'm going out. I'll call you later. That's awesome, though!" He hangs up.

A few hours go by, and I realize nobody has distracted me from the syphilitic imaginings and lonely musings of this mad, German philosopher. So I grab the phone, call the number on the paper, and tell them, "I accept." My words are met by cheers and screeches, and immediately I wonder, what have I done?

○○

At the start of the spring semester, I'm sitting in my quiet dorm room on my army trunk full of belongings. I'm ready to move. I might vomit. Maybe it's the oversteeped tea or the fact that I've just lugged all my stuff out of the building and into my SUV. But most likely, it's something else entirely. I round the roundabout to the exit onto fraternity row. The travel time involved in this move has been approximately three minutes, and now I'm pulling into an empty spot in the parking lot. "This will be good for you," I say to myself in my most self-motherly tone. I look in my rearview mirror at my Mayan braids, then right in the eyes and breathe out. "You've got this."

At the front door, a chirpy sister says, "Welcome!" A slew of girls clap and cheer as I enter the house. There's a big butcher paper sign on the wall. "Welcome New Pledges!" A map detailing the house directs me to my "dayroom."

"Kate! Hi! I'm your pledge trainer, Jessica!" She approached from behind and scared the crap out of me. "You can grab any bunk you like in sleeping porch two. It's on the second floor. We're so excited you're here! Yay!" She claps like a peppy drill sergeant, and I flee up the stairs.

I scope out my dayroom on the second floor and the sleeping porch down the hall. On my way back to the stairwell for my things, I run into a denimed mom and daughter duo. They have coarse, highlighted hair—metallic gold strands like fiber optic wire. They're chewing gum, and their coordinating eyeshadow shades remind me of aquatic life.

"You," says the mom. "Are you the new pledge and roommate, Kate, by any chance?"

"Yup. That's me." She looks me up and down and chomps on her gum. Her eyes widen. I can't help but see the whole thing in slow motion.

"Kasey! This is Kate, your new roommate! Just look at her overalls, aren't they cute? So! You two are in the same pledge class," says the mom. "That's so exciting!" Now her eyes are even bigger, somehow.

"Hi." I shake Kasey's hand.

"Um ... formal!" says Kasey and she giggles. She bites her gum and looks up to her mom, who joins in, laughing. Now, they're just chewing their gum and staring at me.

"So ... Kate, is anybody here to help you move in?"

"Nope. Just me. Excuse me." I manage to get around them to the stairwell and back down to the parking lot for more of my stuff.

Back in the room, I unpack a box of jeans and shirts and hang them in my designated closet. Kasey is chomping on her gum. She places some framed photos and a huge makeup case on her dresser.

"Isn't it adorable?" asks the mom. "Identical dressers and closets!" She sits on the daybed and counts aloud. "One, two, three, four, five. There will be five of you in here. Fun!"

I nod in silent agreement and head back down for another box. On my way back to our room, I see they've multiplied.

"Well, hello!" another mom says as I enter the room. She presents a well-moisturized hand. "Darya Karazi, Naheed's mom," she says kindly. This lady is beautiful and petite with shiny, black hair. She smells like expensive perfume, and her face is painted on with precision. I wonder exactly how long it takes her to get dressed in the morning.

"Hi. I'm Kate." I point to my name on a Post-It note on my dresser and head over to unload my socks into a drawer. Mrs. Karazi informs me, "The sleeping porch is darling! It's just down the hall."

"Uh-huh," I agree, then fervently begin aligning my books on top of my dresser.

I hustle out for another load and run into Kasey in the hallway. She's gabbing excitedly with another girl. We do a do-si-do as I try to make my way past. "Oh my gosh, are you Kate? I'm Naheed and this is Kasey." Naheed is a carbon copy of her mother, delicate with shiny, black hair and big, brown eyes, though she doesn't appear to be wearing any makeup.

"Yes," I tell her. "Kasey and I met." The two girls clutch forearms and make an excited squealing sound.

"We're pledge sisters!" says Naheed.

Woo-hoo! I think to myself. "Yay," I say flatly.

At 5:15 p.m., the house is full and loud. I would leave, except we have this mandatory dinner meeting in half an hour. So, I sit here on the daybed and watch my new roommates unpack. I'm surrounded by their stuff: pink fuzzy slippers and matching bathrobes that are haphazardly flung over doorknobs, mismatched shoes thrown in sloppy closets, and lots of colorful coat hangers. The room has gotten even smaller.

All five dressers are now covered in makeup cases, and junk jewelry hangs from drawer pulls and from ornate mirror frames above each one. I'm greeted by an onslaught of framed family photos—brothers and sisters, parents and grandparents, dogs and cats. I feel betrayed. I thought we got to start over here, to be free of everything we were and everything that held us down. Did they not get the memo?

I take a seat on the daybed and watch as roommate number three enters. She's already met the other two. They talk loudly about where to put things and ask for each other's advice on various aspects of personal organization like it's rocket science. I sit in the corner of the daybed, flanked by pillows covered in eyelet cotton, and try to reserve judgment.

"Do you have any nail polish remover?" The new girl heads straight for my dresser and rifles through a box I have yet to unpack. When she sees I have no nail polish remover, she picks up my favorite book on the beat poets and thumbs through it before flinging it back down. It lands precariously on my dresser top's edge. I breathe out to calm myself and return it to its rightful place: third book in because it's taller than *The Way of Zen* but shorter than *The Catcher in the Rye*.

"Oh … okay. So there's a bubble around your dresser," the new girl says in a friendly but mocking way. "Sun-Mi." She extends a hand for me to shake.

"Kate," I tell her, looking at her dresser across the room. It's absolutely covered in trinkets and framed photos. There's a five-inch cloth doll with black hair and a poofy, kimono-like dress. I head over to inspect it more closely.

"Hanbok doll," Sun-Mi says. "It's a Korean thing."

There's also a little figurine of a garden troll and a brightly painted pottery box with a lid. "So is it Dia de los Muertos? Will you be putting out some fruit?" I ask her sarcastically.

"It's not too much? What's up with the minimalism over there?" She circles the airspace with her finger then lands on my bureau. "No people or dogs of value in your life?"

"No. I do. It's just that my mom died four years ago. I had a stepmom for a few months in high school and a stepbrother, but then she and my dad got divorced. Since I came to college, my dad got married again to a lady with three elementary school kids. She seems pretty nice, but I never see them. I do have two awesome brothers. One moved out when I was twelve. The other one is Brian. He's pretty great." I look at Sun-Mi, apologetic for the ramble. "I guess it's complicated."

Instead of the deer-in-headlights reaction I'm used to, Sun-Mi nods and says, "Yeah. I get it. But belonging is like a lizard's tail. If you let the light in, it can grow back."

I think I might actually like this girl. Then, she walks past my stuff on her way to the bathroom and, with a flick of her index finger, she knocks over my beat poets book, taking Alan Watts and J.D. Salinger with it. In the doorframe, she turns to me with a teasing smile and sticks out her tongue.

Naheed and Kasey watch this exchange like two deer in headlights. Kasey chomps nervously down on her gum and says, "Um … anyways!"

○○

After ten o'clock snack, which is apparently a thing, I tell anyone who cares to know that I'm heading to bed. On the second floor, down two long corridors, is the sleeping porch full of army barrack bunks and my bottom floor mattress covered in a closeout Laura Ashley print comforter from Bed Bath & Beyond.

Some girls are already fast asleep. As I tiptoe in, a few more watch me from their bunks, their feline eyes peering down at me from dark branches where they're perched. We were informed that the California Public Health Code requires us to leave the windows open to fight germs. In preparation, I wear wool socks, sweatpants, and a hoodie tied tight around my face. I enter the cool and slip under my covers. I hear the door open and slap closed as sock-footed girls shuffle like geisha to their own bunks, and the giddy energy of the day falls softly asleep.

Tucked into the quiet company of new friends, the little noises of night become comforts. In this sleeping porch, I take in their energy without being drained of my own. In here, I fall into a deep slumber and dream that the walls are made of rice paper. I awaken momentarily when the morning light streams through an open window, and the gentle motion of a friend in the bunk above stirs me from this sublimity.

Every day at 6:30 a.m., it starts—the staggered call of thirty alarm clocks. Their bells and beeps last for varying durations. I'm able to tune them out pretty well, but a girl must have come leaping off her perch in the bunk room upstairs. It's made just the right bass sound to rattle the room and the windows and startle us awake. In the bunk above me, Nadia calls out, "Huh? What?" She dangles her arm into my airspace and continues to snooze while her alarm beeps incessantly on our shared night table.

By 7:00 a.m., several girls have zombied out of the room, but not as quietly as I might have expected. In the corner, Natalie stretches her arms up to the ceiling and makes an attention-seeking moan. I cover my face, except for one eye, and stare at her. She seems not to notice. Another girl flies down from her top bunk, crashing like a sack of potatoes onto the floor. She must have twisted an ankle. She yells out for all of us to hear, "Crap, that hurt!" My cheek muscles pull. It seems like poetic justice.

Down the hall, "Too Much," by Dave Matthews is playing too loud. And through the open sleeping porch windows, I pick up on bits of conversation from various wings of the house. "Is this shirt me?" "Can I borrow your jeans?" "How should I do my hair?" The hairdryers start up and the talk gets louder. I roll slowly off my mattress into praying formation on my knees, then tiptoe out of the room.

In the dining room, I dish up a stack of spinach from the omelet bar and a small glass of orange juice. In the hallway under the main staircase is the communal fridge where I stashed some marinated tofu from the health food shop on College Avenue. It's apparently been emptied, so I wander like a lost soul into the main kitchen marked "Staff Only."

"Excuse me," I say to a young man who looks up at me from an industrial-size sink full of soapy dishes.

"¡Momento!" (Just a moment), he says and runs around the corner to retrieve a woman. "¡Mamá!"

"Lo siento," (Sorry), I say to them when he returns. "¿Donde está la comida del refrigerador en el pasillo?" (Where is the food from the refrigerator in the hall?)

Their faces relax. The man opens an industrial fridge door, telling me he forgot to put the food back after cleaning the fridge last night. He hands me a can of Coke and my tofu. "Sólo esto," (Just this), I say, taking just the tofu. I see a bottle of Italian salad dressing on the shelf behind him and gesture to it. He hands me the bottle and winks.

They're Ecuadorian, living in Oakland with his mom's sister. Eduardo says my accent sounds Salvadorian, but he thinks he likes me anyway. His mom smiles and winks warmly. For the first time since I moved into this house, it feels a bit like a home.

Back at the table, I slice up my tofu, place it over the bed of spinach, and drizzle some of the dressing on top. It looks delicious. I'm about to take a bite when a girl across the table from me asks, "What's wrong?"

"What?"

"What's wrong? You look sad."

"Huh? Just hungry." I take my first bite, ignoring her bad juju as I would Grandma's.

Getting no satisfaction from me, this girl turns to her right and stares at someone else for a second before saying, "You look tired." This girl looks defeated, and I instantly get this game.

"So do you work here now?" Sun-Mi appears across the table wearing her signature smile. "I saw you yukking it up with the house staff. You tryin' to get favors the rest of us can't have, like that *whole bottle* of salad dressing?" She laughs her glorious, infectious laugh.

"Yes. They're supercool."

Sun-Mi nods and smiles, and another girl slides into the chair next to her. She looks across the table at my plate.

"Ew, what is that?"

"Salad."

"Ew. What's on it?"

I'm about to put a bite in my mouth, but instead, I put my fork down and answer. "It's braised tofu."

"Ew, why?"

"It's protein. I don't eat animal products."

"Why?" Her mouth is wide open. "Does that make you skinny?"

"Um, no. I don't know. I just feel like if it were just me, I wouldn't kill animals for food or harvest their milk or eggs, so why rely on others for my sustenance, you know?" Based on the look on her face, I see that she does not, in fact, know.

Sun-Mi laughs out loud and seems to have my back and says, "She's just blowing around in the breeze." The girl looks away, clearly uninterested in our metaphors.

Instead, she's flagging down Eduardo as he passes with a bin full of dirty dishes. "Eduardo, por favor, queso para la cena," (Eduardo, cheese for dinner, please.) She has one of those offensive Spanish accents that's at once pompous and sounds exactly like English.

Eduardo puts down his tub and comes back with a dish of shredded cheese. "No. ¡Por la cena en la noche!" the girl states authoritatively. He blinks and nods.

"What do you mean?" I ask her. "You're asking for cheese tonight at dinner?"

"Queso, you know. I want them to serve it at dinner."

"Just cheese?"

"No! Queso." It sounds like "kay-soh." "Velveeta with a can of diced tomato and pepper dumped inside. You eat it with chips." She looks annoyed.

"Oh." Okay. "Dice que le gustaria esta noche una salsa de queso como Velveeta con una lata de tomate picado." I try not to make that face where I grit my teeth and open my eyes really big to show my true feelings on the matter. I'm not successful.

"Que horror," (How horrible), Eduardo says under his breath.

"Un invento americano?" (An American invention?) I suggest to Eduardo. "Que horror," I agree, saying it superfast so the girl won't understand it.

Sun-Mi grabs my shirt and whispers in my ear, "The biggest horror is that you think your superfast Spanish is so under the radar. This is California, you moron. And horror, by the way, in either language, means the exact same thing."

◯◯

I spend the rest of Sunday getting used to this big house and this enormous group of girls I share it with. I study the different messages in their looks, the prolonged eye-rapings. I dare myself not to blink or look away.

By the afternoon, I've categorized them by the eye rapist's style and apparent goals. Up and down: "Is she fatter than me?" Straight in the eyes: "Is she happier than me?" In the back of the head: "She makes me reflect on myself, and I don't like it." These are, of course, self-serving theories, and I'm open to the idea that the problem could, in fact, be me. Not everyone is an energy-sucking eye rapist, but most girls seem to take more energy than they give.

After dinner, I exhale my way down the front steps and into the night. I breathe in eucalyptus and sea salt. My fingers tingle, and I regain consciousness in my hands and arms. It radiates through me until my soul is once again full.

At the Wall Berlin café, I grab a vegan brownie and an Americano and just stare out the window. A gray-haired woman strolls slowly by in a long skirt. I swear, it's that lady from the hermitage in the hills. A few fashionable street kids with spiky-collared dogs sit on the curb and panhandle. I like the idea of it—the reliance on the city at large, like humble monks at the mercy of strangers, even if they are just rebellious teens from Knob Hill.

On second thought, maybe this is the grand cop-out—relying on humanity at large. Meanwhile, they skirt the real intimacy of home and close friends. I watch one of them hop into the back of a Range Rover parked on the corner, into a sleeping bag, and retire there for the night. "You phony," I whisper in my best Holden Caulfield voice.

On my stroll home, I pass small craftsman homes covered in layer after layer of paint. At Hildebrand Street, Billie Holiday comes crooning from a house with stained glass windows and a steepled roof. This might have been a church at one time. Today, it houses an earthier spirit. In the kitchen, I see an antique stove. Out here, it smells like sourdough and rosemary.

The authentic life of this town startles me awake. I run straight into neighborhood garden beds planted right in the middle of the sidewalk. Domesticated cats come out through picket fences to greet me. The smell of home cooking wafts from porch stoops and open windows. All the way home, I hear pots clang and evening chatter as I take in this intoxicating mix of flora and urbanity.

I'm barely to the top of the stairs when I hear it, the screeching and singing out loud that comes from our shared dayroom. I tiptoe down the hall to spy on the chaos.

It's eight of them, jumping on the daybed and singing into hairbrushes. I do a drive-by and head toward the bathroom to hide, but it's too late.

"Kate! Kate! Come in here!" yells Kasey. "Yeah!" says Kristina who occupies the room next door. They chase me down and drag me by an arm into to the doorway of our dayroom.

Sun-Mi's wearing pleather pants and a black bikini top. Her hair's in a scrunchie on top of her head. This accentuates her wide-set cheekbones and big eyes. Dressed like this, she looks like an anime character. "Kate! Why so serious? Where have you been? Strolling in a scarf with Sartre? Putting up walls at Wall Berlin?" I would laugh if it weren't true. "Get in here!"

They're taking turns with the solo. Typically shy, Naheed steps up for her turn on the daybed stage. It's all cheers for her as she's about to belt it out, when she trips on a pile of pillows and lands facedown on the carpet. Kasey laughs so hard she falls down next to her and drapes her fiber-optic highlights over Naheed's shiny black hair like a wig.

Shannon occupies the bureau next to mine. She's on the gymnastics team. She appears through the bathroom door, with her controlled sinewy presence, wearing a feather boa. She does a back walkover and the rest of the room cheers. And now, singing in unison, "This is how we do it!" Two hip-thrusting shuffles to the left on the springy daybed mattress, and we lose Jayme. But the girls on the floor keep singing, each with an arm raised, pumping to the ceiling.

Maddie comes bounding in with her university cheer squad pompons. She shakes her hair stripper-style and shimmies up and down the doorframe. "Que horror!" says Sun-Mi and clotheslines me. I join them on the floor in a heap of laughter.

Pinned on the floor under the harsh chandelier light, I turn longingly to the darkened window. The damp soil outside beckons me. The polis down on Telegraph Avenue is easy, anonymous, and free. But not me. I'm stuck here, pinned to the ground, my limbs stretched toward the ceiling and the light, under a heap of relentless friends who have tackled me and made me laugh beyond my will. Grounded and gasping for air, I think this might be real life and that I just might be ready, now, to put down roots.

The Fire Trail

The stoic won't bring us closer to truth. But she, who ventures to lose herself in passion and art brings us one step closer to that celestial spark.

"Can anyone tell me what the central theme is here?" Professor Clark looks out to a blank crowd. He's starting to look irritated. Nobody makes eye contact. The guy to my right starts frantically turning the pages, as if he expects something to jump out at him. By some spark of impulse, I raise my hand.

"Yes!" he points down to me in the second row. "Tell us about the Fire Sermon." He paces to the left with his eyes on the ground, then places a palm on his forehead to swipe his hair from his eyes. I've been loving this moral philosophy seminar, and Professor Clark is my moral hero. I admire the elbow patches on his tweed and think Quinn would agree he's not hot, but his passion for the subject matter and his desire to impart that passion onto us makes him a total beast.

"Well, detachment, basically."

"Yes!" the professor says with his index finger in the air. He paces in front of the chalkboard. "And what's burning?" He steadies his eyeglasses. Before anyone makes a peep, his index finger is raised to the ceiling and he calls out, "Everything!" The room is silent. "And that fact is excruciating … isn't it?" I could hear a pin drop.

"So what is the point of detachment, exactly?" He points to me and then turns to face the chalkboard. I stare at his back. He continues. "To relieve suffering by detaching the mind and the five senses. To lessen the burn by not fueling the fire." The professor returns to the text on his podium and looks out at us thoughtfully. "Do you think that's an easy thing to do? To detach?" The room is silently captivated, but this guy next to me is slumped back in his chair, half-asleep. I laugh out loud, imagining that it's easy for him.

"Is something funny?" The professor is all eyes on me.

I blurt out without thinking, "Isn't connecting … *really* connecting, the hard part?" A few of my classmates laugh nervously. They must think I'm being a smart ass.

"I guess I had never thought of this text in that way." The professor is resigned. He closes his book and stares at the wall clock. "Go spend some time with one another," he says. "Go connect. I'll see you all on Monday."

༃

I drag myself up the grand staircase to our room, where Kasey's sitting on the daybed, grinning. It's annoying. "What?"

"Nothing. Science experiment," she says, tongue in cheek.

"Okaaaay ..." Just then, two doors open on the west wall and Naheed and Sun-Mi come rolling out of their closets with handheld vanity mirrors.

Kasey chomps down on her gum then opens wide to speak. I see the wad of gum in the corner of her mouth. "So ... did you find it?"

"Nope," Naheed giggles.

"Did you lose something?" Half-heartedly, I try again for answers.

"I'm pretty sure it's a myth." Sun-Mi hands me a paper titled "Homework: Find Your G-Spot."

"Is this serious?" Apparently, they're all enrolled in a graduate student-taught seminar titled "Female Sexuality." The fact that they're getting college credits for this blows my mind. "Directions," I read, "Use a hand mirror to locate your vulva. Feel about two inches in for a rough patch on the top wall."

"I've tried a few times, now." Naheed exaggerates her frustration and tosses her mirror on the daybed before crashing down herself. "I hear it's like a religious experience when you find it, though."

"Are you taking Female Sexuality?" Mary pops her head in excitedly. "Such a good class! I took it when I was a sophomore. Did you find your G-spot yet?" In unison, my roommates shrug their shoulders and answer no.

Mary is wearing a gold cross necklace and saving herself for marriage or God or something. She exits the doorframe and I see her navy-blue backpack turn the corner toward the stairs. "Well," she says, "maybe don't look so hard. It's more about … you know …" Her voice becomes faint as she heads down the stairs, "… about who you are and not finding anything in particular."

Just when Mary's out of earshot, Kasey blurts out, "Yeah, or maybe that's what boys are for!" Naheed giggles.

I can't help myself. "So, Kasey, you can't find your G-spot, but a boy can?" I must seem incredibly judgmental right now because the girls have stopped in their tracks. "Don't you think you're giving away too much of your power?"

Kasey chomps down on her gum, then opens her mouth wide, "Huh?"

○○

Just after 10:00 p.m., there's a mass exodus from the third-floor study. The prefunk is on. A hot curling iron is plugged into the wall behind my dresser. The cord blocks the bathroom door. "Are you coming? We're going to the house next door to hang with Shooter." Kasey brushes on some teal eyeshadow, and Naheed blows on freshly painted nails.

Ah, Shooter. It's just a nickname, but his mother should be so proud. "The Greek system's drug dealer? No, thanks. Heading out for a vegan brownie."

"You're a dork," says Kasey.

"Yes, I've been told." The brownie alibi, or the plain fact that I'm a dork, is believable enough to the majority of binge eaters and anorexic exercisers in the house. I just hope to avoid explaining to the codependent socializers why I would ever desire to leave this house alone.

"When are you gonna give in to us and stop running away?" Sun-Mi laughs through her words, but she exposes me gently with her eyes.

"Bye!" chirps Naheed, passive-aggressively.

"Later," says Kasey, just aggressively.

They leave. A minute later I hear the door slam on the first floor. I grab my backpack and a boy's size XL puffer jacket I bought in high school from the Salvation Army Thrift Store. I head out of the house and into the night, relishing my loneliness and hunger. I breathe it in and out, and it builds inside of me. It's painful and somehow incredibly motivating. I get the feeling it possesses an explosive and creative power all its own.

After midnight, I just walk around town, singing Patsy Cline. Back at home, I'm disappointed to hear that everyone's back and awake. I guess they hear me on the creaky stairs, too, and it's too late. "Kate! We're all going to Mexico for spring break. You should come with!"

"Ooh, yeah. I think I'll pass. I don't need to get roofied to spend some time on a beach."

"But we're all going."

I make a face as if I'm seriously considering Mexico, but the fear of missing out has never been a motivator for me. My answer is still no.

"What are you gonna do this weekend, Kate? It's mother-daughter weekend." The other girls look at Sun-

Mi as though she's just committed a major faux pas with this question.

"Thank you for your concern, Sun. It's just like any other weekend, right?"

"Shall I pack you a book and a scarf?"

༺꧁༻

On my way to the sleeping porch, I hear a soft whimper down the hallway. Instead of heading east to bed, I turn right into the south wing. Just beyond the fire door, against the hallway wall, is a cute, little, pink couch that seems to have no purpose at all. But it's the perfect crying couch and that is what Jayme is doing on it.

I'm inclined to give her a quick hug and flee, but I don't. I sit next to her and pull her in. "Hey, baby bear. What's up?"

"I'm so glad it's you."

"Me? Why?"

"What are you going to do tomorrow? All the moms are coming."

"Yeah, I'll just do my own thing."

"Like what?"

"I dunno, take a jog, hit up a museum, grab an espresso. Why?"

"And you're going to be okay?"

"Yes. Why?"

"My mom died too."

I didn't know that. I've been too aloof to know that. We talk for a good half hour about the state of the motherless daughter, about our newfound sisterhood here in this house full of sisters. We hold our inaugural meeting of the unrepresented and bond over how we are lacking in so many intimate ways.

"But you seem so strong, Kate," Jayme says sweetly. I'm surprised by this observation. I must really seem like a hardass.

"That was a gift from my mom," I tell her. "Hey, let's do something. At some point tomorrow, let's say a little mantra to the breeze, something for one another. Let's give each other strength."

There is a place where the fire trail dips into the canyon. I run under a string of prayer flags someone has tied to the trees. Each time I do, the wind picks up, and I feel the pain of humanity in my bones. Though I'm alone, I'm connected by this prayer to the whole of us. "Deal?" I ask Jayme.

"Deal."

Jayme smiles, and so do I. And it's not because I'm reaffirming my vow to be stoic, strong, and detached; it's because I've made a meaningful connection with her. I head to bed elated, thinking about the abundance and the variety of opportunities there are to connect.

༄༅

In the morning, on top of my dresser are *The Stranger* and a scarf. There's also a note: "A scarf, just like Meursault's."

"Damn you, Sun!" I say out loud, "I'm an introvert, not a misanthrope!" But I punch a fist into the sky and half expect a cartoon thunderbolt to appear before a rain cloud. I laugh an evil laugh, fully aware of this irony.

Before the moms arrive, I'm out of here, into the hills in my sweats and my running shoes. I pass through the side yard of Pi Delta and make a left at the alley that leads to Memorial Stadium. I pass my totem, "Sharp Curves Ahead," and exaggerate my step, swinging my hips for a moment in homage to the feminine gods. Then up the stairway I ascend, up old, mossy concrete and past the lofty banisters and bench landings, all the way up to the fire trail.

When the pavement meets the dirt, I'm hungry and out of breath. I pass under the prayer flags, and I become everyone. So I run. I run for my nothingness and to kill this hunger. I run, and my body starts to burn. I feel a spark and a flame, but I can't feel my limbs. I'm unencumbered and free. We are one—the fire trail, everything, and me.

At home, the girls and the moms are in the dining room, having some grown-up version of a tea party. I walk through the first floor to the stairs and keep my head down to avoid eye contact with tea-party stragglers, defectors, or lost moms wandering the house in search of the bathroom. I do a quick change upstairs and duck out the back door.

The rest of the day, I am beholden to no one. So, oblivious to the hours or seconds, I wander. I read Kant by Strawberry Creek and behind a moving wall of books in the main stacks of the library. I browse through the racks at Buffalo Exchange for some preloved clothing, for God-knows-how-long. Under a redwood tree on the edge of campus, I say out loud, "You do not suffer alone." I know that Jayme feels it. At some point I'm hungry, so I head into La Cascada and sit in the corner with a burrito. When I'm done, I stroll home, slip into woolen socks, and head early to bed.

In my twin-size bunk, I stretch. I feel my ribs under my skin. I breathe in the simple, perfect nature of the hills outside. Their energy flows like a river and clashes violently with the urban intellect of the city below. It's an exhilarating crisis that smells like loneliness, eucalyptus, and endless possibilities. And Mr. Caspari is right about the buzz.

I breathe it in and it fills my belly, fingers, and toes. I breathe it out and still it builds. My toes flex and twitch under its spell. I grab my bedsheet. Everything circles uncontrollably around me, building, burning, swirling, until I'm completely overcome and the dam breaks, and the energy spills and cascades back out to the universe.

My toes twitch, my heart pounds. It's clear, I've connected with something much greater than myself. That briny breeze through the palms of my youth, the phosphorescent tide, and the smell of salt—everything has come rushing back. And everything suggests that this great potential has been a part of me all along.

Now, I know. I'm not a rock. I am not an island. I'm a channel. We all are—stewards of the cosmos and conductors of its powers. We decide how to use this potential and just where the energy goes.

Plus, I found my G-spot without even trying. And I didn't need a mirror or a man.

༄༅

"Well, aren't you a good, little Buddha!"

I'm really in no mood for company. I thought I had made this fact clear by choosing this particular bench that faces out toward the parking lot and by placing my grocery bags all around me on the table like a barricade.

I didn't even hear this guy sit down, but here he is, sitting right across from me. He looks like Marvin Gaye, and he's flanked by an angelic, backlit woman on either shoulder. They smile, and I try to ignore them. I take another sip of my juice-bar drink. It's gritty, like rich soil. Probably an acquired taste, but I love it.

"Look at that aura!" the man booms with childlike enthusiasm. The ladies talk around him in hushed voices like woodland sprites until they seem to have agreed on something and are immediately hushed. The man says, "You know, it isn't about your food."

"What?"

"It isn't about your food ... your spirit cannot be helped by such physical things."

When I look at him, a mirage appears, like water vapors that dance and dissipate off his saffron and crimson robes. They circle furiously around his head until, one by one, like synchronized water ballerinas, they drop off into the air. They are, no doubt, life-affirming molecules. I look down at my own hands and suddenly notice them and feel them everywhere. I dare to look this man in the eyes, and I'm surprised because he doesn't siphon from me one single drop.

He seems to speak spontaneously. "Will you come with me to meet the Lama? He is here in Berkeley tonight. I want you to meet him." The man hands me a business card. "Mahtab," he says, opening the floodgate on a babbling brook of laughter. I've only heard this kind of glee from children. That it comes from a grown man is at once unnerving and intriguing.

"Kate." I shake his hand.

The ladies sashay away like petals on the breeze. Mahtab writes an address, a time, and his phone number on the business card. "Please come."

"Sure, yeah. I'll try." I stand to recycle my cup and make my escape back into the grocery store.

In the produce section, I fill a bag with Granny Smith apples. I'm just about at the checkout when I stumble right back into the trio. This time, Mahtab's holding a bouquet of pastel roses. "For you." He hands me the flowers like a giddy schoolboy. The ladies nod approvingly. One puts her hands to her chin in praying formation, locks her eyes with mine, and bows. I laugh and smile and bounce around awkwardly to show my appreciation, but I really just want to get the hell out of there.

At home, the girls are sitting on the floor around the coffee table. A waft of formaldehyde and toluene rudely awakens me from a dreamy, rain-spattered bike ride home in the fresh air. Dave Matthews is playing really loud, and the girls don't even notice me walk in. But I hear his belting over their squeals, "Too much ... too much!"

It looks like pink fingers and glitter pink toes today. I don't get them. They enthusiastically consume just about everything shiny. I want desperately to scale back and rid my life of impermanent, decadent things.

"Where have you been?" Naheed yells over the music. Kasey turns around and stares. I put Mahtab's card on my dresser and crash onto the daybed.

Naheed gets up and waddles on her heels to the bathroom. She's got one of those spongy things between her toes. She does a drive-by and grabs Mahtab's card. "Who's Sri Mahtab?" Her tone is mocking.

"I met him at Whole Foods. He wants me to meet this, I guess, Buddhist leader who's speaking in town tonight."

Kasey looks startled. Naheed's face turns maternal. Sun-Mi laughs through her accusation. "So you're gonna go?"

"Yeah, why not?"

Kasey's eyes look bigger than her wide-open mouth. She's siphoned the liquid out of her chewing gum and says, "Because, sketch!"

༺༻

After dinner, the air is still. I open our dayroom window and wait for the rain. Within a minute, it falls across the street in the shadows and onto our sidewalk in a ray of sun.

It comes in wafts between torrents of breeze. And as quickly as it came, it disappears to the north. I am mesmerized. Jayme grabs a lighter and a box of American Spirits and leads the rest of the girls out the window like a herd of elk to the shingles of our gabled roof. They sit just outside our open window and smoke and chat. This is hardly as inspiring as the fresh air, but a cloud of smoke floats my way on a group exhale, and it smells like a party.

"I'm off!" I tell the cloud.

"Okay!"

"Whatever. Bye."

"Don't get murdered."

"Why would you ever meet a stranger out at night? Be careful!"

I'm back on my bike in the dark and the bitter rain. A half mile down Ashby Avenue, I hop off at an old, turn-of-the-century building. There's a sign that blows around on the door under two pieces of Scotch tape. "Lama, Aryadeva, 4th floor." I climb old, wooden steps and enter a room that's much larger than I expected. There must be a couple hundred people in here. They sit silently on the floor and face their teacher.

Hardly a soul looks at me when I enter, and it feels like the ultimate act of courtesy, especially in light of the fact that they seem so hyperaware of my presence. I spot Mahtab, who tells me with his eyes where to go. I tiptoe down the aisle, apologizing as I bump into people in the row. No one dignifies the suggestion of my embarrassment, so I just let it go.

Once I reach them, I perform an act of contortionism until I'm proudly in the Lotus position. "Never show your feet to the guru," Mahtab whispers. "Your feet are the lowest part of you."

So onto my heels I crouch with all my weight. It's really uncomfortable, and by the time my knees start to ache, I realize I don't even speak the language of this lecture.

The sermon seems to come to an abrupt end, and without the slightest collective outburst, the crowd simply disperses into the foyer. On the landing, a South Asian woman stands by a plastic folding table covered in jewelry made out of hand-chiseled rocks and ore metals. None of it is glitzy or refined, but each piece seems to carry a depth of artistry exemplifying that bond between the spirit of the mineral and the human spirit. I touch a silver amulet that opens with a threaded pin like a screw. On the outside, something is etched in Sanskrit. I have no idea what it says, but I rub the etching with my thumb, and its meaning is quite clear: Mother Earth is consecrated by human devotion.

Mahtab's harem approaches from the west on a breeze that brings with it patchouli incense and the scent of rose petals. The girls' smiles are full of joy and generosity. And behind them, Mahtab laughs joyfully with another robed individual. When the building quiets down, the ladies part the waters by sashaying to opposite sides of the foyer, and Mahtab appears before me.

"Here." He hands me a box. "Open it. Please."

Inside is a locket like the one I just held. This one's on a long, rudimentary chain that's somewhat clumsy, but also exceptionally beautiful because it evokes the rustic quality of the artist's touch.

"Put it on."

"No," I whisper. I blush. I try to hand it back to him, but he refuses it. As a young woman set free in a college town, I'm accustomed to the advances of lecherous strangers. They usually present as a heavy staredown on the sidewalk and a suggestive "hello." They are never this dramatic or ceremonial. Nor are they accompanied by the preapproval of the ladies of court and a showering of gifts. "Thank you," I say, even more anxious to leave. I put the gift in my bag and turn for the door.

"Wait!" he calls. "We're going to have tea. You must come!" I look to the harem. The long-haired ladies nod and affirm his statements. So the four of us walk together down the wood-paneled staircase of the old Bancroft Building where my bike is chained outside to a handrail.

Mahtab urges me toward his large 1980-something car. I shake my head. "Tell me where you are headed, and I'll get there."

After a strenuous uphill ride, I reach the front entrance to the Durant Hotel. I'm wrapping my chain lock to a railing near the steps in the driveway when the valet runs over.

"Are you a guest of the hotel?"

"No, just meeting some people." I feel like a child, handing my bike over by the handlebars. In the lobby, fresh lilies fill a huge vase, lending a sophisticated scent that seems even more exotic in this grungy college town. At the front desk, a woman wearing a navy blazer sees me and makes a gesture toward Mahtab and the ladies, who are waiting near the elevators.

"Hello! You made it!" He sings his words. "Let's head up to my suite." The elevator door opens and I panic.

My presumption that he is a benevolent being clashes violently with everything I know about strange men. If it weren't for the presence of his entourage, I would run. Instead, the four of us enter the elevator together and exit on the third floor.

Just inside room 306, the long-haired ladies hug me one at a time. They bow to Sri Mahtab. One of them looks at me in a congratulatory manner and says, "Have a lovely night." In a puff of white clouds and rainbows, the two are gone.

I'm alone in a hotel room with a strange man. There is no rubric of healthy risk-taking that justifies this. And though it isn't prudent or even smart, I stay.

"Welcome," he says warmly. I scroll through my mental repertoire for possible titles of this episode of *Dateline*. I'm wide-eyed, on edge, just watching for his next move.

"Now, let's attend to that aura," he says in what is suddenly an Indian English accent. He smiles his huge, Cheshire Cat smile. He pats the edge of the bed. I must look terrified because he laughs and says, "Come. Sit. Let's meditate."

In the center of the bed, he crosses his legs and rests his palms downward on his knees. "Lotus is okay," he says instructively, warmly. He laughs and I get the joke. I wrap my heel over my left knee.

"Close the eyes. Let's meditate. Good." At first, I pretend to be into this. I close my eyes and pay attention to my breath, but mostly I listen for any erratic movement he might make. When I hear nothing but his steady breath, I relax myself. His calm presence is somehow facilitating my calm and lulling me deeper into meditation.

For a while, I hover heavily in my gut and I'm anxious. But, then I'm in my heart and I smile. I feel Mahtab smiling with me, and he demands nothing, so I rise deeper into myself. Now, I'm in my throat. I want to scream, but I don't, and the energy builds and floats to my head. Sometime later, I have no idea how long, I realize I'm floating above the bed. I am out of my physical body and into something that feels quite infinite.

I try to make sense of it, and just as I do, I sink back into my head and plummet all the way back down. I am suddenly aware of my body again, and my heart beats fast like after one of those falling dreams I have somewhere between wakefulness and sleep. I open my eyes to see Mahtab staring at me.

"Good!" he cheers like a child. "For one glorious moment, you were meditating perfectly!" And it's true. Never before have I been so entirely within and also without myself. "There's just one thing," he says, and I see his wheels spin. "You are stuck in your crown."

He gets up and starts pacing. This is the first time I've seen concern on his face. "Who do you carry?" he asks me, and somehow, I know exactly what he means.

"Well, I live with some very intensely competitive and superficial women."

Mahtab nods and laughs. "Yes," he says, as if he already knows that. "What about your family?"

"Uh ... my mom died, my dad has moved on with a new woman and her kids. My brothers and I are kind of estranged. They're angry for the loss of our mom and hurt. My grandmother is very manipulative and mean."

"Yes. Exactly," Mahtab says, matter of fact. "And how will you be free of all that negativity without losing sight of your dharma, your path?" I open my mouth to answer, but realize I don't understand the question. "How will you be free to live your true self without disconnecting from meaningful interactions with these people you are meant to be with?"

"Come!" Mahtab urges me to follow him. The man could be fifty, but he hops off the bed like a child and rummages through a black satchel. He pulls out a lighter and a bunch of what looks like kindling or weeds. The lighter and the black satchel are suddenly very off-putting, and I remember I'm alone in a hotel room with a stranger.

Mahtab hops around joyfully, disarmingly, and he calls me into his small hotel bathroom, where he lights the bunch of dried plants on fire. "Take off this shirt," he says, and without flinching, I do. The room begins to smell of burned sage, and I feel the sparks of the kindling on my back and abdomen as Mahtab brushes it up and down my torso. He's singing a prayer that's scribbled onto a piece of scrap paper.

"Om Namo Hanumate Rudra Avataraya. Parayentra Mantra Tantra Trataka. Nasahakaya Shree Ramadutaya Swaha." He repeats it three times, then blows out the flame, pulls my shirt back over my head as if he's dressing a toddler, and calls me back to the bed.

I watch him rummage again through the satchel. He pulls out some silky, red string, fumbles around again for some cuticle scissors that he uses to cut the string, and returns to tie it to my wrist. Wrapping it twice around, he ties it into a knot.

"Don't remove this for two weeks," he instructs. "And don't let anyone look you in the eyes until then. You are even more vulnerable now and also more attractive to others. But you must not let their energy corrupt you. You must build your strength."

He pulls the chain on the bedside lamp, climbs into bed, and says, "Now, my little Buddha, we sleep."

∽

About thirty minutes into "sleep," which consists of me lying in the dark next to a stranger with my eyes wide open, listening to his breath, and calculating his every intention, Mahtab takes my hand. I feel his warm, excited appendage, and I retract.

"See what you do to me?" he asks with a softly desperate tone. I don't react, so he lets go of my hand. A few minutes later, I hear his breath slow, and he falls asleep.

It's 2:17 a.m. I must have actually been asleep. The phone near the bed is ringing. Even at this hour, Mahtab answers it with his usual childlike joy. "Hello," he says sweetly. The red numbers of the hotel alarm clock glow sinister in the dark. I pretend I'm asleep and listen.

"No. She can't come to the phone right now. She's in heaven." I sit up abruptly, shocked by his words. He laughs and holds the receiver in my direction. I can hear a girl or a woman sobbing on the other end of the line. Mahtab says, "It's for you."

"Kate! It's Naheed, I got this number from your dresser."

"Oh, hey ..."

"Are you okay?" Her voice is steady and awkward. I imagine she's reading from a script."

"Yes. I'm good."

Now, her tone changes, and I hear a tremble in her words. "If you're okay, say one. If you are not okay, say two."

"Okay ... one," I say.

"Are you sure you don't want to say two?"

"Yes. Positive."

"When are you coming home?"

"Not sure. In the morning? I'll explain everything tomorrow."

I'm sorry to have worried Naheed, but I fall asleep feeling very nurtured, with my heart chakra thumping in my chest. In my dream, I'm living in a stucco structure in Iran. The world outside rages on under the Ayatollah, and there is uncertainty in the streets. But inside, in here, I'm cradled by my Persian friend or by her Persian mother. I'm not sure which. Motherly love is all I can feel. So I let down my guard and banish the stoic within. With the first light of morning, I'm accepting of this kind of love, and I realize it's everywhere.

☙

"Good morning, my princess!" I'm gathering my backpack and sweatshirt and putting on my sneakers. "Please, write down your telephone number. I will call for you."

I write down the phone number to our dayroom, and he hands me another box. Inside is a rose quartz necklace set in hand-pounded silver. He also hands me a vintage photo in a five-by-seven frame. It's a print of a Victorian woman with pale skin, pink cheeks, and sunny hair the color of mine. "Here. Take this. I found this photo the morning I met you. It led me to you. I was meant to meet you."

I take the photo. Oddly, this is the most disturbing part of our encounter. I feel as if I was typecast, targeted. Suddenly, what was a profound and spiritual meeting feels superficial. Nonetheless, I thank Mahtab and take the photo and another business card he hands me. This one has several phone numbers scrawled on the back. "Call me. You can reach me anywhere. This is my London office. Here is India and New York. I will call for you too."

Yeah, this is probably more of a one-time kinda thing, I think, and I stand to leave. "Remember," he says to me, "you are very receptive. You must not absorb the negative. You must only hear, see, and speak positivity. With more meditation, you will be the channel through which the river flows, I just know it, and also the boulder within."

Is this some crazy universal prank? Did he really say those words? I could have written them myself. "Thank you," I say. "Hey, one more thing … what does your name mean?"

"It is a name given to me by my teacher. It means," and he beams, "the light of the moon."

༺ঞ༻

Back at the house, I keep my head down in case I'm attacked by prying eyes. I feel various energies waft toward me—jealousy, competition, annoyance, and self-doubt—but one feeling surprises me. A junior named Erica passes through the room, and I feel admiration. I let that one in.

A couple of weeks later, I'm feeling lighthearted. Mahtab has faded into that part of my memory reserved for fictional, guiding-light characters like Yoda. I enjoy the folly of my housemates more than I ever thought possible, especially their vindictive, childlike antics. They crack me up because they're so full of passion and lust for life.

On my way to the third-floor study, I'm cornered by a junior named Moriah. We've never had a conversation, but she's always looking me over and making comments about my appearance. "Oh, hey …" Once I'm awaiting the message, it comes slowly. "Cute overalls." She pauses again and looks me up and down. "You look like a toddler." She keeps a straight face in order to pass it off as a compliment but still effectuate the intended injury.

"I was going more for lumberjack." She doesn't expect to get called out by my humor. Or my deflection in the form of flattery: "I'll let you borrow them sometime if you promise to put on some weight so you don't look better than me."

She walks away, looking confused and neutralized. I've converted her negative energy into something positive and sent it on its way.

A week later, I'm able to do this with my eyes only. And people tell me the wildest things now too. From across the dining room, I see Moriah's daggers. I don't look away. I take them head-on with my own look. I've disarmed her, and now she's heading my way. "Did I ever tell you that you look like my sister? I've always been jealous of her. My parents like her more."

"That's flattering. I'm sure she's gorgeous, like you, and that the competition between you two has been good for you both." She looks instantly at peace.

These confessions can be energizing or draining, so I choose to absorb only the good. I refuse to judge, and I send only the positive energy back out there. Now that I've experienced a glimpse of the infinite, everything else is just games.

༻✦༺

After anthropology, I put my things down and crash into the daybed. The girls in the room look menaced.

Naheed's reading *Cosmo* on the floor in her sweats. She sits up tall, crosses her legs under herself, and stares at me.

"What?"

"Um, he called again."

"A few phone calls does not a stalker make, you guys."

Sun-Mi walks by my dresser on her way to the bathroom and messes up my books. "Are you a concubine or something now? You guys! Wait till I get back before you play it!" She skips giddily into the bathroom and throws one of the stalls open. She doesn't bother to close it, and we hear her pee furiously, run her hands under the faucet, and return to the room just as fast as I've ever seen.

"Okay. Are you guys ready? Here it goes ..." Kasey pushes play on our answering machine.

"Hello, Kate, this is Sri Mahtab again. Please, do call me. You must come live with us here in New York. Don't deny your true dharma. This is how you die. Please, do call me. It's your most devoted Mahtab."

Kasey gets her deer-in-headlights face on again. "I'm scared, Kate. I think we should call the police."

Nadia is visiting from the room next door. She sits on the other end of the daybed and hugs one of our throw pillows before beginning her own lecture. "Kate, that was a death threat!"

"No. It wasn't. And why are you even in here? I promise you, that was not a death threat. He's just saying that when you deny your calling, that's when your spirit dies."

"Oh ... is that all?" Sun-Mi is bowled over laughing. She's loving this. Only Naheed seems to have my back.

"He scares me, too, you guys. But, he just talks like that. He told me she was in heaven and he meant asleep, not dead." I nod in her direction to say thank you, but then she chimes in again. "If he keeps calling, though, we're going to have to call the police."

"Fine. Deal. Thank you for your concern, all of you."

I'm home from a run. Everyone's in our room waiting for me. Immediately, I know. This is an intervention.

Sun-Mi speaks for the group. "Kate. It's getting really scary and weird."

"Okay … play it."

"My dear Kate, this is Sri Mahtab. You were sent to me as a test. I will not call you again." The machine beeps.

"Wait … that's it?"

They nod. Nadia has that look of "enough said." But it doesn't seem like nearly enough said to me. I dial Mahtab's New York office and get a beep. I try him in London. Sun-Mi is rifling through her shoes at the bottom of her closet and yells something about paying this month's phone bill. Mahtab picks up.

"This is Sri Mahtab."

"Hi, Mahtab. I've been very busy with school. So, I'm a test?"

"Yes. My guru told me of a dream, an owl on a roof, distracted by a bird."

"Okay."

"I am the owl."

"Okay."

"You are the bird. You were meant to tempt me, to distract me. I failed the challenge, so I will go deeper now into meditation."

I'm doing my best to follow all this, but I'm a little distracted by my sorority sisters, who are standing all around the room, staring at me.

"Thank you for aiding me on my path," he continues. "My guru warned me about you. I cannot believe I didn't see it! When I found that photo of the girl that looked like you, I was already tempted. I desired you and coveted you, and that desire and attachment has brought me pain. Do you understand me?"

"Uh?"

"You are my challenge. I need to let you go."

Then, he's just silent. Before I hang up, I tell him, "Thank you for your passions, your folly, and your fire. Your flaws have brought so many lessons and so much meaning to my life too."

Everyone in the room starts to laugh and Kasey says, "Um ... whatever!"

⊙⊚

Again, Professor Clark is pacing. "What is the point of morality?" Silence. "Is the point to be good for goodness's sake?" Someone in the back row laughs out loud before we all realize he's serious. I wonder how he can do this, day after day, year after year, with so many students. What keeps Professor Clark so passionate about his work? He's already got tenure.

"I have office hours today at two-thirty, and you're welcome to join me for happy hour at Jupiter on Thursday, if you like." He's distracted by the clock. "It's the hour," he says and picks up his worn leather messenger bag and walks out the door.

I check my watch again, confirming with his schedule on the hallway corkboard. It's time for his office hours, but there's no answer. I knock again. This time, I hear a bump and the shuffle of some papers, as if a whole stack of them has gone sliding off a desk. I think I might hear noises from outside his open window, but then I clearly hear whispers and a few deep breaths inside the room. I feel like a loser, but I knock again anyway.

In my toddler overalls, I slide down the wall in the hallway and slump down by his door. I turn the pages of my class notes, making sure I've got my questions ready to go. Anxiously, I sit and wait.

When I've forgotten where I am and why, the door opens. A curly-haired woman, who I recognize as a student from our class, tugs at her pencil skirt and brushes her hair from her face before looking both ways down the long hall. But she doesn't see me sitting on the floor just two feet from the door. She takes off quickly the other way. After she's gone, I scurry as if I'm fleeing the scene of a crime.

Back in our dayroom, I pick up the phone for my once-every-two-and-a-half-week phone call to Grandma. I have this task written in my Rolodex planner, and I'm relieved when I get to cross it off several times in pen.

"Hell-oo?"

"Hi, Grandma. How's it going?"

"Fine, Kate. How are you?" Naheed and Kasey come bounding in and talk over my phone call. "Kate, I can't hear you. Hello? What is that awful noise?"

I drag the telephone cord around our coffee table and into my closet. I close the door to talk in the dark.

"Sorry. It's my roommates."

"Roommates? A lady should have her own apartment."

"Not in college, Grandma."

"Yes, in college. At this rate, you'll end up an old maid!"

"Okay. I'll look into an apartment, but that's expensive."

"Maybe, if you're good, I'll pay for it."

"No, thank you."

"What do you mean, 'No, thank you?' It's in one ear and out the other with you. You are very independent and stubborn, Kate. You know what they'll say about you …"

"No, I don't. What will they say, Grandma?"

She doesn't answer. She lets out a nasal and menacing "I don't know …" and changes the subject.

"Are you still dressing like a little babushka? Dowdy and serious?"

"No. I don't think so."

"Uh-huh," she says and lets it marinate. "Well, put on a little lipstick once in a while. You've gotta create your own joys, Kate."

I hear the girls in the room rush out the door and down the stairs for dinner.

"Hey, Grandma, I've been called to dinner. I'll call you later?"

"Um-huh," she mumbles.

"I love you," I say and try not to hint that I also feel some hate.

"Uh-huh," she answers. "Good-ni-ight."

I hang up the phone and crawl out of the closet. I return the phone to its base and tidy up my dresser. In my mirror, I do look dowdy and serious, so I find a tube of lipstick in Sun-Mi's stuff and dab a little on. I rub my lips together as I do with ChapStick, but I end up looking like a clown. When I wipe away the smudges where I've failed to color between the lines, I see that my face looks bright and cheery. I can't help but smile, but I defiantly say to my reflection, "Whatever, Grandmama."

⁘

After dinner, I lock my bike to a tree on the corner of University and Shattuck and head into Jupiter. It feels like an old English pub. I spot Professor Clark on the far end of the bar at a heavy wooden table, with a bunch of students from our seminar, a graduate student TA, and ... her.

I sit virtually unnoticed as the professor gushes to the curly-haired woman. "Tell them your story." Professor Clark puts his hand on her knee, and she begins to speak. She tells a story about a car accident that took her fiancé's life ten years ago and says that she spent the next eight years in a coma. A wood-fired pizza oven glows on the wall behind me, and I see the warmth of the hearth in the professor's face and that he's entranced by her every word.

"She has the wisdom and grace of an older woman but looks just like the rest of you students," he says. "No expression lines. Just look at that unlined face!" He gazes at her beautiful, youthful face. We all do. "A real sleeping beauty," he remarks. I see the flames of inspiration in his eyes and know just where his energy comes from, and how it is he's still inspired to teach.

"Excuse me, Professor Clark, I have a question about the Fire Sermon before our exam next week. How does it relate to the question of morality?"

He looks irritated that I'm talking shop. Suddenly, I'm that sexless idiot Grandma warned me about. My bookish professor confirms this sad fact. He takes a sip of his beer before looking me straight in the eyes. "Fire! Passion! Desire! It makes life worthwhile, doesn't it?" He slams his pilsner down on the table, and I feel like a little girl who's been dragged into the porn shop.

Now, he's entranced in a rant, and it's all my fault. "Without fire, there is nothing to resolve, nothing to quench. There is nothing left to learn. What did George Washington say?" We all look stumped, as if maybe this is a Socratic moment none of us prepared for. "Morality is that 'spark of celestial fire called conscience.'" I look around the table at blank faces. The professor's voice gets louder. "Your conscience should follow that spark in your gut," he says, and not vice versa.

The professor looks again to the beautiful woman with the unlined face. "Everything is ephemeral. We should follow the spark, don't you think? Follow our passions before the fire burns out, before it's all returned to dust."

The guy who usually sleeps through lecture seems to suddenly wake up. He raises his pilsner and brushes the hair from his face. "Damn, dude! I'll drink to that."

Water

Relationships are fluid. They should flow and easily change shape.

"Feliz Navidad, da da da da! Feliz Navidad ..."

"No, no, no!" Sun-Mi snorts through her laughter. "What's the word for Easter? Kate! Just in time. How do you say Easter?"

I loop my wet backpack on the door pull of my dresser. "Preparing for Mexico?"

"So you're coming?" Maddie slams her margarita-flavored wine cooler down on the coffee table and shows me her most persuasive, head cheerleader, mean-girl face. "Kate, close the door! There are so many snitches in this house—you have no idea!" She gestures her index finger around the room and everyone drinks. What fabulous, ridiculous game is this?

"Snitches get stitches!" snorts Layla, and it's a twofer.

"Rhymes with bitches," explains Nadia, and I'm up to speed.

"I'm going home for spring break." They look at me as if I've answered in Spanish.

"You can't!" Naheed whines with all the drama of a two-year-old. "El Niño will still get you there. Come to Mehico!"

Maddie leaps onto the daybed with her pom-poms and looks out the window at the deluge. "Mean, mean, El Niño!" she says. But I like the rain.

༺༻

At 6:30 p.m., the girls stumble out for dinner. When I'm alone, I pick up the phone. It's been a month or two since we chatted.

"Hi, Dad."

"Daughter ... starting my drive in a few. What's going on?"

"I called Southwest, and they're doing this sixty-dollar fare from Oakland, so I thought I'd come home for Easter week."

"Oh? Is that right?

"I'll be home a week starting on the twenty-ninth."

"I sold the house, Kate. I'm living with Karen."

"Really?"

"Yes ... well, her kids are with their dad on the weekends, so you're welcome to one of their rooms Friday through Sunday. Brian's been taking up the couch in the den, otherwise, I'd say you could stay there. Of course, I won't be around much, but you're welcome for a few days if you want."

"Sounds fun."

"Don't be sarcastic." He's dead serious. Aparently, I'm not serious enough.

"Right. Sorry. Okay, I'll call you back."

Maybe keg stands at Señor Frog's won't be so bad. Maybe the sun and alcohol and cigarette smoke, taking part in a moving target for horny spring breakers and predatory locals could be good for my soul.

I panic. I dial Quinn. "I have nowhere to go for spring break. Can I stay with you?"

"Yeah, sure. In France."

"Crap! I forgot. You don't actually want to do this journalism thing at the Sorbonne, do you? Sounds really stupid."

"Yeah, actually, I do. Why can't you just go home?"

"And where exactly would that be?"

"I don't know. Where does your dad live now?"

"With his new family somewhere in Pasadena."

"Yeah … that would be an awkward spring break. Call your grandmother."

"Do I have to? And isn't El Niño flooding So Cal, anyway?"

"Yeah, it's like years of rain have been saved up and now it's on. But you can't use that as an excuse. Plus, don't you have to vacate the brothel over the break? And, it's La Niña. La … Ni-ña. It's like El Niño but bitchier. Call me if your grandma's is a no-go and you're coming to France."

At dinner, I keep telling myself that life is fluid, attitude just might be everything. I pick the egg out of my vegetable pad thai with expert precision, but before I eat, I head up to our empty dayroom and dial Grandma.

"Hellooo?" she sighs into the phone as if breathing out of her nose takes more enthusiasm than she has for me right now.

"Hi, Grandma. It's Kate." But she knows this; she never picks up the phone without consulting her caller ID.

"Oh?" She's as nasal and put out as ever.

"I was thinking, maybe, I'd come to visit you over Easter."

"You were?" Her words come out on a cold current, slow and full of suspicion.

"Yes. Will you be around?"

"I guess so." She tells me to hang on while she gets her planner and a pencil. When she returns, her voice is oddly chipper. "So, when do you arrive?"

"The twenty-ninth ... for a week?"

"Wonderful! Grandpa and I will pick you up at the airport." And just like that, it seems the tide has turned.

⁂

The wheels of Southwest flight 2234 from Oakland to LAX touch down right on time. I wish we were delayed. I grab my backpack from the overhead compartment and make my way to the curb.

"Kate! Yoo-hoo! Over here!"

My grandparents are in the terminal. I never expected to be one of those people who are awaited in the terminal. I have envied those people, sort of hated them. Now, I might have to find something else to hang my bitterness on. I do a quick glance of the space to make sure they're actually here for me.

In the back seat of Grandma's car, I amuse myself by imagining that my brothers sit on either side of me. They throw out protective arms when she stops hard at the red lights and when she brakes really close behind the car in front of us. Of course, Grandma always drives.

"How was your flight? How's the weather in San Francisco?" Grandma makes small talk as if she's charming a stranger. "We're having the Niño," she says. "Just look at our sky. *Hawrible*!"

"Ugh," I tell Grandma in patronizing agreement, but secretly I love it.

"Can you believe it? You come for sun at the beach and you get El Niño."

"Barb!" grumbles Grandpa. "It's La Niña this time. Get it right."

"Enough, Robert!"

I think, *It's like El Niño, but bitchier.*

⁓

Before I can drop my bag in the guest room, Grandma comes barging in. "Kate! Go. Two doors south. Nice gal, Angie. She's giving you a massage. She'll do you then me. Go!"

"Right now? I was going to work on my term paper for a few minutes. I'll go after you?"

"Kate! Do as I tell you."

I see outrage in her face, and it's transporting her to the bad place right before my eyes. She's following me with her pupils, but her body is paused in place. I drop my bag and head immediately out her front door and down the boardwalk. Nevermind that I still need to pee.

Angie's house is tall and white with gingerbread trim like a Bavarian townhome. I'm not actually sure it's Angie's place until a plump, frizzy-haired woman with glowing skin answers and gives me a robust hug.

"Welcome. Welcome, Kate! I'm Angela." She puts her hand out for a shake, and I can feel that her fingers and thumbs have been worn thin from oil and friction.

I'm already in the swim of obeying, so I do as she says. I hang my clothes on the hook inside her massage studio and slide under the sheet. For five glorious minutes, she's kneaded the knots and worked the worries out of my back. I think I might be asleep, but then I think I wouldn't think that if I were.

Regardless, the door flies open and startles me awake.

"Wakey, wakey!" Grandma's shrill voice rings out as she rips the sheet off my body. I look over at Angela, who has moved aside with a gasp.

"Barbara! What are you doing?" Angela squeals.

"She's done. She was disobedient. My turn." Grandma glares at me. "Go write your school paper. Didn't you say you had to write a school paper? Go!" She points, so I grab my jeans and sweatshirt from the hook and stumble out the door.

On the other side, I hear her making small talk with Angie as if nothing ever happened.

༶

"White or red?"

"Me? I'm not twenty-one, Grandma."

"Don't be ridiculous. White or red? Robert! Pour her some of your wine."

Grandpa shuffles dutifully into the kitchen. He looks how I imagine one would in a communist regime when the neighbor suddenly disappears. Of course, he knows. She left the house early and in a rage. Now, he's acting as though nothing happened.

Once the Maltese is on Grandpa's lap and the scotch is swirling in Grandma's fist, she starts. "So ... why aren't you at your dad's?" Her voice is menacing. Surely, she knows.

"I guess he sold the house."

"Yes. He's an idiot. He practically gave it away. Can you believe it? He was so desperate to move in with the girlfriend." I realize she doesn't know he's married for the third time. "Frankly," I brace myself. "I think the wife, the one with the baby, she was in the picture long before your mother was even dead. It's his child, for God's sake! Everyone know's it. And he had the audacity to parade it down the boardwalk in front of my friends. The new wife and a baby, just a year after Linda was dead!"

I raise my eyebrows and make big, dramatic eyes, signaling that I'm not into drama. "I have no idea."

"What?"

"I have no idea. I don't know."

"You don't have any ideas about that? You think your dad is so great he wouldn't carry on with another woman while your mom was dying?"

"I just don't know."

"Eat the meat." She points to some ham cold cuts wrapped around spears of asparagus.

"I don't eat meat."

"So ... you're a *vechetarian?* That's ridiculous." I take a sip of wine to avoid the obligation of an answer. "So ... have you talked to your brothers? I hear that Doug is in a cult and frankly ... I think Brian's on some sort of drugs."

"Hmm. No. I haven't talked to either in a while, but I doubt those things are true."

"Then how would you know, Kate?" Grandma incites, waits, and stares. I shrug my shoulders. "Would you like to hear the truth about your parents? Your mother was never happy, you know."

"Not really, Grandma."

"You say you have no ideas. I thought you were supposed to be smart. You must have *some* ideas."

I swirl Grandpa's red. He keeps it in the refrigerator, so the cold and slightly rancid wine casts a layer of condensation on the outside of the glass. "Actually, Grandma, I do."

"Well then, let's hear it!" This is an invitation to brawl.

"None of that stuff is very positive, or about us, or about now. Let's have some fun." She's silent for a minute, and I think this could go either way.

"And, you're here all week?"
"Yes."
"And, you want fun?"
"Yes."

The sky opens up, and the rain falls like a sheet onto the boardwalk out the window. A flock of seagulls takes off to the east. What takes seconds seems like minutes. I watch Grandma's face as she watches the birds fly toward us and into the wind shear that sweeps them over the house. It's as if a switch has been flipped, and whatever negativity Grandma has harbored, she's just decided to let it go.

"Well, then let's get out of this rain. Robert!" Grandma claps twice as if she's talking to Pico. "Kate and I are going to the rock house. You'll be fine here without us."

Within half an hour, we've thrown our bags into the trunk of her white Mercedes and kissed Grandpa goodbye. We're barreling east on the 91 toward Phoenix. The rain spatters our windshield and the wipers flap erratically. They remind me of Grandma's crazy driving. We're bats out of hell, and it's already fun.

༄

At the turnoff for Riverside, the car in front of us spins out of control and nearly collides with the car to our right. "Grandma! Watch out!"

"Kate. Get a hold of yourself!" she says and continues driving as if nothing ever happened. Grandma is fatalistic and free, and she doesn't give a damn.

"When did you stop sweating the little things?"
"Forty."
"Seriously?"
"Yes. For women, it happens at forty."
"Like, that exact number, forty?"
"Yes, Kate." She's irritated. "Or whenever you've seen enough. You either stop caring about anything at all, or you choose to follow the fun. But either way, you enter the world of an old lady. Then, you get to lecture the *yonge*." Grandma laughs and I'm surprised she's this introspective. But mainly, I can't shake my obsession with her pronunciation, so I repeat the word over and over in my head.

"When Grandpa Frank died, I'd seen enough. I could either start dying myself or I could live every moment to the fullest." She looks over at me, and for the first time, maybe ever, I see clear to the bottom of those icy, blue eyes. What I had thought was unwitting materialism and nihilistic self-absorption is suddenly a very meaningful will to joy.

"You have to have some hobbies, Kate. You have to do something with your hands that connects you to this world. Your mom's generation made a mistake by not teaching you girls how to cook and garden and sew."

"Mom didn't cook and stuff because you said she was too fancy to!"

"Yes, to scrub toilets and tend to the kitchen all day in bare feet!"

"I don't see the difference, Grandma. Crouching down in the garden all covered in dirt, scrubbing the toilets—it seems the same to me."

"One is ladylike, Kate, the other is not. I don't get you. Don't you want to rise above? Don't you want to be better than other people? Be competitive, be ambitious. You're too nice," she practically spits, and I see that her quest for superiority has made her very lonely.

I smile over at my platinum-blonde grandmother. She sighs and grumbles, "Either way, you have to use your talents to create something. You'll never find yourself by contemplating your navel. You've got to engage the world, to manipulate it."

And boy, does she. Grandma manipulates and engages fully in the material. She's got one hand on the steering wheel and rubs her arm again with the other.

"Have you ever seen an old lady like me with lovesick goose bumps? It's absurd. And boy, did Grandpa Frank and I have passion. We would dish it to each other, Kate, and argue and fight. One time, I pushed him out of his new Corvette and sped right off into the night. You should have seen his face! Good relationships need tension, Kate, struggle!"

"Sounds ... fun?"

"Oh, it was. And you ... you need a man who can take it. You aren't the kind of gal to back down. Boy, your mother made sure of that. You need someone who can deal with your feisty nature." And I realize that mom gave me exactly what I'd need so Grandma would eventually meet her match.

"Well, that was long ago. And since your birth grandpa had money, you know what I do?" She grins and shows me her perfect dental implants. "I enjoy it! I travel and shop!" She looks like a greedy kid in the candy store, and I think maturity doesn't necessarily come with age. But neither does that childlike joy.

We pass an industrial park and an Uwajimaya. "Look. There! That's where Grandpa and I go for our little oriental gifts, like house slippers and dishes. Cute stuff. They sell sushi in there too. Can you believe it?"

"Slippers and sushi, why not?" Grandma laughs in a lighthearted way that I'm not accustomed to hearing from her. It seems like a safe time to engage deeper in conversation. "Okay, I get living your life to the fullest, but what about giving back? What about making the world a better place, Grandma?"

"Bah!" she sounds like a sheep. "Don't be ridiculous! We made a mistake raising you kids here in California. Don't be a hippie. What do you know of the order of things, or of God, for God's sake? The truth of the world shows up in goosebumps, just flashes and sparks, those little aha moments of beauty. That's all I know about the spiritual world. And who cares about it, really? I don't." Suddenly, she sounds very New York, and all I can think is, *Forget about it* …

Before the windmills come the dinosaurs. I scan the landscape for them, the sand-colored, thirty-foot-high *Tyrannosaurus rex* and his long-necked, herbivore companion. They're the gatekeepers of this arid land. Inside one is a gift shop full of roadside whimsy. I bought some tumbled tiger eye there when I was eight.

But they're nowhere to be seen. Instead, the earth is carved and flattened and scraped. A new world of tract homes smothers the landscape. There's a Texaco station and a Costco and behind the Circle K, my dinosaurs, now dwarfed, like remnants from another time, only this one I remember fondly.

"Grandma! What happened? They've ruined the dinosaur habitat with all those buildings. It's awful!"

"Kate. Have a pulse! The world evolves. If you fight change, you'll be old before your time!"

"It's not the change, Grandma, it's how they built urban sprawl on that beautiful land."

"With the concrete dinosaurs?"

"Yes."

"You want to preserve the grass around the concrete dinosaur buildings? Good Lord. Well ... I couldn't care less. Go tie yourself to a tree like that Julie the Moth. Don't bathe. It doesn't bother me." Her white knuckles grip the wheel at nine and three, and I know it bothers her deeply.

"Well ... as stupid as the whole thing is, I believe you'll do it. You will preserve the dirt around your beloved dinosaurs. I know you will because you have passion for it!" These actually sound like words of encouragement. "And remind me to take you shopping because you look like a bum."

Just when I've about lost my dirt-loving religion, Grandma says something else. "Just believe in something, Kate. I don't care what. Be certain. Be passionate. Create beauty and joy." My religion is restored.

"Welcome to Palm Springs." The sign comes right out of my midcentury dreams. Some chic, double-wide trailers reside in an adjacent park, with plastic, pink flamingos and what looks, from afar, to be plastic, green grass. Under the highway bridge, a few dirt bikers kick around sand. And above it all, the San Jacinto Mountains rise off the desert floor. They block the sun of the late afternoon, offering mercy and a mystic retreat via the aerial tramway to a place that is cool and alpine and where, as a child, I saw a Native American hatchet left driven into a stump. These sand-colored mountains, speckled in various shades of brown boulders and green weeds, are the home of the Easter Bunny, I was told. I still believe.

"So …" Grandma's apparently being nonchalant. "Do you have a boyfriend?"

"Nope."

"Well, you know … they're all the same in the pants."

"What?"

"It's what's in their wallet that matters."

"Grandma, I can make my own money."

"Sure you can. Your dad gave you a good work ethnic." I flinch, but I don't correct her. "Being rich makes life easier." Grandma gets super nasal here to denote that a dark truth is coming. "And marrying rich is the easiest waaaay." Carbon dioxide hisses through her teeth on the word "rich," like a tire losing pressure.

"I guess so. But Grandma, I'm not looking for the easiest way through life. I sort of think that the beauty of life is in the struggle."

"Don't be an idiot. You've never been poor or lived through war. I remember the Depression!"

Grandma readjusts her grip on the steering wheel, as if she's manually reducing her blood pressure. I guess she hasn't achieved good health at her age by driving herself into a tizzy. "Well, you'll do what you want, but after you get your serious degree, you can opt out. They're all doing it, you know. There was an article in *Vogue*. All the *yonge* mothers are staying home. And the rich ones have nursemaids and mom's helpers too." Grandma grins and studies my face for what I presume would be jealousy, desire, or some other sign that I'm interested in what she's selling.

"You shouldn't lift a finger, Kate! No granddaughter of mine will run around ragged. I simply won't have it!" Suddenly, we're in Grandpa Frank's 1956 Corvette convertible with updos, silk headscarves, and big, dramatic sunglasses. We're pouty and adamant dames on the run, bitches not to contend with.

"Well, I think that finding my passions might take getting lost in the trees. You can't rush me through my lessons, Grandma. I think I have to find my own way, no matter how clear the big picture is to you. Plus ... I feel like life is about the journey, you know?"

"Life is a destination!" Grandma declares. "But, if that's what you really want." The word want comes out slow, like a threat. "If that will make you happy, then I don't care what you do."

But clearly she cares. And that she cares might be all that matters. We drive on silently for a while, and I think that time for an older lady runs at a completely different tempo than it does for a young one, and that's exactly the way it should be.

⁓

At the end of Palm Canyon Drive, we make a right. We pass Liberace's house with the gaudy, naked statues and Sonny Bono's house and his watchdogs and their really great blowouts. They bark at our sedan as we wind up the hill to where the view opens up, and I see Bob Hope's mushroom-shaped roof across the ridge. Into the gates and onto the rubble we roll, to Grandma's cheerful yellow house on the edge of the mountain. The sound of our tires on the rocks recalls the delight of my childhood visits here, and when we open our doors, the desert heat envelops us like a sauna. The air smells like hot herbs and cactus.

"Welcome to the Rock House!" says Grandma. We look out at the kidney-shaped pool and the paths full of grapefruit trees and orange and lime and one tree that's a tangerine grafted with a lemon. My brothers and I would lie under it on a chaise and peel the thick, fragrant rinds. We'd savor the warm, sweet fruit one section at a time. "I guess we don't call it that anymore." Grandma giggles. "Not after the Colombians came with all their cocaine. Now, people think we sell drugs here. Isn't it a riot?"

It is. And Grandma's a riot. She's no porch-rocker. She's the owner of the Rock House, which is sometimes mistaken for a crack den, the woman who filled her kidney-shaped pool with bright, plastic Easter eggs and sank them with driveway rubble and quarters so we kids would wake up on Easter morning to a pool full of jewels. All so we could dive for them, and blinded by flares of sun in the water, we would believe in magic.

We carry our bags up toppled boulders of sedimentary rock, past the succulent garden steps to the front door. A lizard basking on a rock scurries away, and a hummingbird flaps furiously at a flowering palm that clings to the hillside where we stand on the landing. Grandma fumbles for her keys, and I wander out to the railingless deck that overlooks the drive and the desert below. "Look!" I point to the iridescent green-and-blue bird.

"Yes! She visits often." Grandma pops open the door. The house is warm from the steady desert heat. It smells sweet, dusty, and familiar. "Hang on. I'm turning on the swamp cooler!"

She runs to the thermostat, and I drop my bag on the floor. I crash onto the cream-colored, midcentury sofa in her sunny, yellow living room. I put my Adidas up on the yellow lacquer coffee table under an inch of glass. The vent in the ceiling above me roars to a start and purrs cool air. I exhale.

"Put your things in your room!" Grandma barks. I jump for my bags and head down the hall to the little room off the jacuzzi deck with the twin beds. The rectangular windows are framed oblong, like a ladder, and outside the boulders of the hillside hover over the house in a mystical way that makes me feel small and comforted at the same time. These hills lead to mountains and miles of nothing but high desert.

This room is where the boys would sleep. I would roll the hideaway into the spacious hallway, where I'd sleep alone. Still, my brothers would shuffle down the hall in socks, with arms outstretched like zombies, trying to shock one another with static that builds in this dry, desert air. Then they'd come for me. Between the spark and the thrill of the chase, I'm not sure which was more electric.

"No!" yells Grandma from down the hall. "The guestroom! You're of age now, and you are my guest, after all!" I stumble out of the room, suddenly overtaken by the loftiness of being Grandma's invited guest. To what do I owe this honor? Was calling her and inviting myself all it took?

At the end of the hall, in the room that overlooks the pool deck and the fruit trees, is the room where Mom and Dad would sleep. The rattan desk chair and wooden desk are covered in small objets d'art. A white porcelain hand serves as a ring holder for Grandma's esteemed guests, and there's a vanity mirror and beaded trinket box. The queen-size bed is made in cream and brown elephant motif sheets. Slow-moving ripples of sunlight reflect on the ceiling from the pool outside. I watch one amorphous shape meld into another. I could watch these webs of light all day.

"Yoo-hoo! Knock-knock!" Grandma comes waltzing in. She's wearing a chiffon, multicolored, ankle-length robe and a huge straw hat. "These are for you. Here we sun in style." I realize this is not a choice, so I take them and dress myself up like a French aristocrat on the Riviera. "Bain de Soleil?" she asks, and it's just like the commercial. Grandma squirts some orange gel from the tube. With two hands, I catch it and slap it on my face and arms.

We're watched by lots of faces as we make our way down the hall to the back door. We pass a painting of a mustachioed man in a beret who stares out as if we are the canvas. He holds his brush toward us in anticipation of some inspiration. There's a DeSimone vase with a Picasso-like face that gazes out from the bulb, a statue of a giraffe, and an African mask. "Grandmama, I've always loved the décor in this house."

"You know the trick, right? My house reflects me, who I am. I live with my home and gather my things in time. It tells my story and no one else's. Only the girls who don't know what they like pay an arm and a leg for the interior designers. These are things you should do yourself, Kate. It's fun and saves you money, and because you're my granddaughter, of course, you have taste! Enough inside," she demands. "My house is meant for basking in the sun."

With our brightly printed chiffon robes dancing around our ankles, we head out. Grandma shoves a pair of flip-flops at my chest. "Put them on. You can't walk barefoot on the rocks!" I put on the two-sizes-too-big flip-flops and pull the brim of this enormous straw hat over my eyebrows. I follow her down the path, past the grafted fruit trees, and past that spot under the porch where my brothers and I believed the snakes waited to strike us as we passed. This is Grandma's house, after all. I don't let the sunny façade lull me into a false sense of security.

A cheerful, yellow thermometer on the wall reads eighty-eight degrees. "Isn't it perfect, Kate?" We lie here in the sun in our hats and orange gel Bain de Soleil, listening to the desert birds and letting the cares of the world melt away.

Twenty minutes into her *Cosmo*, Grandma barks simultaneous and contradictory orders. "Kate! Go for a swim! Read this. Here. Here!" She shoves the magazine at me. Enjoyment is serious business for Grandma. She's the foreman making damn sure I'm having it her way.

After an article that promotes sleeping your way up the corporate ladder and a couple of paragraphs into an article on Lisa Marie Presley, Grandma says, "Up, up, let's go!"

"What?"

"Let's go! Time to grocery!" Grandma is constantly careening toward her next big plan. She barks orders. She orchestrates her next project or acquisition, how she'll get away with it. Expanding ever outward, she leaves nothing to chance.

"Okay." I breathe out and ground myself from within. I peel myself off the chaise—grin and bear it—and think maybe she's like one of those sharks that has to keep moving to survive. Before I know it, we're cruising with the spring breakers on Palm Canyon Drive. The road's blocked at the intersection by a police officer. A squad car with its lights on marks the barrier. We have to detour several blocks to get to the market.

"Isn't this fun!" Grandma grins and looks over at me for my approval.

"Uh-huh," I say dryly.

"Kate! Look at all the hard bodies. Take your cover-up off. We're cruising. You're *yonge!*"

"No, thank you." I look off to the left side of the street. "I didn't know there was a museum here."

"Oh, yes. Some of my art hangs in there. Can you believe it?"

"Really?"

"Yes, it's a riot. Some of my paintings."

"Let's go see!"

"Don't be silly. They're nothing." But the traffic stops cold as we get to the museum's drive, so Grandma pulls her white Mercedes into the lot and parks. "Okay, just a quick stop."

At the front desk, she fumbles through her *pock-a-book* for her *lonk* wallet. This goes on for a little while. Eventually, the lady at the desk asks instead for Grandma's name. We enter the first-floor gallery full of bronze yard sculptures in cactus and Native American themes.

We get out of the elevator on the second floor where the plaque on the wall says, "Local Artists." Grandma is super nasal and nonchalant. "Well ... here we are." In the grand entrance to the gallery, there are several paintings of a river and what look like floodlands and savannah. "Isn't it ridiculous?" Grandma practically spits.

"What is?"

"These paintings of the Nile, right here in the entry to the wing. They aren't even very good."

I see the titanium white reflections on the water and adjacent flood lands and the depth of the landscape. "I think they're amazing!"

"Well ... you don't know art, then. They're by Doris, down my hill. She's a pitiful, no-talent ninny." Grandma's jealousy is comical in its transparency. She grabs a strand of my hair. "Why do you have so many colors in your hair?"

"Sun, chlorine, a sneaky little product called Sun-In."

"Yes, but why is the base so dark?"

"That's probably my actual hair color, Grandma."

"Strange," she says with a completely straight face. "I have never known anyone in our family to have such dark hair."

"What? What about my mom, your daughter? She looked like Snow White."

She looks at me blankly and says, "Hmm, I don't remember." And then, "I'm sorry for certain things in the past that I cannot change." It comes out of nowhere. Then, she flicks and releases my hair.

"So, what are you sorry for, exactly?"

"What? I'm not sorry for anything. Good Lord! I just wonder why you have such dark strands in your hair." Grandma shrugs and stares at her archnemesis's art in a place of honor on the gallery wall. "It's pitiful," she says, and I think jealousy is deep, and the Nile isn't just a river in Africa.

⁓

The rest of the gallery is full of abstract expressionist works. Some are bordered in artist-made frames that are rubbed in stain or weathered by the sun. The awkward, off-kilter ones are my favorite, the perfect complements to organic forms.

On the far wall, two paintings reside side by side. I step closer to see they're Grandma's. One looks like a gathering of pots and vases in Southwestern stripes. The other is straight abstract expressionism—a blob, really, in taupe and sand and muted blues on a backdrop of midnight. It seems to jut out at me like a shooting star. It's spectacular.

"Well, you've seen them. Shall we go?"

"Not yet, Grandmama. Tell me about them."

"There's nothing to tell! You feel, Kate, that's all!"

Grandma is showy with her jewelry and handbags. She wears her fancy labels like nametags. But I ask her again to tell me about her fancy art in the art museum and she refuses. To my shock, she just stands there, looking embarrassed and sort of exposed. She's all feeling and no rationality, all venom and no fur. She doesn't pause to analyze herself or her emotions; she just lives them, and they become her art.

Around the corner is a third piece by Grandma. It looks like a human figure surrounded by plumes of fire. The brushstrokes are dramatic and somehow full of doubt. The figure gazes out, secular, afraid, and alone. This one gives me chills, so I rub the goose bumps from my arm. "Ooh, Grandma, what is it?"

"It's me."

∽

In the morning, I watch a web of light on the ceiling until I hear the coffee grinder out in the kitchen. I follow the wall of art that follows me, past all the eyes and through Grandma's house that reflects her, even if she refuses to reflect on herself. I find her glitzing by the breakfast-room window and reading the paper. Her diamond rings flash at me as she folds over the page. "Well, well, look what the cat dragged in."

"Good morning, Grandmama."

"Did you sleep well? I boiled you an egg." And there it is, a solitary egg, in its stemmed white plastic egg holder. I sit down in a matching white swivel chair with a yellow cushion, feeling as if I've stumbled into an episode of *The Jetsons*.

We drink our coffee. Grandma turns a page. I eat my egg and fresh-picked grapefruit with one of her serrated grapefruit spoons. After breakfast, she barks, "Pool!" and claps one time in the air. Those are my orders.

By the pool, I listen to the birds in the orchard and the soothing tick of the insects. Grandma sashays in with a floatie lounger. "Oh! The *wuata's* wonderful!" It makes a warm splashing sound. I wonder if the temperature and the light make the splash sound more jubilant here under desert skies than it does under the marine layer. I feel a sense of guilt for liking it, and I wonder if I'm getting soft by turning my back on the gloom that has been such a steadfast friend.

After an hour, Grandma peers out from the brim of her ridiculously large hat. "Up. Up!" She claps with no warning. "Let's have some fun!"

"I thought we were having fun."

"I mean real fun!" She shows me her greedy-little-kid grin that I guess I'm supposed to find cute, but unbeknownst to Grandma, I don't actually like kids very much. "Let's go shopping!"

She flip-flops through the kitchen and shakes her keys at me. She's applied pink lipstick to match her toenails and thrown on a Pucci dress. We careen down the hill in her white Mercedes, past Sonny Bono's house and Liberace's naked Greek statues. After a stop-and-go ride, we land in the parking lot of Neiman Marcus.

"I'm going to teach you how the real rich witches shop." She smiles dryly, showing me her teeth, and I'm not sure she's not actually one of them.

"Why ever would you do that, Grandma?"

"You can outsmart them." She grins. I have no idea what she means.

Grandma holds open the door to Neiman's. "Come. Come!" She yanks on the first thing she sees hanging. It's a yellow skirt printed with blue flowers. She grabs the tag. "Kate! Look. Versace … it's good." Again, I have no idea what this means. Good because it's a nice skirt? Good simply because it's Versace? Good because we will pass among the rich witches?

The shopgirl beelines our way. "Hello! Are we finding what we are looking for?" I wish I had a spare arm to throw and fend her off, though I realize she's just doing her job. I like to shop alone. I guess I fear I'll become one of the robots if I take advice from the shopgirl. I fear losing my identity to the royal "we."

"Are we looking for anything in particular?" I chuckle because I've wanted to ask my shopaholic grandmother this very question for as long as I can remember.

"I have some ideas for you, if you're looking at skirts," she says to Grandma. The shopgirl is well-trained, but Grandma says, "No, thank you." She grins a big, dismissive grin and shakes a diamond-encrusted hand on its Rolex-clad wrist. Again, she says, "No, thank you," this time with an amusing heir of authority. She brushes her fingers outward and shoos the woman in a flicker of bling. The woman nods and walks away. I think this is Grandma's spare arm to throw, a brilliant, diamond-encrusted defense mechanism. She hides behind her shine as I hide behind the rain. To the shopgirl, Grandma feigns that we are *they*, and the whole thing is just embarrassing.

When she's gone, Grandma grabs my shoulder with her talon-like nails, and it feels like abduction by an osprey. She points to the tag on a Moschino shirt and whispers hot and loud in my ear, "Look at the kind of money they spend on T-shirts at Neiman Marcus!" She holds up a plain white T-shirt, made in China but with the Italian label, and grins like the Cheshire Cat. She points to the price tag. "Two hundred sixty-nine dollars."

"So why are we even here, then?"

"To see what they are all wearing."

"Who?"

"Everyone! This is the height of style. This is all the rage, Kate!"

"Okay. But why do you care? I actually don't want to be a follower and conform to some canned idea of what's cool."

"Don't be stupid!" she says. "That's just your problem. To really be in the world, you need to join humanity. You need to keep a finger on the pulse of life. Fashion is a language, Kate! It keeps you connected to other happy people. Come on and join the land of the living and stop acting like a zombie."

I look over at her—glitzy and ritzy, wearing a white Louis Vuitton Murakami shoulder bag that's monogrammed in every color of the rainbow. I can't help but smile because, for all her insults and all her drama, Grandma sure is fun.

"Okay," she says instructively. "Did you get a good look?"

"Um, yeah, I guess."

"Then let's go!" She heads to the door. "Out, out!" I'm shooed through as if I'm Pico.

It's ninety-eight degrees. I'm sweating in the passenger seat, and I've got a headache. I don't know how she continues like this. It's as if she's younger than I am. Where does she get the energy? "Buckle," Grandma says dryly. We stop and go through a few lights. We do a California roll at a stop sign and park abruptly. "Here we are! Ross Dress for Less. Out!"

"Now, you're smart. Put together one of those trendy outfits you saw at Neiman's." If I didn't already have a headache, I certainly would by now. I look out through fluorescent lights at a sea of disheveled garments. On the upside, there is no shopgirl.

I take off looking for a pair of shoes to end all shoe-buying. They must be appropriate for day and night, rain or shine, shoes for all time. It's a utilitarian and almost religious quest for me, one I hope will halt frivolous materialism and the need to buy shoes ever again. I pick up a ridiculous pair of gold, kitten-heel sandals to get to what look like sensible tennies underneath.

"Good girl," says Grandma approvingly. "You'll knock their socks off when you get back to school!" But she rolls her eyes when she sees what I'm really digging for.

Grandma stops at a huge bin full of wallets and shoes tied together with stretchy, white string. She sucker punches me in the stomach with the heel of a black patent stiletto. "Live a little. How are you ever going to get a man?" I think to argue, but she's moved on.

In the back of the store, there is a designer section that Grandma seems to know all too well. I hide behind a rack of Lilly Pulitzer dresses in the hope that she'll just leave me alone for a bit. "Kate! Here! Color!" she says, pointing to the shift dresses.

"Yeah, they're a little spastic."

"What does that mean?"

"Maybe good for New York in summer."

"That's exactly my point, Kate. That's your problem. Your mom and I made a big mistake raising you in Los Angeles. There's no change of seasons, no cause for celebration. Plus, everyone cares more about looking skinny than they do about being joyful. It's a shame."

Around the rack, I see it, the undulating waves of an artisan yarn. Before I can utter a sound, Grandma's all over it. "Oh!" She acts out her most dramatic role of the day. I'm expecting her to tell me it's "good" because it's clearly the trademark of an expensive designer, but she doesn't.

"Look at this hand-dyed yarn! Hold it, Kate. Hold it!" I take the Missoni dress, and Grandma and I say something in unison, maybe for the first time ever, "It's a work of art!"

Grandma's obsessions are the very things my ascetic tendencies would have me avoid. She dives deep into her insecurities, her jealousy, and her greed. They energize her and stoke her fire. But we are united by this thing of beauty.

Maybe there aren't any shoes to end all shoe shopping, just the burning desire to keep searching for the next trendy pair of beautiful shoes. I watch her scan the racks for something to fill up her cart. She's agitated and incomplete, and there might not be anything more fantastically human than that.

"You're evolving. I'm proud of you," she says, just before she's distracted by a cute pair of flats. She pulls me in by the talons for a shoulder-to-shoulder hug. "Maybe, you'll tune in to the pulse of humanity after all. Maybe, you won't be left behind."

It comes out as if she fears for my life, as if trendiness is essential to our survival. It's evolution at work. Those subtle cues that whisper to my subconscious—the hairstyle, brow shape, pant length du jour, that particular hue of pink on which we concur. We wink, we bond, we agree. We ants go marching cooperatively, and maybe, that's not such a bad thing.

"Look at us," I say to Grandma over the Missoni dress, "swooning together over material!"

"Isn't it all just material?" she asks, no pun intended.

⁓

"Wakey-wakey!"

"Good Lord, Grandma, where do you get the energy?"

"We don't want the other girls to get our deals now, do we?" Oh, yeah. Right. "I thought we'd check out the outlet mall on our way home. Get up, get up!"

Under the windmill-covered hills of Cabazon, we stroll the outdoor mall. I find a great bag in Yves Saint Laurent, but even outlet prices aren't affordable for me. I might be "of age," but I'm a college student, and Grandma agrees, "It's ridiculous what these designers are asking for a leather bag these days."

After lunch at the greasy Chinese joint in the food court, we continue home on the 10 Freeway. We exit onto Artesia for Grandma's little beach town.

"Pull over at the light, Grandma."

"What are we doing?"

"You'll see. It's my turn."

"I'm intrigued," Grandma says with a grin.

"Good," I tell her, but I'm nervous. This could go either way.

Inside the Salvation Army Thrift Store, Grandma stumbles behind me in awe. I can't tell if she's disgusted or inspired.

We thumb through racks of old, musty clothing and I catch a glimpse of her eyeing a full-length mink. "Kate

… come, look! I can easily sew this hole in the seam, and it's brand new and only costs twenty-five dollars!" I raise an eyebrow in an I-told-you-so way.

"You should buy it and insure it and invite PETA to throw red paint all over you," I say. Grandma chuckles. We are two peas in a pod, and I realize where I get my dark sense of humor.

"Oh my God, I've got to try this on!"

She takes a long, silver sequin gown over her head into a dressing room behind a mirrored wall. I take my stash into a stall on the opposite wall behind an opposing mirror and start trying things on. Within a minute or two, I hear giggling … well, evil chuckling. So I come out in a yellow shift dress to see what's so funny.

"Good Lord, aren't I the glamour girl!" Grandma says. "I'm gorgeous. They won't believe their eyes!"

And I don't believe my eyes. I'm closing the door to my dressing room behind me, but before I turn around to look at Grandma, I see a succession of me that seems to extend into infinity. It's me in a mirror through a mirror, and the whole scene is lit with flares of light that ricochet from Grandma's sequined dress. On the far left, I'm shrunken and infantile in my yellow shift. With each incarnation, I'm taller and appear more mature, until I'm a full-grown adult beside Grandma, who is glitzing in her sequined gown.

"You're a good little shopper, Kate. You might not need my money after all. And boy, did you get my style! I guess I'll lose you now that I have nothing really to offer you."

"What do you mean, lose me?"

"I'll be irrelevant to you if I'm not already. You'll go on with your life, and you won't need me."

"Need you? Grandma, I don't need anyone! I've been playing your hurtful games all my life. Oh ... you've taught me to stand alone." I hold my breath, but she doesn't argue.

I feel a jab in my chest. I'm holding back tears. It's not just that she's a toxic gaslighter. Maybe I've been afraid of letting her in, of getting too close to another mother figure I can lose. This one is unique and antique and so much older than my own mother was.

"Damn you, Grandma. I love you," I say, and I'm not even acting.

"Uh-huh," Grandma says dismissively, but I feel Mom's spirit in the flares of her silver sequins, and they rejoice.

After a minute, I lose Grandma to the other end of the store. I head to menswear and look for plaid trousers. I catch up to Grandma amid a rack of coats. She's wearing a leather jacket and posing for the mirror. She holds a brown, suede belt to her hip and drapes some feathers from a headband over her shoulder and admires herself. "Isn't it a riot? They will think I spent an absolute fortune!"

"They will, now, won't they?" *We're getting away with it,* I think. They won't know what hit them. Plus, we're having an absolute *bawl.*

Back at Grandma's, the dogs bark to alert Grandpa of our arrival. He comes out to the garage and helps us with our bags. "Well, well, looks like you've been shopping." He flinches at the big, black trash bag from the thrift store.

After lunch, Grandma gets out her sewing machine. We take in the waist on a floral dress and hem a pair of button-front, chambray sailor pants. They might be Navy surplus, the real thing, but their irony is vague and this nuance appeals to me. Grandma finishes bedazzling a canvas jacket she's picked up for four dollars. Like paying witness to a happening, I watch as she grabs a dish of watered-down oil paint from her easel and splatters it onto a dingy, white sweatshirt. It becomes 1980s ... or Eastern European. I can never tell which, but it's fabulous. Before I can comment, she tells me the hem of my skirt should be shorter. "Show some leg, Kate! Live a little. Fashion is for the *yonge*." But I disagree.

I watch her carefully darn some feathers to the shoulder of her new leather jacket. She cinches the suede belt tight around her waist and pulls a straw bucket hat that's rounded in grosgrain ribbon over her brow. The ensemble looks like some military regalia, reserved only for the most polished matriarch. Grandma's no waif in someone else's art. She's her own art, with the experience and certainty of a woman who's been there.

"See ... couture!" she says with a grin. "They will be floored."

"Indeed, they will."

I'm sorry the week is over. I shower and pack and come downstairs to a pile of junk awaiting me at the back door. "What's all this, Grandpa?" He just shakes his head and grumbles. "I don't know. Talk to Mama ..."

"Oh, you know," says Grandma, sounding manic as ever, "I thought you could use some more sweaters up north. God … I have three closets of them!"

"Hmm. Okay. I guess I'll have to check that big box." I roll my eyes but suppress a smile. I'm happy for her aesthetic to clash with my ascetic, for her hoarding and the fire of her disorganized emotions. They bring life to my disciplined and ordered self. Grandma's obsession with the stuff of earth is inspiring to me, so I'll take her crap anytime.

⁓

I'm home to greener hills and cleaner streets. It seems the rain is over. "Hola!" I say to my girls as I enter our room. I'm surprised by how much I've missed them, unnerved that I've let their sunny dispositions into my dark, stoic heart. They're sunburned and bleached. And I'm changed too.

I drop my bag and my big box right in the middle of the room. I throw myself onto the daybed and listen to tales of the Swedish stalker and a false alarm on a hammerhead shark. I laugh until my stomach hurts as they recount exactly how it was that Naheed fell asleep and got the most sunburned of all.

At my dresser, I unpack Grandma's big box. There's an old photo of my brothers and me stuck under the cardboard flap at the bottom. We've got our arms wrapped around one another. We look so happy and whole in our togetherness. I think to toss it, but instead,

I find that frame with the photo of the Victorian woman from Mahtab, and I stick us hermanos right on top.

On the finial of my mirror, I hang a really stupid raspberry beret Grandma and I made even stupider by bedazzling it.

Sun-Mi comes to inspect. "So … I like your new shrine."

"Thanks."

"You know, I, too, had some revelations while on break."

"Oh, yeah?"

"I'm thinking of dying my hair blonde—you know, going blasian." She tosses her hair like a valley girl.

"You should."

She picks the frame up from my dresser and looks close at the photo of my brothers and me. I wait for her to toss it aside and make a snide comment about it. Instead, she puts it back gingerly. Sun-Mi beams me a smile, and I let it in.

At One

An old soul's job on earth is to become new.

☙

The money was the weirdest part. It looked so monotone and green and long.

If I had ever thought I was really an introvert, ever thought I could truly be happy alone, my junior year studying in the Basque country of Spain knocked that right out of me. Coming home, I was happy to flee the piety of the cathedral on the town square and the paseo of multigenerational families that strolled past me each night, those impenetrable units of belonging that made me feel even more alone.

"In God We Trust," it says, and I think that's a very American thing to print on money. At the ATM in Newark, I am so happy for our odd green and beige currency and to be back in the US, where being part of a family doesn't have to define me. Here, I'm free to create meaning and traditions for myself.

I found an ad on the wall at the University campus center—"Room for Rent in the Gourmet Ghetto." I interviewed in a white cotton sweater to suggest I'd be a great housemate—meticulous and clean, maybe even angelic. Magill has lived here all her life and rents rooms to Kimberly, Kadir, and me. Mine is the small sunporch, street-side, on the second floor. Here, I live with civilians, not students, but real-life residents of the city of Berkeley.

The large window in my sunporch room opens to the tree-lined intersection below. Its dozen panels of antique glass sweep inward, dwarfing what little space I've got. But when the window's open, the energy sweeps down from the hills and into our little house, making it expansive like the wide world itself. My room doesn't have any heating vents or a radiator, just thin panes of glass that magnify the sun and radiate its warmth. In winter, it's cold in here, and I hunker down on my futon under a comforter of down as if I'm camping.

I'm at my little school desk from the Habitat for Humanity ReStore, reading my environmental policy textbook. The phone rings and scares the crap out of me. Fueled by adrenaline, I jump up to answer it. And I know exactly which boards to avoid, averting the creak of these weathered floors. Hopping over a section of flooring with two steps, then box-stepping to the right, I grab the phone before it rings again. I'm careful not to wake Kadir, who might be asleep in the next room.

"Kate ... I'm watching *The Today Show*. They are all excited about Dads and Grads. When are you graduated from your university?"

"Hi, Grandmama. In six weeks."

"Instead of coming up, I'm giving you what it would cost me to get there. I'm giving you what I would have spent."

"But I'd rather see you, Grandma."

"Don't be crazy. I'm very proud of you up there at your university. I'm sending you a check."

I hang up and recount this conversation to myself in Spanish. I imagine the confusion it's causing, the generations congregating on the cathedral steps and the chatter getting louder. An old-timer in a black beret with a heavy Basque accent throws his hands up in outrage. "How can this be?" he asks me.

"Where do you put your faith, your highest value?" I respond. He points to the almighty steeple and all around him to the people. It's an outrage, he says. "Yes," I nod. I agree. And all I can think to say is that it's a very American thing to put on money.

༄

Magill's boiling water in her house robe and shooing the cat away from her omelet. "Kate, congratulations. It's your graduation day!" She opens the refrigerator and pulls out a small cake. "I made this for you." It's pink and round, and I instantly think of Strawberry Shortcake. I take a whiff, and Strawberry's here with us, with her strawberry plastic skin and scented Saran hair; Pony and She-Ra and G.I. Joe are here too.

"My brothers are on their way!"

"Oh, how exciting, your brothers?" Magill's fifty-one years old and has a son my age in Oregon. But she's timid and sweet, just like a child. She's rainbows and butterflies and connection and community, and I feel so lucky to rent the tiny sunporch room in her quaint, little house from the turn of the century.

Back at my desk, I hear them calling from the street below. "Kate! Come out!" I pop open my large window and swing it into the room. It screeches and creaks. I duck under it and come up to the most beautiful sight. My brothers are taunting me, calling me out from the middle of the four-way stop. Brian throws a pebble that flies right over my head and lands with a clatter on my floor. "You idiot!" Doug laughs. I bound down the stairs and into the street.

On the porch, I introduce them to Magill and to Kadir, who passes us on his way to work at the Montessori school. He carries his bike down the steps and flies on two wheels down Spruce Street, waving good-bye. Magill approaches sheepishly. She does an awkward curtsy and giggles. "Is it too early for cake? Can we celebrate?" In the kitchen, she pours tea into butterfly teacups and slices the homemade strawberries and cream confection. "Oh, it's so special to have you here," she says to Doug and Brian like a little girl.

Magill is right. It's awesome to have my brothers here among the family that I choose. Doug graduated from USC last year and sells software for Oracle in

Los Angeles. Brian's still finishing high school and lives with Dad. After a few years of stability, the three of us realize that the bonds between us are stronger than the negativity our circumstances can breed. And with the darkness subsided, I think about that photo of the three of us, how I placed it on my dresser in darker times—a prayer for the return of light, now manifested.

Kimberly peeks in from the hallway on her way downstairs and says, "Hello." She's shy and meek and usually walks with her head down as if she's deep in thought. When her bedroom door's open, I see stacks of chairs and boxes, but I can never find her in there. She's damaged and barricaded from years of physical abuse at the hand of her father. We, the family she chooses, protect her fragile sense of security as if it were our own.

When Magill's head is in the cupboard searching for napkins, Brian manages to wedge himself between the wall and her little, round table to eat. Doug checks to see she's still out of sight, then exaggerates the tightness of the space with his six-foot-four body. "You look like a giant," says Brain, and the three of us chuckle quietly.

Before I realize it, they've devoured their cake and each given Magill a hug. They follow me down the hall with a look of having just taken communion, that slow, contemplative stroll back to the pew.

But as soon as we get to my little room, the outside is calling. "I made you guys a reservation at the Faculty Club. I'll take you there. Wanna walk?"

Doug lies down on my futon, looks up at my plastered ceiling, and crunches right back up. "Let's roll!"

It's been a long time since the three of us were all together. It's been even longer since it was to celebrate anything. But nothing really changes. And when we're together, we're giddy, and there's a hilarious subtext to just about everything. Our chitchat comes out in Brian's broken baby talk, and Doug's big brother torture tactics lace his every utterance with an exhilarating menace. The world is once again the walk-street beyond our magnolia tree. Our interactions with outsiders are again those first childhood impressions that have imprinted on our minds. They remind us how incredibly amusing people really are. When my brothers and I are together, it's us against the world, and we see it through the eyes of children.

Down the stoop onto Spruce, I make a left. "Are you guys hungry? Well ... welcome to the Gourmet Ghetto!"

"What's that?" Brian laughs and flashes me a made-up gang sign.

"Not that kind of ghetto. You'll see."

At the corner of Vine, we pass the original Peet's, where Alfred Peet once lived upstairs and brewed his unusually strong Dutch blends that wafted through the neighborhood and caused some controversy before eventually acquiring a cult following of beatniks. This is where I work part-time.

Next door at the Cheese Board Collective, I order the black bean polenta. It comes out smothered in cilantro salsa. It's delicious. I devour every morsel from a red gingham hotdog bowl with a compostable spoon. We ramble on down the road to the corner of Shattuck, where the boys get slices of gruyere pizza from the

Cheese Board co-op, and we sit on the grass in the center divider and eat.

Doug has his rolling Tumi suitcase, fitting of his position in software sales. We reach the edge of campus at the Genetics and Plant Biology building and his cell phone rings. Neither Brian nor I have a cell phone. This is a fact we attribute to still owning ourselves and not being a pawn of "The Man." Doug answers the two-by-three-inch device, which sets Brian and me off. We tease him about his tiny flip phone, that old corporate ball and chain. Undeterred, Doug talks shop like a pro. He hangs up and, immediately, Brian's in a headlock.

Over the Faculty Glade, we walk in the sun and shadows of redwood trees. We pass the garden beds so lovingly cultivated, and I think of the university employee who loves each day because he shows love to his garden. Or vice-versa. I confuse myself again and just admire the flowers.

On the quiet, wooded edge where Piedmont Avenue graces the base of the hills lies an overgrown Craftsman cottage with stained glass windows and carved wooden beams. I've wandered by and looked in at its majestic fireplaces and dark wood paneling with awe. I think it looks like a secret meeting house for the understated and meek, those little-known leaders who shall inherit the earth. But really, it's a university-operated boarding house, a little bohemian refuge for guest scholars and friends of the university. I lead Brian and Doug inside, like, "Watch this."

"Can I help you?" asks the lady at the desk. Brian looks nervously at me, as if maybe I'm mistaken. But I put down $106.30 and get them the keys to room 102. Doug reaches for his wallet before I tell him there's no way I'm taking his money.

"Meet me back at my house at three o'clock? The ceremony's at four o'clock." My brothers nod, and Brian, with his backpack, and Doug, with his rolling Tumi, head down the dark hall. I hear Brian laugh evil and funny. I hear Doug talk Transylvanian. I head back down the hill in the shade of the redwoods.

At home, I put on a dress and brush my hair. I take a beaten-up copy of *Walden* to the front of the house and lie down on my belly on the concrete that's been warming in the sun. Magill's sunflowers, now five feet high, line the fence where the sweet peas grew all winter.

At three o'clock, I see the boys strolling my way. Doug's got on a muted purple shirt and black, flat-front pants with a leather belt. Brian's in dressy surfer clothes: short-sleeved, button-down plaid shirt and khakis.

"So," Doug says and plops down on the step next to me. "Dad called. I guess Karen might not be ready in time. He said they'll meet us there or at dinner."

"Or at dinner? Very committal," I say sarcasticly. I've learned not to expect any different. "How's the room?"

"Um, creepy, dude."

"Yeah, Kate ... thanks for those tiny twin beds," Doug gibes. "My feet hang over the front."

Brian laughs out loud. "Remember that story Mom told us about how she and Grandma showed up to Uncle Frankie's high school graduation with cowbells because they were so proud of him?"

"Yeah, well, that's saying more about Uncle Frankie than anyone else."

"True," says Brian.

"Well, we're here for you with cowbells, right, Bri?" My big brother gives me a side hug from where we sit here on the stoop. "Mom would be so proud of you."

We're silent for a while, just enjoying the warmth of our togetherness and the sun on the stoop. Magill comes home at 3:45 p.m. She returns to the stoop with a jug of lemonade. She wants to know all about Doug's big, grown-up corporate job and how Brian's doing in high school down in Los Angeles. She says "Los *Angel-es*" as if it's a mythical place, and I remember she's never really lived anywhere else. I imagine for a second that Magill runs a rest home for weary travelers, and she's just starved for news of the outside world. In exchange, she offers some creature comforts and loads of sustenance for the soul.

Kadir rolls up and leans his bike against the house. He sits next to Brain on the step and starts twirling one of his dreadlocks in his right hand. "How's everyone?"

We sit, chat, and laugh about nothing. We drink Magill's bittersweet lemonade as the sun sinks low on the west side of the house. A beam of light shines straight through the windows from the west side and warms the back of my head.

Kimberly comes out with her typical look of concern. She pushes her glasses up and stares at us. "Um ... isn't your graduation, like, now?"

But none of us budges.

∽

At 6:30 p.m., we vacate the porch stoop and stroll down the hill to my graduation dinner. We enter the darkened room with colorful tin lights in star shapes. Perforations in the fixtures create a constellation of celestial light on the midnight blue walls and ceiling.

At a wooden table for ten, we see the Casparis and Dad and Karen. Ami and her girlfriend, Ruth, come in right behind us. "I can't believe you and Quinn graduate on the same night," Ami says, out of breath from a brisk walk. "We were going to Quinn's, but rapid transit to get here is *way* cheaper than two plane tickets." Ami pauses and pulls me in for a hug. "Just kidding!"

Ruth rolls her eyes and smiles. "Hey, are we late? We had to transfer in Oakland."

"Not at all! Thank you for coming!" I'm so happy to see them.

Mrs. Caspari waltzes up and grabs my hands. "Sorry we missed your ceremony, dear. Mr. Caspari had a work meeting." With only our eyes, my brothers and I say to each other, *Let them think we were actually there.* I hope, just for kicks, that someone lies and says how great it was to see me receive my diploma.

"Yes, dear," says Mr. Caspari, "congratulations on your graduation. What a sweet choice of restaurants! Just like a Costa Rican cantina!"

We order a round of sangria and some chips and salsa. I look to the four corners of the table under the starlight. I'm amazed that all these people are here for me. I surprise myself by liking the attention, and I crack myself up by imagining they're all complicit in the creation of a self-absorbed monster. But as we await our dinner, I soak it all in. Connections form in my neocortex, my neurons grow. Moment by moment, I'm more accepting of love and feeling more capable of giving it. Moment by moment, I'm becoming a better person.

"Excuse me ... how long will our dinners take?" Dad asks the waitress. He looks down at his watch. "We have a ten o'clock flight out of Oakland."

Mrs. Caspari turns to Dad. "What? You can't leave, are you crazy?"

"No. Our flight's at ten. We've got to get the kids from Ron. He only has them Wednesday through Friday."

"Well ... I'm sure he'll keep his kids another day so that you can see yours. Call the airline. Change it!" Mr. Caspari's now talking with his hands, and through my sangria haze, I forget if this place is Italian or Basque or a Costa Rican cantina. But I see that to Mr. C., this is an outrage.

Halfway through my enchilada, I watch Dad and Karen stand. They walk around the table and shake hands with everyone like you would at a business meeting. "Good-bye, children," Dad says to us. "Good-bye, daughter. Well done." Dad gives me a stiff WASPy hug, and they leave.

Mrs. Caspari moves in to the chair next to me. "Hey. Well ... that was odd. I guess he feels like he has more important things to do right now."

Mr. Caspari laughs. "Oh, Diana, well-put! Well-put. You tell it like it is, my dear." Mr. C. looks me sharply in the eyes. "Well, sweetheart, lots of people love you and are proud of you, and we aren't leaving until they drag us out of here."

Mrs. Caspari looks across the table at Doug and Brian and gathers all our hands in hers. She pulls us in really close and says, "I feel a special energy between you three. Never forget that you've got each other." She's not a particularly religious woman, but this sounds like a prophecy, and I look over at Brain, who's nodding, like, amen.

It's about ten o'clock when Mrs. Caspari practically drags Mr. C out of Café Luna. He gives me dos besos. And now that I've lived in Spain, I don't fumble it one bit. I give Mrs. C. a hug, and she kisses me on the cheek.

The boys and I walk Ami and Ruth to the BART station. My brothers drop me off at my front porch stoop. "You guys know how to get back to your creepy, little room with the two tiny beds, right? Oh, and you're welcome for that."

"We got it," Doug assures me, and they head east. "Good-night!"

In my room, I lay my head down. I feel the glorious bay breeze creep its way under the frame of my old, swinging window. Then … nothing but sleep.

Sometime after midnight, I'm awakened by a feeling that someone or something is watching me. I sit up with a start and wipe the sweat from my forehead. The light from a car outside at the four-way stop illuminates my walls for just a second, and I see it's nothing.

But I lie back down and can feel it still. I pull my comforter up just below my eyes. Maybe I'll see it, but it won't see me. I don't see it, but I feel it just outside my window, hovering, requesting permission to come in. It's intense and weighty, and I'm exhausted and happy, so I tell it, "No, thank you. Not tonight."

⁓

It's barely light yet, and my phone's ringing. That damn phone.

"Hello?"

"Hey, Kate, it's Doug. What are you doing? Can you come up here?"

"Sleeping. It's, like, five o'clock in the morning!"

"I know. I know." He sounds like he's had five espressos. "Sorry. Brian and I need to talk to you. We need to tell you something."

"Jesus ... what? Okay ... so tell me."

"No. In person. Can you come up here now?"

"Now? No. I'm going back to sleep."

"Are you sure? It's really important."

"Are you guys okay?"

"Yes. We're better than okay. Okay ... just call us as soon as you wake up."

"Okay. I will." I go back to sleep for about an hour, but as the light grows brighter, I'm stirred by curiosity, and I don't want to waste a single moment that my brothers are in town. So I jump up, shower, and head for the Faculty Club.

On my way up Virginia Street and into the hills, I smell the morning dew on the soil. I'm light and airy, just like the leaves that rustle on this tree-lined street. I hear the chain clank on a bicycle as someone rides by, and the birds singing only to me.

I knock on room 102. Immediately, Doug answers.

"Hey. Come in. Hey, actually, do you want to get coffee? Let's go somewhere."

"Um, sure, but don't you have something you want to tell me?"

"Brian, you start. No … wait, let's get coffee first."

"Jesus. Are you guys serious?"

At Intermezzo, I get an Americano. My brothers order latte drinks. It makes me think they don't actually like coffee. I wait for them on a small bench for what seems like forever. Finally, they crash onto chairs around me.

"Okay, so, are you guys gonna tell me?"

Doug is giddy and scattered like a child. "No. Just wait. Let's go somewhere else. Do you know of any good walks around here? Hikes?"

I lead them up behind Memorial Stadium and behind my old dorm to a trail with views of the Golden Gate Bridge. We walk up and up until we're huffing and puffing. We stop and climb the front face of a huge boulder on the side of the trail. Up here, we look out to the bay and the sea beyond the Golden Gate. "Is this a good place?" I ask, really hoping it is this time.

"Yes," says Doug. "Brian, you start."

"No. You."

"Jesus … one of you, just tell me!"

"Okay, so … you know how Grandma always says that Mom comes to her in the form of a hummingbird?"

"Um, no. No, I didn't."

"Oh. Well, she tells Doug and me that all the time. So … last night we were at that place, the hotel, and I asked Doug if he believed that whole thing about Mom being the hummingbird."

"Okay … "

"Then … Doug, you tell her."

"Okay, okay," says Doug. "All of a sudden, I started to feel like I stuck my hand in the electricity socket, you know, but not, like, painful, just tingly. Then, my arms and legs got that way. I lay on my bed for a while, and I felt super light and energized."

I look over at Brian, whose eyes are wide and glazed over. He nods.

"So," Doug continues, "I said, 'Hey, Brian, I feel super weird right now, like I'm floating,' and Brian said he did too. And then, we lay there on our twin beds for, like, forty-five minutes feeling this electricity. Then, I felt like I was hovering above the bed, and there was this sound, like a really beautiful … like ringing … a vibration … music."

"Um, me too." Brain nods again. He doesn't blink.

"Okay … so … what does this mean?"

Doug tears up, then laughs and says, "It was the most beautiful feeling I've ever felt. If I can just remember this feeling … I'll never worry again."

I look over at Brian, who nods slowly. All he says is, "Yup." I look to Doug and shake my head because I don't really get it.

"It was Mom, Kate. She came for your graduation … she brought the cowbell."

At dusk, I'm home in my room wondering why she didn't come to me. I'm the old soul, after all. I look out the window and up to the hills. I throw open the swinging frame and it's twelve panes of leaded glass. Maybe, if I had been with them, I would have felt it too.

I had promised to not be afraid. I'm not afraid. So why did I tell her to go away?

Downstairs, I hear Kadir and Magill laughing hysterically to the stupid antics of the *Absolutely Fabulous* ladies on TV. No doubt, they're injecting themselves with Botox and making sure their designer labels accidentally show. *Youth, money, and insecurity—they're all earth,* I think, *that delicious spice of life.* And so is this glorious smell, Kimberly's Saturday salsa, the pepper and tomatillo tang, and the sound of Magill's cat landing on the hardwood from her bannister perch. They suit me now, so happy in this house.

The breeze rustles the poplar tree in our front yard. I smell sweet brine and soil and dew and eucalyptus. I hear the leaves flutter on the wind. I take a deep breath and realize I'm all earth now. I'm grounded and content. I catch a glimmer of light on a leaf. I taste the salt of my own tears. I close my eyes and just feel. "Some other time," I say to myself. I'm so touched by the bitter sweetness of this ephemeral world. The eternal can wait.

༺❀༻

They're smoking pipes, and Grandma's lit a cone of incense inside the head of each one. A pungent cloud is building over my head.

"German," she says.

"Ah."

"We sold them at Fancy This. Aren't they cute?" Grandma grins at me, and this is my cue.

"Oh, yes, Grandma, they are!"

Brian looks disgusted. "So why do you have your Christmas trolls out if tomorrow's only Thanksgiving?" Doug flickers him a high five with his eyes.

"They are Santas! They celebrate everything all at once now. You're not keeping up with the times. At Macy's, they've got Thanksgiving casseroles right next to Santa Claus aprons. It's a riot." She takes a bite of pâté on cracker. "So, Kate, where do you go next week? You will work for the dirt conservatory?"

"Yes, Grandmama. It's a land trust in San Diego County, but it's just an interview. Wish me luck."

"To work for the dirt company? Good Lord, what kind of luck would you need?"

"Yes. The land trust. Wish me good luck. I want this job. They protect natural places in perpetuity."

"You need to accept change! Though, I guess you look the part." She wags a finger up and down at my khaki, Army surplus jacket. It's not flattery. "Do you still live at your commune? You'll wind up an old maid living there, you know. No eligible man will look at you twice."

Brian makes his eyes big and suppresses a laugh. He rolls his neck to the right.

"I still rent a room on the north side of campus. Yes."

"With other unattached people?"

"Whether they are attached or not is irrelevant. But, yes. There are other renters, and the landlady lives there too."

"Uh-huh," she says and takes a sip as if she's keeping score and I'm losing. "So is your dad still sleeping on the girlfriend's couch? They do that, you know, to make the man marry them. All of a sudden, they find their religion and won't have the sex anymore."

Nobody's told her that Dad is married again. Still nobody does. Grandma scans the room. She calculates over her plate of pâté. "Brian, are you running with a bad crowd? My friend down in San Diego says all the university kids run with a bad crowd. It's the drugs." Grandma takes another bite of pâté, making her eyes really big and never taking them off Brian.

"Um … no." Brian sits down on the floor and pets the dog. "Hi. Hi!" he says, roughing up Pico's replacement Maltese, Bonsai. It's a good diversion tactic. But I feel we can do better.

"Dougie, are you in a cult? I hear you go to a church, and now you have church friends."

"Nope," he says. Grandma shakes her scotch glass, and the ice jingles like evil sleigh bells. Doug heads to the piano and starts playing a glorious diversion of Christmas carols. We all sing along merrily, even Grandpa. Brian and I grit our teeth through the melody in relief.

Doug's back in his interrogation chair by the coffee table. I ask, "So what have you been up to lately, Grandma?"

"Oh, not much, you know …"

"No. Tell me." The boys look stunned, as if they didn't know we were allowed to ask questions too. We've been so conditioned to just sit and play the victim. I see that they're nervous.

"Well, my neighbor, Syd, nice gal ... she and I are crocheting sleeves and having denim and wool jackets made in a factory in China. We've got the costs all figured out. It's big business."

"Seriously?" asks Doug.

"Really?" laughs Brian.

"Yes." Grandma gets up and heads to her little office behind the kitchen. She comes out with some crochet legwarmer-looking things with wrist cuffs sewn on. She puts on the denim vest and holds the sleeves in place. "See?"

They're cheesy jackets, but they might actually sell somewhere. We model them, and Grandma and Grandpa applaud and laugh. Doug does a particularly good go at the catwalk, turning dramatically and taking the jacket off, one unattached sleeve at a time.

"Well," Grandma sighs and smiles, "you kids head out for some fun. I'll leave the key under the mat for you. Remember, though, I'm putting you to work with the turkey early, so don't be tired in the morning." Before we know it, we're shooed out under the streetlamps on the boardwalk.

༄

We head north toward the pier and the local bars, toward the inevitable inebriation and homecoming of everyone we ever knew who's visiting family and those who, for whatever reason, never left.

Into the The Mermaid, we escape the blustery, salty air. The door is weathered like driftwood and has a porthole for a window. It slams behind me, and I expect to find a sea witch or Popeye the Sailor in here. Instead, we're met by a very South Bay scene. It's the usual surfer boys in trucker hats and girls wearing low-cut tops and low-cut jeans. This never was my scene, so I head for a pub table in the back and watch as my brothers make their way to the bar.

I look down at the floor sprinkled with sand. It's gotten in between the floorboards and is stuck to the bottom of my shoes. I found a sprinkling of it under the floor mat of my Jeep when I moved to San Francisco. I still find it at the bottom of my handbags and in the pockets of my backpack. The sands of my youth; I can't escape them. They permeate everything.

The boys arrive with their beers and a club soda. "Dude, how weird was it when Grandma was being so cool tonight? We were actually having fun."

"It was a choice," I tell them. "We chose to have fun."

"What?" Brian demands.

"We stopped being afraid of her and just moved on. She knows we don't necessarily like her, you guys, and it hurts her feelings. And by the way, you both really need some acting lessons. Try to find that person inside of you who truly likes and appreciates her. If you don't, she'll smell your fear, and it's all over."

A girl from high school whose name I can't remember waves in my direction. I pretend to be wasted and give her a vague wave back, then stare off into space. Just as I planned, her attention is sucked back into the crowd of faces. I assume I've pulled this move from my reptilian brain, where it resides alongside the instinct to bleed or to play dead.

I saw a monk seal one time on the PBS channel. As it floated listlessly in the tide, the British guy explained that the seals often appear sick or dead, but they're just acting to fend off the sharks. There was also this Abaco boa constrictor that bleeds without ever being harmed. *Ay-yai-yai*, I think, *well-played*. I'm not in the mood for one-upping or small talk tonight. If my listless stare hadn't worked, I'd consider a little bloodletting so this girl would just leave me alone.

I swing my leg over a tall, wooden stool. I feel as I did as a child struggling to stabilize my butt on Santa's lap, thinking, even at that age, there was something perverse about perching myself over the inner thigh of a stranger.

Doug leans in. "So what part of you likes and appreciates Grandmama, exactly?"

"Well, she demands loyalty from us and dedication. It sort of feels like love, doesn't it?" Doug stares at me. "I think that she won't run away, and she won't give in. She'll load you up with crap so you have to contend with her. I like that she's not afraid of a little friction in a relationship or a little clutter. And it's not just because she's a loud, hand-talking New Yorker, you guys. She's passionate about her relationships, and she wants to mean something to us." They're both silent, then they break down in mocking laughter. I don't care.

"Plus, she gives awesome old-person advice. You know, those backhanded comments that sting but can mold you into a better person." Doug's practically falling off his chair. "It's just the game she plays, you know, her act. Did I ever tell you about the monk seal?" Now Brian's staring at me in disbelief. "Okay, whatever. But she's sort of fun, no?"

"Um ... no," they say in unison.

Most of us could use some acting lessons. Our intentions are selfish, awkward, and transparent. But truly great people are fantastic actors. They dig deep into their authentic selves for goodness, and with faith in humanity, they gather the muster to lead us away from the toxicity of our own inadequacies. It's all games, all acting, and it's as natural as the cosmos.

As for the bad actors, we have a choice with those toxic people. They can break us or make us who we're destined to be. But each one of us is some sort of actor. We act to convince others, to convince ourselves. We act for attention, for reverence, or for love. Grandma is a great intimidator jockeying for her own worth. She acts to feel needed and important ... and, when all else fails, feared.

I'm a great avoider, a snarky and distanced nonparticipant. I act to avoid getting hurt and to compensate for my loss. But, I'm learning to like games and constructs. When my old soul drags its heels and goes boneless, now I say yes. I act and connect. Maybe I *can* fake it till I make it; surely, I'm younger than my old soul now.

As for the chicken or the egg, the nurture versus nature, they never did reopen the Paranormal Psychology Lab. But what I do know is that demanding silence and avoiding others does not serve me. I'm not a boulder or a rock or an island. I'm a channel, etched by cold waters and opposing views. We all are. Our sandy shores are eroded by the friction of our relationships and softened by the efforts of love that never give up. Eroded beings, we wax and wane and grow, our seepage shoring each other's banks.

I stare off into space at the blur of beach bots who make up my hometown. I look out at the collective whole until I can no longer see faces, just a past that makes up the tapestry of who I am. I am better for it, for all of it. For my elders and my hometown, my first and forever teachers, ever-present parts of me I can't escape with time or distance. They stick to me like sand and travel far and wide in my baggage.

The pumice of Earth seeps into my soul and gathers spirits on the seas. I delight in the fact that when I immerse myself, really engage in the seemingly superficial, really agitate the sand and dirt of the material world, it greets me in celestial flashes and sparks.

"So …" says Brian quietly. Doug and I wait for a statement or a confession. I hope it's a confession because I'm learning to really dig drama. "It happened again."

"It? Like, the energy?"

"Yup. Once, over the phone, when Doug and I were talking about your graduation." Doug nods. "And once, when I was alone on the beach checking out the surf."

"Wow. I'm jealous. I'm happy for you, but I'm jealous. That's cool." Just then, a guy in a trucker hat comes up and smacks Brian upside the head.

"Wuzzup, dude!" They hug and two more douchey surfer-looking guys join in the huddle. I lose Brian to the shuffleboard table. Then, Doug is sucked into a crowd at the bar. It's just as well because I'm almost late to meet Quinn.

༺༻

Just before nine o'clock, I walk up the hill toward Java Man. Quinn's at a table outside with her Earl Grey.

"Um, hello! Late much?"

"What do you mean? It's five after!"

"I got you a nasty black coffee for here. So ... how's your grandma? I forget, are only the good still dying young?"

"Yup."

"Oh, crap, it's Sarah Chen and her crony, Briana. Duck." Down the sidewalk come our two high school classmates and a small child.

"Yeah, so, I'm not going to duck. Wait ... whose kid?"

"Briana's. Apparently, she's an early breeder."

We talk quietly. I'm careful not to change my mannerisms or do anything that will call attention to us. I'm not in the mood to make googly eyes for Briana's kid or pretend I'm happy for her having procreated before any of us got our first real job. When they're inside and the door slams, I relax again. "I have a new obsession. It's bad people speaking freely ... my new favorite thing."

"Okay."

"Bad people don't even know they're bad. That's why it's so funny. My Grandma told Brian that he should always pay cash because it makes women 'interested in the sex.'"

"No!"

"Yup."

Sarah flings open the door behind me. Quinn slouches, buries her face in her tea, and pretends to take a sip. I watch covertly as Briana grabs the little boy's wrist and pulls him down the step. "Mommy! Ouchie!" he whines.

"Sam, be quiet. Sarah ... I'll meet you at Brad's!" Briana yells enthusiastically, though Sarah's just ten feet away.

"Totally," Sarah responds halfheartedly. She's still the cold, mean girl, and amazingly, people are still kissing her ass. Sarah hops into a black Range Rover and backs out of her parking spot faster than I've seen anyone drive in a parking lot. It looks as if she's burned herself on her coffee and now she's pursing her lips to swear. One-handed, she pulls forward and makes the turn to leave the lot. The little boy jets down the sidewalk and over the driveway apron right in front of her.

"Sam!" calls Briana. When Sarah's stopped ten feet away from him, Briana runs out and pulls him by the arm back to her white Honda. "Oh my God, Sarah, I'm so sorry!" she calls to her friend, who looks miffed.

Sarah's now wiping off her center console with a beach towel. "It's okay. I just didn't want to be responsible." She tosses the towel aside and speeds away.

Quinn's practically squealing. "Did she really just say that?"

"Um, yes. Prime example."

"Well, it's kind of reassuring to know that people don't really change. And they'll usually show you exactly what you need to know about them." Quinn watches as Briana drives off, yelling something at her kid, who's strapped down in his car seat.

"No, they don't change. Relationships evolve, though. Plus, it's the superflawed people who add that spice to life."

Quinn puts her mug down and stares at me. "Wait, are we not misanthropes anymore? I didn't get the memo."

༶

My eyes are peeled for Exit 133. They said it would be easy to find. First right at the exit, then follow the sign all the way west. San Diego County's different from LA: more grass, more hillsides, and more open space. In the evening glare, I feel like I'm driving in a wheat field.

When the grass on the side of the road turns suddenly manicured and the road a little bit brighter, I see it: "Montage Laguna Beach."

"Welcome to the Montage. May I park your car?"

"Um … no thanks. I'm just meeting my brothers here for a drink." I never have cash for the valet, so I'd rather just avoid the awkwardness. But it's already weird. I park and walk back past him like I'm doing the walk of shame.

In the lobby, they're waiting. The hostess at the bar turns to me. "Welcome! Your brothers are sure happy you found us! I'm still working with the floor staff to get you three a table." Is she an old friend of my brothers, or are the boys actually this charming?

After a few minutes of stalking tables of patrons who seem poised to leave, Doug grabs a huge club chair from the lobby and slides it over to a side table with two chairs in the hallway between the lobby and the bar. Brian and I crash down while Doug alerts the bartender that we'll be ordering in the hallway.

We're clearly being ignored, and Brian's pretty sure it's because we're dressed in flip-flops and jeans. Not Doug, of course, who always looks appropriate. I start to wonder when we'll be asked to leave, then I look over at the hostess table. She's apparently impressed by our advanced seating move and gives us a thumbs-up.

Doug took a new job negotiating software contracts with the Navy. The boys are now sharing an apartment in La Jolla. "I'm excited to see your new place. What time do you think I'll have to leave in the morning to get to my interview?"

"Umm, nine?" says Brian. "That address you gave me is pretty close, for sure." Hearing this, I have a sudden feeling of warmth. I think for a second I might land this job, get to follow my passion of fighting urban sprawl, and be near my brothers again.

"I think we're the castoff stepchildren over here," says Brian.

"No way!" Doug argues. "The hostess digs us, just wait."

Sure enough, our old friend shows up. "You three are cute. I just got our best table cleared off if you want it."

Doug winks at us, like, "See?"

Outside on the stone patio at the best table in the house, we're snuggled right in the middle of the cove, right where brown rock crumbles into the Pacific. The sun sinks low. It hovers over the ocean, turning everything to gold. Waves boom, and salt spray fizzes. I hear the clang of dishes, the clink of wine glasses.

When the sun is half-immersed, it hovers salmon pink. "Fall sunsets are the best!" I say, and the three of us look out to the sun setting on the horizon. "Remember those red tides we got when we were kids, how the ocean and the wet sand would flash and spark, how it would glow?"

"Yeah, so?" Brian demands the summary.

"They're awesome."

"What are?"

"Spirits, I guess. They take so many different forms."

I gaze out again, just as the sun immerses itself in the sea.

"Hey," says Doug, "So ... you know how Mom comes to Brian and me and gives us those amazing positive vibes?

"Yeah?"

"What's Grandma gonna do after she's gone?"

I swallow so I don't spit out my drink. But, before I can even laugh, my arms start to tingle.

"You guys," says Brian, "it's happening ... it's Mom."

I feel a soft pulse of electricity radiating through me. I realize I've felt this sensation in little flickers throughout my adult life. I have called it "intuition," and when I've allowed it to, it has led me to countless joys. "What does this mean, you guys?"

Doug holds his palms to the sky. He looks like he's praying. I see emotion wash over him like salvation. "We're all connected," he says, "Mom is always guiding us."

Brian looks startled. "Dude ... I think she liked your joke."

Acknowledgments

Thank you to the fates for unravelling the lessons of my life in such creative ways. Thank you, Andrew Gifford, of the Santa Fe Writers Project, for your dedication to indie literature and giving so generously of your time. Thank you, Robert Long Foreman, for your willingness to share your talent. Thank you to the enchanting Carmen Maria Machado, for pulling my manuscript from the awards slush pile and giving me a reason to finish it. Thank you, Melissa Long, for reading between the lines, and to Amy Ashby and Mindy Kuhn at Warren Publishing.

Thank you, Dad, for your encouragement, for laughing at my jokes, and for passing on these crazed writer's genes. Gracias, Maria, por la generosidad de tu amor. Thank you to my Cal girls, to my STS mommies, and to Marika and Brook. Ellie, Charlotte, and Tommy—I love you. Tom, I love you most.

www.ingramcontent.com/pod-product-compliance
Lightning Source LLC
Chambersburg PA
CBHW022000100426
42738CB00042B/973